2018

SAT®
WRITING:
Advanced Level

ies
TEST PREP

10 LESSONS

ADVANCED
PRACTICE
SERIES

525 QUESTIONS

THE MOST CHALLENGING SAT WRITING QUESTIONS

♦ **Punctuation Usage**
♦ **Difficult Transitions**
♦ **Sentence Placement/Deletion/Addition**

5 WRITING TESTS

Authors
Khalid Khashoggi, CEO IES
Arianna Astuni, President IES

Editorial
Patrick Kennedy, Executive Editor
Christopher Carbonell, Editorial Director
Rajvi Patel, Senior Editor
Cassidy Yong, Assistant Editor

Design
Christopher Carbonell

· ·

Published by IES Publications
www.IESpublications.com
© IES Publications, 2017

ON BEHALF OF

Integrated Educational Services, Inc.

355 Main Street

Metuchen, NJ 08840

www.iestestprep.com

We would like to thank the IES Publications team as well as the teachers and students at IES Test Prep who have contributed to the creation of this book.

The SAT* is a registered trademark of the College Board, which was not involved in the production of, and does not endorse, this product.

ISBN-10: 1548897388

ISBN-13: 978-1548897383

QUESTIONS OR COMMENTS? Visit us at iestestprep.com

TABLE OF CONTENTS

Practice Tests

Key

 Pay attention to anything near this graphic. Information accompanied by this pencil is crucial to understanding this book's techniques.

 These tips are provided to give you additional knowledge of essential SAT Writing and Language Techniques.

Dear student,

When the Redesigned SAT was first administered in 2016, we at Integrated Educational Services knew that a process of evolution and adaptation had been set in motion. Between major re-designs, tests can change direction and emphasis over time. This is exactly what happened with the SAT Writing and Language Test: while the College Board has not added new concepts or formats, it has put difficult new spins on existing question types in a few specific areas. Questions involving punctuation, sentence transitions, and logical content choices have proven remarkably difficult for even the most advanced test-takers, and may only become more difficult as more and more tests are administered. We soon discovered that we need a specialized book, one  that could—depending on the test-taker—both work as an independent crash course and complement our other volumes.

That is where this latest volume in the IES Advanced Practice Series comes in. The *2018 SAT Writing: Advanced Level Practice Book* can indeed be deployed as part of a larger curriculum, much as we use it on IES campuses. In particular, this volume offers an in-depth look at topic areas that are explained in the IES *New SAT Grammar Practice Book*, expanding these areas outward with editing, multiple-choice, and mastery review exercises. However, this new volume can also stand on its own for seasoned test-takers. If you are aiming for the highest possible score, there is a good chance that you have already mastered the fundamentals of subject-verb agreement, parallel structure, style, and diction. Yet there are trickier matters—whether to use a colon or a semicolon, whether or not to insert that extra sentence—that require their own kind of practice. You will find that practice right here.

Regardless of your familiarity with the SAT, this book is designed to take what you already know and expand upon it. Every time you write an essay of your own, you must make the kind of careful content, transition, and punctuation choices that the SAT Writing and Language sections require. This book will show you how to adapt some of what you know to any question that the College Board can devise, and will give you the confidence that you need to take control of an increasingly dynamic SAT.

Wishing you the best of luck in your test-taking endeavors.

-Arianna Astuni

Chapter One
Colon Usage

Colon Usage

Colons for Introducing Items and Lists

Often, writers use colons to quickly and efficiently introduce items and lists. Sentences that function in this manner, however, must follow a specific structure.

    1) The part of the sentence BEFORE the colon must be a stand-alone sentence (or "independent clause") and must contain a noun that indicates what will appear after the colon. We call this noun the "content clue."

    2) The part of the sentence AFTER the colon must only consist of items designated by the "content clue."

With these guidelines in mind, observe how the following two sentences use content clues to coordinate lists and items.

CONTENT CLUE  ITEM

Only a <u>single member</u> of the team raised objections: <u>Dr. Padmanabhan</u>.

CONTENT CLUE ➡ LIST

The company purchased <u>new equipment</u>: <u>jackhammers, shovels, and pickaxes</u>.

Note that the use of a colon makes any further transition or introductory phrase unnecessary in introducing an item or a list. Avoid errors such as those below, which create sentences that are grammatically incorrect and needlessly wordy

Only a single member of the team raised <u>objections, as:</u> Dr. Padmanabhan. ✕

Only a single member of the team raised <u>objections: it was</u> Dr. Padmanabhan. ✕

Only a single member of the team raised <u>objections:</u> Dr. Padmanabhan. ✓

Note also that a semicolon can NEVER introduce an item or a list, while a colon always can.

The company purchased new <u>equipment; jackhammers</u>, shovels, and pickaxes. ✕

The company purchased new <u>equipment: jackhammers</u>, shovels, and pickaxes. ✓

 However, there are cases in which a colon (somewhat like a semicolon) CAN introduce independent clauses, as will be explained in the next lesson.

COLONS FOR INTRODUCING EXPLANATIONS

A colon can be used to structure a sentence that consists of two major parts: an idea and an explanation. Colon sentences of this sort will all follow roughly the same structure.

1) The part of the sentence BEFORE the colon must be an independent clause, and must present a fact, thought, or opinion that requires some elaboration.

2) The part of the sentence AFTER the colon must ALSO be an independent clause, and must clearly refer to some part of the content before the colon.

The structure is very similar to the colon sentence structure for introducing items and lists. You may even notice that the explanation sentences below have content that functions much like the "content clues" mentioned earlier.

In many cases, the second part of the sentence will also answer a question that is raised, implicitly or explicitly, in the first part of the sentence.

What had happened?

Idea ➤ Explanation

Finally, she understood <u>what had happened</u>: <u>a kicked-over lamp had started the fire</u>.

Why did nobody want to debate him?

Idea ➤ Explanation

<u>Nobody wanted to debate him</u>: <u>his ideas were simply too vague to be worth discussing</u>.

Make sure, of course, that such explanation sentences include independent clauses both before AND after the colon. While an item or a list is (technically) a sentence fragment, the second part of a colon explanation can NEVER be a sentence fragment of this sort.

Nobody wanted to debate <u>him: if his</u> ideas were simply too vague to be worth discussing. ✕

Nobody wanted to debate <u>him: his</u> ideas were simply too vague to be worth discussing. ✓

EXERCISES: COLON USAGE

CREATING THE BEST PLACEMENT

DIRECTIONS: Read the sentence and determine how the sentence should be coordinated using a colon. In some cases, you will need to eliminate awkward and inappropriate transitions when inserting the colon. Then, choose whether the colon is used to introduce a list or used to introduce an explanation.

Example

The rules of the game are quite clear, they are explained in detail in the appendix.

↓

The rules of the game are quite **clear: they** are explained in detail in the appendix.

Sentence Type: EXPLANATION

---

1) I always carry two items a wallet and a phone.

LIST OF ITEMS / EXPLANATION

2) Before he died, he spoke a few simple words "my shoes are untied."

LIST OF ITEMS / EXPLANATION

3) Bobby's hair is soaking wet and he had walked for an hour in the rain.

LIST OF ITEMS / EXPLANATION

4) Never do this when you are driving text.

LIST OF ITEMS / EXPLANATION

5) The party was great there was a live band and free food.

LIST OF ITEMS / EXPLANATION

6) The Cheetah has just been declared an endangered species when there are fewer than ten thousand left in the wild.

LIST OF ITEMS / EXPLANATION

7) There is a way out of this mess to tell the truth and make amends.

LIST OF ITEMS / EXPLANATION

8) Allow me to make a long story short, he left his house without his keys.

LIST OF ITEMS / EXPLANATION

9) Let me say it again if nobody is allowed to use my office.

LIST OF ITEMS / EXPLANATION

10) I need you to buy the following for me, a guitar, a piano, and a violin.

LIST OF ITEMS / EXPLANATION

11) I can't stand rap music and it unsettles me.

LIST OF ITEMS / EXPLANATION

12) There are problems with the new device less sturdy and water-resistant than we had hoped.

LIST OF ITEMS / EXPLANATION

13) He had a few ideas, hire an editor, find a publisher, and add a new author photograph.

LIST OF ITEMS / EXPLANATION

14) The procedure is extremely simple where all you need to do is move this lever at set intervals.

LIST OF ITEMS / EXPLANATION

15) Shackleton's assistants, eventually, devised a way to escape from the island, they would send one man in a small boat to seek help.

LIST OF ITEMS / EXPLANATION

16) A large room at the Metropolitan Museum contains rare medieval instruments, lutes, harps, and flutes.

LIST OF ITEMS / EXPLANATION

17) African-American author Nella Larsen published two novels in her lifetime, such as *Quicksand*, which records a young woman's quest to find social acceptance, and *Passing*, which many critics regard as her masterpiece.

LIST OF ITEMS / EXPLANATION

18) Creating a strong retirement fund depends on a simple tactic to stay calm despite market fluctuations.

LIST OF ITEMS / EXPLANATION

19) It did not take long for controversy to arise, although the participants had simply been masking their irreconcilable differences of opinion.

LIST OF ITEMS / EXPLANATION

20) The researchers could not accept this result, striking them as suspiciously predictable.

LIST OF ITEMS / EXPLANATION

21) There was, however, one man who had faith in such nonviolent methods, Henry David Thoreau.

LIST OF ITEMS / EXPLANATION

22) Some visitors may not be sure how to interpret the sculpture in the courtyard as a distracting and regrettable decoration, or as a daring aesthetic statement.

LIST OF ITEMS / EXPLANATION

23) Automotive history is a field well worth studying, if it brings together such diverse disciplines as engineering, cultural history, and economics.

LIST OF ITEMS / EXPLANATION

24) It is arguable that these restaurants make most of their profits from a single item being buffalo wings.

LIST OF ITEMS / EXPLANATION

25) That was the essence of Christopher Hitchens's style, as thorny, erudite, and brutally honest.

LIST OF ITEMS / EXPLANATION

ANSWERS ON THE NEXT PAGE

ANSWERS: Colon Usage

Creating the Best Placement

1) I always carry **two items: a wallet** and a phone. (List of Items)

2) Before he died, he spoke a few simple **words: "my shoes** are untied." (List of Items)

3) Bobby's hair is **soaking wet: he had** walked for an hour in the rain. (Explanation)

4) Never do this when you are **driving: text**. (List of Items)

5) The party was **great: there was** a live band and free food. (Explanation)

6) The Cheetah has just been declared an **endangered species: there are** fewer than ten thousand left in the wild. (Explanation)

7) There is a way out of this **mess: tell** the truth and make amends. (Explanation)

8) Allow me to make a long **story short: he left** his house without his keys. (Explanation)

9) Let me say **it again: nobody is** allowed to use my office. (Explanation)

10) I need you to buy the following **for me: a guitar**, a piano, and a violin. (List of Items)

11) I can't stand rap **music: it** unsettles me. (Explanation)

12) There are problems with the **new device: it is** less sturdy and water-resistant than we had hoped. (Explanation)

13) He had a **few ideas: hire** an editor, find a publisher, and add a new author photograph. (List of Items)

14) The procedure is extremely **simple: all** you need to do is move this lever at set intervals. (Explanation)

15) Shackleton's assistants, eventually, devised a way to escape from **the island: they would** send one man in a small boat to seek help. (Explanation)

16) A large room at the Metropolitan Museum contains rare medieval **instruments: lutes**, harps, and flutes. (List of Items)

17) African-American author Nella Larsen published two novels in **her lifetime:** *Quicksand*, which records a young woman's quest to find social acceptance, and *Passing*, which many critics regard as her masterpiece. (List of Items)

18) Creating a strong retirement fund depends on a simple **tactic: stay** calm despite market fluctuations. (Explanation)

19) It did not take long for controversy **to arise: the participants** had simply been masking their irreconcilable differences of opinion. (Explanation)

20) The researchers could not accept **this result: it struck** them as suspiciously predictable. (Explanation)

21) There was, however, one man who had faith in such **nonviolent methods: Henry David Thoreau**. (List of Items)

22) Some visitors may not be sure how to interpret the sculpture in **the courtyard: as a distracting** and regrettable decoration, or as a daring aesthetic statement. (List of Items)

23) Automotive history is a field well **worth studying: it brings** together such diverse disciplines as engineering, cultural history, and economics. (Explanation)

24) It is arguable that these restaurants make most of their profits from **a single item: buffalo wings**. (List of Items)

25) That was the essence of Christopher Hitchens's **style: thorny**, erudite, and brutally honest. (List of Items)

Chapter Two

Combining Sentences: Commas and Transitions

COMBINING SENTENCES: COMMAS AND TRANSITIONS

HOW TO COMBINE TWO SENTENCES

On the SAT, you will frequently encounter questions that require you to combine two sentences using commas and transitions—and that also require you to address a few different criteria simultaneously. You will need to determine the correct transition AND the correct punctuation for such sentences. With these requirements in mind, consider the following example

Professor Sun praised the initiative. Professor Morris had strong reservations.

Professor Sun praised the initiative, although Professor Morris had strong reservations. ✓

Before you combine the sentences, make sure that you perform two steps:

1) PREDICT the needed transition relationship. The sentences above require a contrast (positive to negative), so that a word such as "yet" or "although" will be an appropriate linkage.

2) DETERMINE the proper punctuation. When using commas, always make sure that the comma occurs just BEFORE the transition.

If you do not watch for these two requirements EVERY TIME, you will create sentences that commit clear errors.

Professor Sun praised the initiative, and Professor Morris had strong reservations. ✕ (WRONG TRANSITION)

Professor Sun praised the initiative although, Professor Morris had strong reservations. ✕ (WRONG PUNCTUATION)

In other cases, you will be asked to combine a sentence with a fragment. Questions of this sort can be answered in one of two ways:

1) By treating the fragment as a descriptive phrase, then combining

2) By transforming the fragment into a full clause, then combining

Consider, for instance, the two options for creating an effective single sentence from the sentences and sentence fragments provided below.

The coach overreacted. Canceling the game immediately. ✕

The coach overreacted, canceling the game immediately. (Descriptive Phrase) ✓

OR

The coach overreacted, and he canceled the game immediately. (New Clause) ✓

 Make sure, however, that you do not introduce an illogical transition AFTER correcting the sentence structure properly. For instance, the above combined sentence involves two ideas that are BOTH negative and should be connected by a transition (such as "and") that indicates similarity. Transitions that create fairly good sentence structures, but faulty sentence relationships, must be eliminated.

The coach overreacted, <u>although</u> he canceled the game immediately. ✕

The coach overreacted, <u>and</u> he canceled the game immediately. ✓

NUANCES OF CORRECT PUNCTUATION

 When combining two sentences, always make sure that a comma appears BEFORE the transition into the second sentence. Placing the comma after the transition will create a conjunction that is not clearly connected to any idea, as can be seen in the examples below.

Each lunar vehicle is quite difficult to <u>manufacture yet, each one</u> is also quite sturdy. ✕

Each lunar vehicle is quite difficult to <u>manufacture, yet each one</u> is also quite sturdy. ✓

In some cases, however, you may be required to deal with a different transition error. When you are coordinating transitions, commas and semicolons CANNOT be used interchangeably: a semicolon creates a stronger stop that can eliminate a comma splice, while a comma ALWAYS needs an accompanying transition. Nonetheless, semicolons often will be coupled with accompanying transitions of their own, as in the cases below.

First Clause ➡ Transition ➡ Second Clause

The jurors adjourned for <u>the day; nonetheless, they</u> convened in the parking lot and continued to discuss the case.

First Clause ➡ Transition ➡ Second Clause

Some of these computers have had <u>technical difficulties; fortunately, the flawed</u> devices are now in the process of being recalled and replaced.

To address some of the most common sentence constructions that are based on this structure, just keep in mind the following advice.

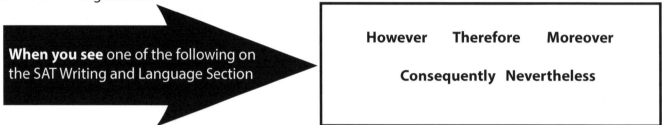

When you see one of the following on the SAT Writing and Language Section

However   Therefore   Moreover

Consequently   Nevertheless

<u>**CHECK to make sure**</u> that the word is preceded by a semicolon if it begins an independent clause.

The grammatically correct progression for sentences such as these will always be the same:

first independent clause ➡ **semicolon** ➡ **second independent clause**

Any deviation will automatically be incorrect; indeed, the transition must always introduce the clause AFTER the semicolon.

Some of these computers have had technical <u>difficulties fortunately, the flawed devices; are</u> now in the process of being recalled and replaced. ✗

Some of these computers have had technical <u>difficulties, fortunately, the flawed devices are</u> now in the process of being recalled and replaced. ✗

Some of these computers have had technical <u>difficulties; fortunately, the flawed devices are</u> now in the process of being recalled and replaced. ✓

EXERCISES: COMMAS AND TRANSITIONS

PART 1: CORRECTING ERRORS

DIRECTIONS: Read the sentence, underline the problematic section or sections, and then correct the sentence as needed.

Example

The rules of the game are quite clear although, some students claimed otherwise.

⬇

The rules of the game are quite **clear, although some** students claimed otherwise.

---

1) The cleaning service began by focusing on rugs and carpets but, now extends to tubs, showers, and bathroom tiles.

CORRECTION: _____

2) These cats are bred to endure cold weather, yet can survive months in sub-arctic temperatures.

CORRECTION: _____

3) Nobody believed the mathematician's explanation yet, nobody defended his theories at the conference.

CORRECTION: _____

4) Critics found the early portion of the opera delightful, however; the second half was a major disappointment.

CORRECTION: _____

5) The theory is plausible, if I am not sure that it can ever be fully validated.

CORRECTION: _____

6) August Wilson is a revered playwright, so; it is natural that several of his dramas have been slated for big-budget film adaptations.

CORRECTION: _____

7) They decided to leave the premises, until their wait had been futile so far.

CORRECTION: _____

8) The governor declared a state of emergency in the flooded regions; in contrast, she exhorted citizens across the state to send food and clothing to the hurricane victims.

CORRECTION: _____

9) Librarians provide valuable services, in large part although these professionals help non-experts to locate resources that might otherwise be overlooked.

CORRECTION: _____

10) As these educators argue, educational methods are shifting; but are not really, being disrupted by the creation of new e-learning platforms.

CORRECTION: _____

PART 2: COMBINING SENTENCES

DIRECTIONS: Read the sentences, determine the proper relationship, and create an effective single sentence using a comma and a transition.

Example

The rules of the game are quite clear. Some students claimed otherwise.

↓

The rules of the game are quite **clear, although some** students claimed otherwise.

---

11) I realize that this is futile. I will still try.

REVISION: _____

12) I finally gave in to her. She was persistent to the point of exasperation.

REVISION: _____

13) She dislikes her co-workers. The young man who works the reception desk is an exception.

REVISION: _____

14) I have time to spare. I will go for a walk.

REVISION: _____

15) I am always willing to help a friend. I draw the line when it comes to money.

REVISION: _____

16) Dr. Flock argued that such practices were currently unpopular. They would continue to decrease in popularity over the coming decades.

REVISION: _____

17) The steamboat reached its destination safely. There had almost been a collision with a small barge during the trip.

REVISION: _____

18) I decided not to return your call yesterday. It was already past 11:00 p.m.

REVISION: _____

19) You should always stand to the side of the elevator door. Don't obstruct those who are exiting and may have urgent business to address.

REVISION: _____

20) We believe Mars was once a wet planet. No supporting evidence has been found.

REVISION: _____

21) Eating peanut butter can help you lose weight. Peanut butter contains less fat than comparable sources of protein.

REVISION: _____

22) Playing shortstop requires outstanding instincts. Playing catcher requires a much keener ability to read the signs and signals given by a pitcher or coach.

REVISION: _____

23) It is too early to declare this squid an endangered species. Recent population statistics have not been verified.

REVISION: _____

24) He excelled as a pianist. He was also remarkably skilled as a violinist.

REVISION: _____

25) The entire royal family had reservations. The king decided to proceed and make the best of the situation.

REVISION: _____

ANSWERS ON THE NEXT PAGE

ANSWERS: COMMAS AND TRANSITIONS

PART 1: CORRECTING ERRORS

PLEASE NOTE THAT THERE MAY BE **MULTIPLE WAYS** TO CORRECT A SINGLE SENTENCE USING THE PRINCIPLES IN THIS CHAPTER.

1) The cleaning service began by focusing on rugs and **carpets, but now extends** to tubs, showers, and bathroom tiles.

2) These cats are bred to endure **cold weather, and can** survive months in sub-arctic temperatures.

3) Nobody believed the mathematician's **explanation, and nobody** defended his theories at the conference.

4) Critics found the early portion of the opera **delightful; however, the second** half was a major disappointment.

5) The theory **is plausible, yet I am** not sure that it can ever be fully validated.

6) August Wilson is a revered **playwright, so it is natural** that several of his dramas have been slated for big-budget film adaptations.

7) They decided to leave **the premises, since their** wait had been futile so far.

8) The governor declared a state of emergency in the **flooded regions; furthermore, she exhorted** citizens across the state to send food and clothing to the hurricane victims.

9) Librarians provide valuable services, **in large part because these** professionals help non-experts to locate resources that might otherwise be overlooked.

10) As these educators argue, educational methods **are shifting, but are not really being** disrupted by the creation of new e-learning platforms.

PART 2: COMBINING SENTENCES

11) I realize that this **is futile, yet I** will still try.

12) I finally gave in **to her, since she** was persistent to the point of exasperation.

13) She dislikes her **co-workers, although the** young man who works the reception desk is an exception.

14) I have time **to spare, so I** will go for a walk.

15) I am always willing to help **a friend, but I** draw the line when it comes to money.

16) Dr. Flock argued that such practices were currently **unpopular, and that they** would continue to decrease in popularity over the coming decades.

17) The steamboat reached its destination **safely, even though there** had almost been a collision with a small barge during the trip.

18) I decided not to return your **call yesterday, since it** was already past 11:00 p.m.

19) You should always stand to the side of the **elevator door, so that you don't** obstruct those who are exiting and may have urgent business to address.

20) We believe Mars was once **a wet planet, yet no supporting** evidence has been found.

21) Eating peanut butter can help you **lose weight, because peanut butter** contains less fat than comparable sources of protein.

22) Playing shortstop requires **outstanding instincts, while playing** catcher requires a much keener ability to read the signs and signals given by a pitcher or coach.

23) It is too early to declare this squid an **endangered species, since recent** population statistics have not been verified.

24) He excelled as **a pianist, and he was** also remarkably skilled as a violinist.

25) The entire royal family **had reservations, yet the king** decided to proceed and make the best of the situation.

Chapter Three

Commas and References

COMMAS AND REFERENCES

ESSENTIAL REFERENCES

Once you have mastered the basic rules of comma placement—using commas to coordinate lists, and avoiding commas that awkwardly separate subjects and verbs—you will need to master a group of more difficult guidelines. Yet all of these guidelines are linked to a core question: when should you use commas to separate nouns from reference phrases, and when SHOULDN'T you? Answering this question will be the purpose of this chapter.

On the SAT, you should watch out especially for nouns linked to reference phrases that begin with one of the following pronoun transitions:

who   **whom**   **which**   **that**

First, consider the cases in which you should NOT separate nouns and the phrases that refer back to them with commas. In these cases, the references are essential to the meaning of the sentence. Consider the following.

The man, who was talking to her, turned out to be her grandfather. ✕

With the exception of the comma placement, the grammar of the sentence is correct. But the phrase between the commas contains information that is essential to the sentence's MAIN TOPIC. Look, for instance, at how the meaning changes if the phrase "who was talking to her" is deleted.

The man, ~~who was talking to her,~~ turned out to be her grandfather. ✕

The man turned out to be her grandfather. ✕

Now, the man cannot be easily identified. Fortunately, this example indicates some of the main rules for when you should NOT use commas to separate a reference from a noun.

1) If the reference contains content that is absolutely necessary to the present MEANING of the sentence

2) If the reference is linked to another portion of the sentence by an extremely obvious contextual or grammatical CLUE

For instance, in the case above, the phrase "who was talking to her" is necessary to the meaning of the sentence, because otherwise the situation is extremely ambiguous. The reference to "her" also links to the later reference to "her grandfather." Thus, rules 1 and 2 are both satisfied.

Keep in mind, however, that some essential references will be much longer but should STILL be linked to the sentence without commas.

There was little that the professor could say to calm the many <u>people who</u> had arrived at his lecture early and were eager to engage him in a heated debate over his recent, controversial remarks. ✓

INESSENTIAL REFERENCES

Nonetheless, there are times when commas ABSOLUTELY should separate references from nouns. The rules for such inessential references are the EXACT OPPOSITES of the rules for essential references.

1) If the reference, though related to the overall topic of the sentence, can be eliminated without significantly changing the MEANING of the central clause in the sentence

2) If the reference does not contain prominent CLUES other than the pronoun ("who, whom, which") that links it to the rest of the sentence

Consider the following example.

There was little interest in trying to reinvent Professor Charlton's device, which had failed safety inspections in the 1980s and had thus lingered in obscurity for many years. ✓

Notice, first, that eliminating the phrase beginning with "which" does NOT significantly change the meaning of the sentence. This portion of the sentence simply introduces a new negative explanation: the overall situation and negative tone have been established and are not in any way compromised. Furthermore, there are no indispensable grammatical references to ANY earlier sentence content (aside, of course, from the word "which"). The phrase is appropriate but not ESSENTIAL, and should thus be set off using commas.

AN IMPORTANT NOTE ON "THAT"

Only in rare cases will the word "that" be accompanied by a comma if it is introducing the kind of reference that we have discussed above. Splitting "that" from earlier content creates a choppy construction that has some of the appearance of a comma splice, since "that" can be the subject of a full sentence. ("That is correct.") Avoid this error almost automatically. Only if there is an intervening phrase does a comma after "that" become needed.

She was <u>convinced, that</u> further reforms would not be necessary. ✗

She was <u>convinced that</u> further reforms would not be necessary. ✓

She was <u>convinced that, in the</u> absence of a truly catastrophic reversal, further reforms would not be necessary. ✓

EXERCISES: Commas and References

Inserting Commas

Directions: Read the sentence and determine whether any commas should be inserted. If so, insert as needed. If not, circle "No Commas Needed."

Example

She was convinced that the game, which originated in the 1800s would not be difficult.

⬇

She was convinced that the game, which originated **in the 1800s, would** not be difficult.

---

1) He began his career by working in the field of comparative literature which was transformed significantly as the 1970s progressed

No Commas Needed

2) The architecture of Frank Lloyd Wright which is a point of pride for many Americans today was in many ways based on a purposeful rejection of industrial styles that had become popular in Europe.

No Commas Needed

3) Among the greatest items of consensus that emerged from the conference was a new sense of resolve in defending the local bison population.

No Commas Needed

4) Few of the people who were waiting for the ferry were interested in purchasing tickets for multiple trips.

No Commas Needed

5) His belief that the parrot would come back if allowed to fly about freely was proven to be based on principles which were completely erroneous.

No Commas Needed

6) A desire for day-to-day independence is one of the two most important psychological premises that experts often put forward to explain why freelance employment is on the rise.

No Commas Needed

7) It was his belief that due to the current rate of technological advancement in the aerospace industry affordable flights to Mars would be viable within 200 years.

No Commas Needed

8) Some of us are convinced that universities have not been aggressive enough in incorporating new works by African authors into core curricula, even though Native American authors are now well-represented.

No Commas Needed

9) These clay pots which were only discovered few years ago resemble Pueblo artifacts that have been in museum collections since the 19th century.

No Commas Needed

10) It was certain according to the new emperor that anybody who saw the opulent parade would be too intimidated to oppose the change of regime.

No Commas Needed

11) All of the employees who are involved in the strike believe that expanding health benefits should be the company's first priority.

No Commas Needed

12) Only Senator Dinton who is more averse to compromise than his peers has declined to endorse the legislation that emerged from the bipartisan committee on television violence.

No Commas Needed

13) Dr. Tsu is best known for advertising a brand of water bottles that originated in his hometown.

No Commas Needed

14) Over the course of several years, students flocked to her private library which was the pride of this small and otherwise little-known college in rural Maryland.

No Commas Needed

15) The preeminent poet of the Harlem Renaissance, Langston Hughes crafted poems which even in the rapidly changing world of today encourage students to think anew about the struggle for racial justice in the United States.

No Commas Needed

16) He asserted, however, that the officials who had created the new system for classifying rare invertebrates had glossed over the inconsistencies which their scheme would inevitably raise.

No Commas Needed

17) The California Condor which was brought back from the brink of extinction in the late 1990s has reclaimed much of its former range in the American West.

No Commas Needed

18) One major marketing asset of these chairs is their use of elegant yet low-cost fabrics which are discussed at length on the company's website.

No Commas Needed

19) It was decided that Tarrytown Village which had been a beloved tourist attraction for almost three generations would stay open every day during the long Thanksgiving weekend.

No Commas Needed

20) The otter is an animal which many people find amusing but which few biologists have studied seriously.

No Commas Needed

21) The man to whom I was speaking was a tour guide at the museum; with his help, I located exactly the gallery that I had been trying to find.

No Commas Needed

22) As most medical historians would readily admit, the breakthroughs which psychiatric medicine has achieved in the past several years would have been unimaginable only a few decades ago.

No Commas Needed

23) An award of some sort was given to each team which competed in the pinewood derby on that memorable Tuesday morning.

No Commas Needed

24) Those two women whose names unfortunately have slipped my mind in the years since were the first to introduce me to the unexpectedly vibrant cuisine of Upstate New York.

No Commas Needed

25) Although James Garfield served as president for a remarkably short time, William Henry Harrison who had served as president decades earlier in fact had the shortest tenure of any American Chief Executive.

No Commas Needed

ANSWERS ON THE NEXT PAGE

ANSWERS: Commas and References

Inserting Commas

1) He began his career by working in the field of comparative **literature, which** was transformed significantly as the 1970s progressed

2) The architecture of Frank Lloyd **Wright, which** is a point of pride for many Americans **today, was** in many ways based on a purposeful rejection of industrial styles that had become popular in Europe.

3) **No Commas Needed**

4) **No Commas Needed**

5) **No Commas Needed**

6) **No Commas Needed**

7) It was his belief **that, due** to the current rate of technological advancement in the aerospace **industry, affordable** flights to Mars would be viable within 200 years.

8) **No Commas Needed**

9) These clay **pots, which** were only discovered few years **ago, resemble** Pueblo artifacts that have been in museum collections since the 19th century.

10) It was **certain, according** to the new **emperor, that** anybody who saw the opulent parade would be too intimidated to oppose the change of regime.

11) **No Commas Needed**

12) Only Senator **Dinton, who** is more averse to compromise than his **peers, has** declined to endorse the legislation that emerged from the bipartisan committee on television violence.

13) **No Commas Needed**

14) Over the course of several years, students flocked to her private **library, which** was the pride of this small and otherwise little-known college in rural Maryland.

15) The preeminent poet of the Harlem Renaissance, Langston Hughes crafted poems **which, even** in the rapidly changing world of **today, encourage** students to think anew about the struggle for racial justice in the United States.

16) **No Commas Needed**

17) The California **Condor, which** was brought back from the brink of extinction in the late **1990s, has** reclaimed much of its former range in the American West.

18) One major marketing asset of these chairs is their use of elegant yet low-cost **fabrics, which** are discussed at length on the company's website.

19) It was decided that Tarrytown **Village, which** had been a beloved tourist attraction for almost three **generations, would** stay open every day during the long Thanksgiving weekend.

20) **No Commas Needed**

21) **No Commas Needed**

22) **No Commas Needed**

23) **No Commas Needed**

24) Those two **women, whose** names unfortunately have slipped my mind in the years **since, were** the first to introduce me to the unexpectedly vibrant cuisine of Upstate New York.

25) Although James Garfield served as president for a remarkably short time, William Henry **Harrison, who** had served as president decades **earlier, in fact** had the shortest tenure of any American Chief Executive.

Chapter Four

Dashes

DASHES

HOW DASHES FUNCTION

On the SAT, you will encounter the unit of punctuation known as a dash (always written as "—") with some frequency. Dashes will typically serve one of two functions:

1) A dash may set aside descriptive or explanatory content, much in the manner of a comma. Often, the content will be too long or involved for effective coordination with commas alone. Two dashes will normally be used in this case.

2) A dash may indicate a sudden shift in the tone or topic of a sentence. A comma can serve a somewhat similar function, but not as effectively, since a comma will create weaker emphasis. One dash will tend to be used in this case.

You have probably noticed that dashes are somewhat similar to commas, regardless of usage. When coordinating ideas, you can return to the rules of effective comma placement; however, it will quickly become clear that comma usage (where dash usage would be more appropriate) will create awkward or confusing constructions.

Consider the use of commas and dashes, respectively, to set aside the descriptive content below.

This miniature <u>tree, which</u> will only grow to eighteen, perhaps nineteen inches when kept indoors in a small <u>bowl, can</u> reach a height of four feet in its natural habitat. ✗

This miniature <u>tree—which</u> will only grow to eighteen, perhaps nineteen inches when kept indoors in a small <u>bowl—can</u> reach a height of four feet in its natural habitat. ✓

As you can see, the dash version is easier to read, process, and understand, while the over-abundance of commas in the comma version is disorienting.

Now, consider the use of dashes and commas to indicate shifts.

He created sculptures of ravishing beauty by utilizing everyday <u>materials, but</u> did anybody notice, or care, before his death? ✗

He created sculptures of ravishing beauty by utilizing everyday <u>materials—but</u> did anybody notice, or care, before his death? ✓

In this case, only the dash version clearly separates the sentence into two distinct segments, one of which is positive, the other of which is negative in tone.

Ensuring Proper Dash Placement

Once you have determined that a sentence needs a dash, you must carefully determine WHERE exactly the dash must be placed. Each type of dash content has its own straightforward rules, which must be carefully observed.

For dashes that set aside descriptive or explanatory content, simply apply the rule familiar from comma usage for interrupting phrases: the sentence MUST make grammatical sense if the portion between the dashes (essentially, the interrupting phrase) is disregarded.

 Return to the example above.

> **This miniature ~~tree—which will only grow to eighteen, perhaps nineteen inches when kept indoors in a small bowl—can~~ reach a height of four feet in its natural habitat.**

> **This miniature tree can reach a height of four feet in its natural habitat.** ✓

This sentence remains coherent and grammatically correct even after the portion between dashes has been removed. Consider, however, that moving a dash even slightly can create an improperly constructed sentence.

> **This miniature tree which ~~will—only grow to eighteen, perhaps nineteen inches when kept indoors in a small bowl—can~~ reach a height of four feet in its natural habitat.**

> **This miniature tree which will can reach a height of four feet in its natural habitat.** ✗

 For a dash that indicates a shift, you must check for two criteria:

> 1) The two portions of the sentence separated by the dash are clearly and distinctly different
>
> 2) One portion (normally the first) is a stand-alone clause

 Consider again the example given above, and look at how it diagrams out using a dash:

He created sculptures of ravishing beauty by utilizing everyday materials Clear Positive

—

but did anybody notice, or care, before his death?   Clear Negative

 However, look at the confusion that results when the tones in the sentence are not separated out in this manner.

He created sculptures of ravishing beauty by utilizing everyday materials, but did anybody notice—or care, before his death?

He created sculptures of ravishing beauty by utilizing everyday materials, but did anybody notice   Some Positive, Some Negative

—

or care, before his death?   Clear Negative

A dash that more clearly calls attention to the two different, separate tones in the sentence avoids such problematic overlap.

ONE FINAL NOTE

Do not always assume that two dashes are used for setting aside a description or an explanation. Sometimes, only one dash is needed if the descriptive or explanatory content occurs at the end of a sentence, as in the sentence below.

Modern furniture stores have recently capitalized on a popular new trend in importing a miniature Japanese <u>tree—which</u> will only grow to eighteen, perhaps nineteen inches when kept indoors in a small bowl.

However, for the sake of clear and effective coordination, SAT Writing sentences will typically use ONLY a single dash to indicate a change in tone.

EXERCISES: Dashes

Part 1: Correcting Errors

Directions: Read the sentence, underline the problematic section or sections, and then correct the sentence as needed.

Example

The rules of the game—which, initially, had seemed quite clear turned out to confuse all involved.

↓

The rules of the game—which, initially, had seemed **quite clear—turned out** to confuse all involved.

---

1) The members of the committee—were in agreement, except, of course, for a few vehement holdouts who were determined to vote in protest of an inevitable policy.

Correction: _____

2) Of the different books in his library—which included large sections devoted to the Middle Ages, the Renaissance, and the early Enlightenment, there were—perhaps only two or three that he truly treasured.

Correction: _____

3) After three straight seasons of stunning losses, the girls hockey team, having enlisted a new coach and under the leadership of two ambitious junior-year captains—finally seemed poised to return to its earlier renown.

Correction: _____

4) The architecture was based—on questionable engineering principles—but the trustees nonetheless expressed complete confidence that the new student center would be a masterpiece.

Correction: _____

5) He spent years struggling to hone his voice, master different inflections, learn the nuances of Verdi's compositions, and finally—concluded that all his opera training had been a complete waste.

Correction: _____

6) Nobody—not the local townspeople, not the scholars at the nearby university, not the visiting journalists could convincingly explain how—the rumors of werewolf sightings first emerged.

CORRECTION: _____

7) Shelley normally needs to wait a long time—every afternoon, at least on those foggy afternoons when visibility near the lighthouse is relatively poor.

CORRECTION: _____

8) Although John Barth often tried to maintain his composure, his disdain for the marks of poor writing—stock characters, creaky plotting—stale metaphors would normally break through even the most polite facade that he could muster.

CORRECTION: _____

9) These coral reefs—the first of their kind to be found growing in the submerged remains of ships—or on any sort of corroded metal surface, will soon be protected by California state law.

CORRECTION: _____

10) Air traffic control may seem like an unexciting profession, that is, if you somehow find high wages—and life-and-death decisions "unexciting."

CORRECTION: _____

PART 2: INSERTING DASHES

DIRECTIONS: Read the sentence and determine whether a dash or dashes should 1) set off explanatory or descriptive content or 2) signal a shift. Then, insert the dash or dashes as needed.

11) For the better part of fifteen years, her company prospered by selling designer-style furniture all designed to channel the latest trends, but crafted from remarkably sturdy and inexpensive materials to families and young homeowners who might not have invested in attractive chairs and couches otherwise.

EXPLANATORY OR DESCRIPTIVE CONTENT / SHIFT IN TONE OR MEANING

12) At the age of 73, he won a lifetime achievement award for his collected symphonies badly belated recognition but recognition nonetheless.

EXPLANATORY OR DESCRIPTIVE CONTENT / SHIFT IN TONE OR MEANING

13) Some readers see the protagonists of Ishiguro's *Never Let Me Go* as emotionally stunted other readers, as sympathetic and vital individuals.

EXPLANATORY OR DESCRIPTIVE CONTENT / SHIFT IN TONE OR MEANING

14) It is hard to see how such claims could be accepted by anybody aside from the most rabid partisans, of course.

EXPLANATORY OR DESCRIPTIVE CONTENT   /   SHIFT IN TONE OR MEANING

15) Georgia O' Keefe's best-known paintings depictions of lush flowers, ominous livestock skulls, and mysterious landscapes can be taken as a private network of symbols and preoccupations, or can simply be enjoyed for their ravishing colors.

EXPLANATORY OR DESCRIPTIVE CONTENT   /   SHIFT IN TONE OR MEANING

16) In an attempt to compete with word processing programs such as Google docs and Microsoft Word, Apple has begun including Pages an app that creates basic text documents, and that utilizes Apple's famously minimalistic design language on every Apple personal computer that is sold.

EXPLANATORY OR DESCRIPTIVE CONTENT   /   SHIFT IN TONE OR MEANING

17) I have spent years studying Mary Wollstonecraft's writings, years more tracking down her letters, reading biographies of her contemporaries but does any non-expert really care?

EXPLANATORY OR DESCRIPTIVE CONTENT   /   SHIFT IN TONE OR MEANING

18) These pictures of cats every cat you can think of, from majestic Maine Coons to sinuous Siamese cats, to endearing tuxedo cats and tabbies are much richer in aesthetic value than a casual viewer might expect.

EXPLANATORY OR DESCRIPTIVE CONTENT   /   SHIFT IN TONE OR MEANING

19) The market for English as a Second Language courses is growing rapidly not rapidly enough, though, to be truly profitable just yet.

EXPLANATORY OR DESCRIPTIVE CONTENT   /   SHIFT IN TONE OR MEANING

20) Almost every prospective investor declined to buy into the company, laughing off its product as ridiculous and then looking on in disbelief as the firm's value quadrupled in the space of a few months.

EXPLANATORY OR DESCRIPTIVE CONTENT   /   SHIFT IN TONE OR MEANING

21) He's a cantankerous yet genuinely talented composer in short, anything but a small-minded egomaniac.

EXPLANATORY OR DESCRIPTIVE CONTENT   /   SHIFT IN TONE OR MEANING

22) Students were advised to use three readily-distinguished colors red, yellow, and green as preferred by the instructor.

EXPLANATORY OR DESCRIPTIVE CONTENT   /   SHIFT IN TONE OR MEANING

23) When Bob Dylan won the Nobel Prize, some critics particularly those who had for many years advocated the work of celebrated elder novelists such as Philip Roth and Joyce Carol Oates penned editorials critical of the Nobel Committee's choice.

EXPLANATORY OR DESCRIPTIVE CONTENT   /   SHIFT IN TONE OR MEANING

24) The United States is apparently not ready to elect a president committed to raising taxes as a central policy at least not yet.

EXPLANATORY OR DESCRIPTIVE CONTENT   /   SHIFT IN TONE OR MEANING

25) Modern menswear is indebted to Beau Brummell, an English man-about-town who in the course of accumulating a large social circle and running up daunting debts developed the progenitor of today's two-piece suit.

EXPLANATORY OR DESCRIPTIVE CONTENT   /   SHIFT IN TONE OR MEANING

ANSWERS ON THE NEXT PAGE

ANSWERS: Dashes

Part 1: Correcting Errors

1) The members of the committee were in **agreement—except**, of course, for a few vehement holdouts who were determined to vote in protest of an inevitable policy.

2) Of the different books in his **library—which** included large sections devoted to the Middle Ages, the Renaissance, and the early **Enlightenment—there** were perhaps only two or three that he truly treasured.

3) After three straight seasons of stunning losses, the girls **hockey team—having enlisted** a new coach and under the leadership of two ambitious junior-year **captains—finally seemed** poised to return to its earlier renown.

4) The architecture was based on questionable engineering **principles—but** the trustees nonetheless expressed complete confidence that the new student center would be a masterpiece.

5) He spent years struggling to hone his voice, master different inflections, learn the nuances of Verdi's **compositions—and finally** concluded that all his opera training had been a complete waste.

6) **Nobody—not** the local townspeople, not the scholars at the nearby university, not the visiting **journalists—could** convincingly explain how the rumors of werewolf sightings first emerged.

7) Shelley normally needs to wait a long time **every afternoon—at least** on those foggy afternoons when visibility near the lighthouse is relatively poor.

8) Although John Barth often tried to maintain his composure, his disdain for the marks of **poor writing— stock characters**, creaky plotting, **stale metaphors—would normally** break through even the most polite facade that he could muster.

9) These **coral reefs—the first** of their kind to be found growing in the submerged remains of ships, or on any sort of corroded **metal surface—will soon** be protected by California state law.

10) Air traffic control may seem like an **unexciting profession—that is**, if you somehow find high wages and life-and-death decisions "unexciting."

PART 2: INSERTING DASHES

11) For the better part of fifteen years, her company prospered by selling designer-style **furniture—all** designed to channel the latest trends, but crafted from remarkably sturdy and **inexpensive materials—to families** and young homeowners who might not have invested in attractive chairs and couches otherwise.

EXPLANATORY OR DESCRIPTIVE CONTENT

12) At the age of 73, he won a lifetime achievement award for his **collected symphonies—badly belated** recognition but recognition nonetheless.

SHIFT IN TONE OR MEANING

13) Some readers see the protagonists of Ishiguro's *Never Let Me Go* as **emotionally stunted—other readers**, as sympathetic and vital individuals.

SHIFT IN TONE OR MEANING

14) It is hard to see how such claims could be accepted by **anybody—aside** from the most rabid partisans, of course.

SHIFT IN TONE OR MEANING

15) Georgia O' Keefe's best-known **paintings—depictions** of lush flowers, ominous livestock skulls, and mysterious **landscapes—can be** taken as a private network of symbols and preoccupations, or can simply be enjoyed for their ravishing colors.

EXPLANATORY OR DESCRIPTIVE CONTENT

16) In an attempt to compete with word processing programs such as Google docs and Microsoft Word, Apple has begun including **Pages—an app** that creates basic text documents, and that utilizes Apple's famously minimalistic **design language—on every** Apple personal computer that is sold.

EXPLANATORY OR DESCRIPTIVE CONTENT

17) I have spent years studying Mary Wollstonecraft's writings, years more tracking down her letters, reading biographies of **her contemporaries—but does** any non-expert really care?

SHIFT IN TONE OR MEANING

18) These pictures **of cats—every cat** you can think of, from majestic Maine Coons to sinuous Siamese cats, to endearing tuxedo cats **and tabbies—are much** richer in aesthetic value than a casual viewer might expect.

EXPLANATORY OR DESCRIPTIVE CONTENT

19) The market for English as a Second Language courses is **growing rapidly—not rapidly** enough, though, to be truly profitable just yet.

SHIFT IN TONE OR MEANING

20) Almost every prospective investor declined to buy into the company, laughing off its product as **ridiculous—and then** looking on in disbelief as the firm's value quadrupled in the space of a few months.

SHIFT IN TONE OR MEANING

21) He's a cantankerous yet genuinely **talented composer—in short**, anything but a small-minded egomaniac.

SHIFT IN TONE OR MEANING

22) Students were advised to use three readily-distinguished **colors—red**, yellow, and green as preferred by the instructor.

EXPLANATORY OR DESCRIPTIVE CONTENT

23) When Bob Dylan won the Nobel Prize, **some critics—particularly those** who had for many years advocated the work of celebrated elder novelists such as Philip Roth and **Joyce Carol Oates—penned editorials** critical of the Nobel Committee's choice.

EXPLANATORY OR DESCRIPTIVE CONTENT

24) The United States is apparently not ready to elect a president committed to raising taxes as a **central policy—at least** not yet.

SHIFT IN TONE OR MEANING

25) Modern menswear is indebted to Beau Brummell, an English man-about-town **who—in the** course of accumulating a large social circle and running up **daunting debts—developed** the progenitor of today's two-piece suit.

EXPLANATORY OR DESCRIPTIVE CONTENT

Chapter Five
Parentheses

PARENTHESES

PARENTHESES FOR EXPLAINING IDEAS

Often, writers use parentheses to coordinate information about specific words (most often nouns). This information can include definitions, qualifications, and helpful examples. Although such information is important, it may be too detailed or involved to organize using commas. Parentheses, which can more clearly offset a portion of a sentence, here become valuable.

 In cases that involve parentheses for explaining ideas, the statement in parentheses MUST refer to a specific noun in the sentence, as in the following example.

IDEA  EXPLANATION

Tuberculosis (a disease of the lung) is expected to be eradicated by 2020.

The phrase "a disease of the lung" directly refers to "Tuberculosis". The sentence thus follows proper rules for coordinating nouns and references.

A sentence that uses a parenthetical phrase must also be grammatically correct WITHOUT the parenthetical phrase. Block out or temporarily disregard the information in parentheses, then check for grammar. In the case below, the grammar clearly falls apart.

Tuberculosis ~~(a disease of the lung is expected)~~ to be eradicated by 2020.

Tuberculosis to be eradicated by 2020. ✗

 However, the correct placement of parentheses will result in excellent grammar once any parenthetical phrases have been eliminated, as demonstrated below.

Tuberculosis ~~(a disease of the lung)~~ is expected to be eradicated by 2020.

Tuberculosis is expected to be eradicated by 2020. ✓

Parentheses for Secondary Information

Sometimes, a writer will use parentheses to designate information that is related to the topic of the sentence, but does NOT clearly refer to a single word or noun. This secondary information will normally be introduced by a transition, as in the example below.

> **It is important for a juror to remain detached (since emotional involvement blurs reality) when deciding the outcome of a trial.**

Keep in mind that the phrase in parentheses does not actually define a "juror"; instead, it states a condition.

Note, however, that using commas to offset this information would create a sentence structure that (though somewhat acceptable in grammatical terms) is stylistically awkward and confusing.

> **It is important for a juror to remain detached, since emotional involvement blurs reality, when deciding the outcome of a trial.** ✕

The parentheses make such secondary phrases easier to coordinate. As always, though, make sure that the sentence is grammatically correct WITHOUT the information in parentheses.

> **It is important for a juror to remain detached ~~(since emotional involvement blurs reality)~~ when deciding the outcome of a trial.**

> **It is important for a juror to remain detached when deciding the outcome of a trial.** ✓

EXERCISES: PARENTHESES

CREATING THE BEST PLACEMENT

DIRECTIONS: Read the sentence and determine which section or sections should be set off using parentheses. Each sentence will involve AT LEAST ONE parenthetical phrase. You should also provide any other coordinating punctuation that the sentence requires.

Example

The rules of the game thanks to a misprint in the directions confused all involved.

⬇

The rules of the **game (thanks to a misprint in the directions) confused** all involved.

---

1) The police officer who shot Mr. Jones in an incident that still defies consensus was charged with manslaughter.

NOTES: _____

2) The right-on-red rule allowed everywhere except in Manhattan stipulates that a driver must make a complete stop before turning.

NOTES: _____

3) My sister called out of the blue to my great surprise, naturally and asked me to lend her some money.

NOTES: _____

4) Barack Obama is the first U.S. president if you don't count Jimmy Carter, who was no longer acting president when he traveled to Havana in 1996 to visit Cuba in fifty years.

NOTES: _____

5) In the game of Poker, a player must ante bet before he receives his hand set of cards.

NOTES: _____

6) They decided to wait at first yet were forced due to the length of David's absence and the cost of inaction to begin the vote without all board members present.

NOTES: _____

7) The College Board has eliminated all vocabulary that it considers obsolete words, for example, like "extemporaneous" and "serendipitous" from the SAT.

NOTES: _____

8) Weather forecasters now believe that barring any unforeseen circumstances the snowstorms will only increase in severity in the course of the next five to seven years.

NOTES: _____

9) Dr. Hsu feared controversy and who indeed wouldn't? under the circumstances.

NOTES: _____

10) The nocturnal tapir has a nose that is prehensile or that is capable of moving and curling freely, much like an elephant's trunk or a monkey's tail.

NOTES: _____

11) Most residents of New Jersey are incensed about the newly-instituted gas tax, which as nobody seems to realize is nonetheless the only way to fix the state's infrastructure problems.

NOTES: _____

12) Of course Adobe's products InDesign, Acrobat, and Photoshop among them are popular: they are both affordable and for professional graphic designers and design hobbyists alike essential.

NOTES: _____

13) Nobody no, not even the University of Colorado researchers can explain the origins of these wildcats.

NOTES: _____

14) This new pilot training program was seen as a major success at least until some South Korean journalists, indeed, voiced dissenting opinions.

NOTES: _____

15) Today, Marie Curie is best remembered for her role in the discovery of two elements polonium and radium and for her efforts to combat cancer.

NOTES: _____

16) Of course, museum visitors may find these photographs which also feature rabbits, cats, and chimpanzees in elaborate costumes to be a poor investment.

NOTES: _____

17) In the sentence "red is the color of fury," "red" usually an adjective, as in "my red car" is a noun.

NOTES: _____

18) Despite or perhaps because of the lack of information, readers are often eager to form their own ideas about Emily Dickinson's political beliefs.

NOTES: _____

19) People are likely to believe even an outrageous marketing claim until, of course, they don't.

NOTES: _____

20) Corporations especially pharmaceutical companies, seeking reputable endorsements for their products, will often pay universities which need the money to perform research on the benefits of such products.

NOTES: _____

21) The creation of such exquisite tapestries was a painstaking process, one that could require a single weaver by the estimates of some scholars to spend months creating but a few square feet of the image.

NOTES: _____

22) A man is relentlessly hunted down by his *doppelganger* "double" in Edgar Allan Poe's famous short story "William Wilson."

NOTES: _____

23) Adored by her contemporaries but adored even more by posterity, Josephine Baker is an icon of the performing arts.

NOTES: _____

24) We strive for a place somewhere between expression necessary for personal growth and stoicism necessary for character development.

NOTES: _____

25) "Gloaming" a word which means dusk was completely unfamiliar to the class, as were the words "neophyte" a beginner and "virago" a disagreeable woman.

NOTES: _____

ANSWERS ON THE NEXT PAGE

ANSWERS: Parentheses Use

CREATING THE BEST PLACEMENT

1) The police officer who shot Mr. Jones **(in an incident that still defies consensus)** was charged with manslaughter.

2) The right-on-red rule **(allowed everywhere except in Manhattan)** stipulates that a driver must make a complete stop before turning.

3) My sister called out of the blue **(to my great surprise, naturally)** and asked me to lend her some money.

4) Barack Obama is the first U.S. president **(if you don't count Jimmy Carter, who was no longer acting president when he traveled to Havana in 1996)** to visit Cuba in fifty years.

5) In the game of Poker, a player must ante **(bet)** before he receives his hand **(set of cards)**.

6) They decided to wait at first yet were forced **(due to the length of David's absence and the cost of inaction)** to begin the vote without all board members present.

7) The College Board has eliminated all vocabulary that it considers obsolete **(words, for example, like "extemporaneous" and "serendipitous")** from the SAT.

8) Weather forecasters now believe that **(barring any unforeseen circumstances)** the snowstorms will only increase in severity in the course of the next five to seven years.

9) Dr. Hsu feared controversy **(and who indeed wouldn't?)** under the circumstances.

10) The nocturnal tapir has a nose that is prehensile **(or that is capable of moving and curling freely, much like an elephant's trunk or a monkey's tail)**.

11) Most residents of New Jersey are incensed about the newly-instituted gas tax, which **(as nobody seems to realize)** is nonetheless the only way to fix the state's infrastructure problems.

12) Of course Adobe's products **(InDesign, Acrobat, and Photoshop among them)** are popular: they are both affordable and **(for professional graphic designers and design hobbyists alike)** essential.

13) Nobody **(no, not even the University of Colorado researchers)** can explain the origins of these wildcats.

14) This new pilot training program was seen as a major success **(at least until some South Korean journalists, indeed, voiced dissenting opinions)**.

15) Today, Marie Curie is best remembered for her role in the discovery of two elements **(polonium and radium)** and for her efforts to combat cancer.

16) Of course, museum visitors may find these photographs **(which also feature rabbits, cats, and chimpanzees in elaborate costumes)** to be a poor investment.

17) In the sentence "red is the color of fury," "red" **(usually an adjective, as in "my red car")** is a noun.

18) Despite **(or perhaps because of)** the lack of information, readers are often eager to form their own ideas about Emily Dickinson's political beliefs.

19) People are likely to believe even an outrageous marketing claim **(until, of course, they don't)**.

20) Corporations **(especially pharmaceutical companies)**, seeking reputable endorsements for their products, will often pay universities **(which need the money)** to perform research on the benefits of such products.

21) The creation of such exquisite tapestries was a painstaking process, one that could require a single weaver **(by the estimates of some scholars)** to spend months creating but a few square feet of the image.

22) A man is relentlessly hunted down by his *doppelganger* **("double")** in Edgar Allan Poe's famous short story "William Wilson."

23) Adored by her contemporaries **(but adored even more by posterity)**, Josephine Baker is an icon of the performing arts.

24) We strive for a place somewhere between expression **(necessary for personal growth)** and stoicism **(necessary for character development)**.

25) "Gloaming" **(a word which means dusk)** was completely unfamiliar to the class, as were the words "neophyte" **(a beginner)** and "virago" **(a disagreeable woman)**.

Chapter Six

Difficult Transitions

DIFFICULT TRANSITIONS

UNDERSTANDING TRANSITION ERRORS

Some of the most challenging transition questions on the SAT require only a few steps; though fairly concise, these questions are especially demanding because they require outstanding logic and attention to detail if you are to address them successfully. For instance, see if you can detect what is wrong with the following sentence.

> **Ms. Amador argued that the parking area should be expanded to invite and encourage local commerce. Likewise, Ms. Clay argued that the larger parking area would simply alienate local residents by disrupting the picturesque appearance of the downtown area.**

The problem is the transition "Likewise". Although both women are making arguments, they are arguing for fundamentally DIFFERENT positions; "Likewise" would only be appropriate if the women were on the same side. A proper transition should call attention to the overall logic of the sentence in a much more accurate manner.

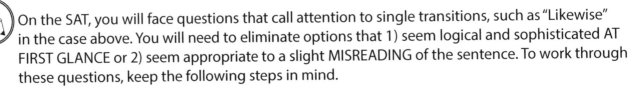 On the SAT, you will face questions that call attention to single transitions, such as "Likewise" in the case above. You will need to eliminate options that 1) seem logical and sophisticated AT FIRST GLANCE or 2) seem appropriate to a slight MISREADING of the sentence. To work through these questions, keep the following steps in mind.

1) Read the sentences carefully, and temporarily disregard the provided transitions

2) Determine the major relationship between the sentences

3) Determine any minor and possibly FALSE relationships between the sentences

4) Provide a transition of your own based on the major relationship

5) Consult the answers; use the FALSE relationships for process of elimination and the major relationship to validate your choice.

Most importantly, NEVER allow yourself to pick an answer based on wording that "sounds good." The example above is open to this error: "Likewise" is a seemingly sophisticated transition that fits a misreading, but is not the BEST PREDICTED answer by any means.

TRANSITIONS AND STANDARD PHRASES

For complete mastery of SAT sentence transitions, you will need to consider a second broad group of errors: problems with transitions known as "standard phrases." Below are a few examples of standard phrases that you have probably encountered in more preliminary SAT prep:

"Either . . . or"   **"Both . . . and"**

"Neither . . . nor"   **"Not only . . . but also"**

Such standard phrases effectively pair off specific ideas, as the sentences below demonstrate.

> **The allegations were <u>not only shocking</u> to the candidate <u>but also humiliating</u> to his supporters.**

> **<u>Neither the head</u> of the research team <u>nor his immediate subordinate</u> wanted to take complete credit for the discovery.**

In these cases, it is easy to see how a standard phrase pairs two descriptions ("shocking . . . humiliating") or two nouns ("head . . . subordinate"). More difficult standard phrase transitions will involve pairings of ideas, often with interrupting phrases and more difficult sentence relationships. For instance, see if you notice what is wrong with the following sentence.

> **In assessing the results of such surveys, researchers have determined that students prefer the later-in-the-day class times introduced by the Iowa district against the earlier-in-the-day times that prevail in much of the Great Lakes region.** ✕

The error DOES involve a standard phrase: "prefer . . . against" is an incorrect version of "prefer . . . to". However, the phrase is hard to detect for two reasons.

1) The standard phrase is less noticeable than a basic standard phrase such as "either . . . or"

2) The standard phrase appears to fit the OVERALL relationship described in the sentence, even though the SPECIFIC wording is completely incorrect

Dealing with such standard phrase errors requires heightened attention to detail, along with a new strategy. When you are figuring out a sentence relationship, ALWAYS determine whether you are dealing with a transition that involves TWO PARTS. If so, check for tricky standard phrases such as the following:

"as much . . . as"   **"just as . . . as"**   **"more a . . . than a"**

"so . . . that"   **"prioritized . . . over"**

As you complete SAT sections (or simply work through independent reading) add more standard phrases of your own. You will find that some standard phrases are similar in meaning: the pairing "preferred . . . to" and "prioritized . . . over" is but one example.

IMPORTANT TIP

Keep in mind that the overall meaning in a sentence may seem intact, but that the STANDARD PHRASING may still be INCORRECT.

EXERCISES: DIFFICULT TRANSITIONS

PART 1: CORRECTING ERRORS

DIRECTIONS: Read the sentence or sentences, determine the proper relationship, and then correct the sentence or sentences as needed. Please keep in mind that transition choices may vary, but should reflect the same general relationship.

Example

The game pleased most of the class, and Susan did not enjoy this diversion.

↓

The game pleased most of the **class, but Susan** did not enjoy this diversion.

---

1) Despite the many difficulties that they knew they would face, the explorers decided that they would not rest while they had traveled at least five more miles.

CORRECTION: _____

2) I decided, at a relatively young age, that I would begin collecting stamps. Paradoxically, my brother created a coin collection when he was in grammar school and continued to pursue this passion as an adult.

CORRECTION: _____

3) It was agreed that further inquiries would be undertaken only if absolutely necessary. The sensitive nature of this work had, however, made the researchers wary of drawing public attention to their enterprise.

CORRECTION: _____

4) The work of Agnes Martin differs in a variety of aesthetic and affective respects from the compositions of even her most famous contemporaries; likewise, while genuine "minimalistic" artists limited themselves to industrial colors, Martin delved into the possibilities presented by luminous pastels.

CORRECTION: _____

5) He argued that an entirely new program for creating spreadsheets would be necessary. Nonetheless, it would be absolutely essential to disregard the most widely-accepted public presentation software and devise a completely new platform.

CORRECTION: _____

6) The feral raccoon population near the abandoned buildings only continued to grow, posing a more and more serious threat to public health; the town council, surprisingly, decided to bring in pest control specialists from a larger, neighboring municipality to begin devising a solution.

CORRECTION: _____

7) These microorganisms can break down some of the rarest metal alloys, and are somehow incapable of breaking down an especially common industrial metal: steel.

CORRECTION: _____

8) Perhaps no one community exerted as great an indirect influence on the creation of nineteenth-century sign fonts except a small village located several miles from Frankfurt.

CORRECTION: _____

9) The new music subscription service was limited to the Pacific Northwest, was run by a novice entrepreneur, and faced significant funding difficulties during its first two years. For instance, it grew rapidly, and soon boasted a stable of promising young artists.

CORRECTION: _____

10) Saving this capybara population is such a priority for environmentalists of all leanings as a series of video conferences was recently held, bringing together experts from across three continents.

CORRECTION: _____

PART 2: IDENTIFYING THE CORRECT TRANSITION

DIRECTIONS: Read the sentence or sentences, determine the proper sentence relationship, and choose a transition that is logically appropriate. Please keep in mind that transition choices may vary, but should reflect the same general relationship.

11) Cindy's mature style of sculpture was the product of a painstaking process of creative evolution. _____ , she began experimenting with industrial metals and slowly adapted her earlier, miniaturistic manner of working to large commissions.

12) _____ he inspired confidence in the other miners, he nonetheless led his stalwart companions into a series of difficulties that nearly brought about their demise.

13) Among the architects who most admired Louis Sullivan was Frank Furness, who shared Sullivan's taste for ornate decoration. _____ , Furness was also interested in structural innovations, while Sullivan's buildings were mostly rectangular and, thus, mostly conservative in layout.

14) Many people mistakenly assume that tea originated in England, which is indeed famous for its citizens' consumption of the beverage. _____ , tea originated in China, and was imported into Europe during centuries of exploration.

15) There are thousands of different fonts available on most graphic design programs, and skilled typographers can see the small distinctions between these fonts. _____ , most non-specialists think of fonts in terms of two simple categories: serif and sans-serif.

16) It is true that some of these measures are ethically suspect. Yet supermarkets that do not embrace such marketing tactics, _____ , may be doomed to failure in today's competitive world of commerce.

17) It may seem unlikely that two major American artists would form a harmonious student-and-mentor relationship. _____ , Edward Hopper and Robert Henri worked in a collaborative manner, with Hopper absorbing insight after insight from the older painter.

18) Newly-opened cafés often find themselves obligated to focus on serving beverages and light snacks instead of serving a full menu of warm meals. This choice, _____ necessary, can make it difficult for a new café to earn the ready loyalty of customers who are eager to settle in for gourmet dinners.

19) Captain Linnaeus Tripe created remarkable black-and-white photographs of temples in India and Southeast Asia. _____ , museum-goers today are astonished by the command of atmosphere and shadow that these photographs evince.

20) The foundation has decided to bolster its efforts to raise money for science scholarships for young women, _____ it is becoming clear that gender discrimination needs to be more aggressively confronted in disciplines such as biology and engineering.

21) In his novels, Sherman Alexie depicts the enduring power of Native American tradition in a confusing modern world. _____ , Leslie Marmon Silko has written about characters who find tribal tradition a healing and therapeutic influence, even in the face of twentieth-century forms of cultural disorientation.

22) _____ she is perhaps best known as the love interest of master singer and songwriter John Lennon, Yoko Ono was an original and daring artist in her own right.

23) Sea cucumbers may be capable of surviving in extreme environments, but they can be easily injured by human touch; _____ , visitors to the aquarium are advised to be especially gentle if they are ever given the privilege of handling a sea cucumber.

24) Some college graduates find freelance employment such an isolating and potentially disheartening experience _____ they have begun banding together in shared workspaces.

25) A breathing exercise of this sort is designed _____ a means of calming the nerves than as a means of imparting any measurable health benefits in terms of digestion or respiration.

ANSWERS ON THE NEXT PAGE

ANSWERS: DIFFICULT TRANSITIONS

PART 1: CORRECTING ERRORS (ANSWERS MAY VARY.)

1) Despite the many difficulties that they knew they would face, the explorers decided that they would not rest **until** they had traveled at least five more miles.

2) I decided, at a relatively young age, that I would begin collecting stamps. **Similarly**, my brother created a coin collection when he was in grammar school and continued to pursue this passion as an adult.

3) It was agreed that further inquiries would be undertaken only if absolutely necessary. The sensitive nature of this work had, **indeed**, made the researchers wary of drawing public attention to their enterprise.

4) The work of Agnes Martin differs in a variety of aesthetic and affective respects from the compositions of even her most famous contemporaries; **in particular**, while genuine "minimalistic" artists limited themselves to industrial colors, Martin delved into the possibilities presented by luminous pastels.

5) He argued that an entirely new program for creating spreadsheets would be necessary. **Moreover**, it would be absolutely essential to disregard the most widely-accepted public presentation software and devise a completely new platform.

6) The feral raccoon population near the abandoned buildings only continued to grow, posing a more and more serious threat to public health; the town council, **consequently**, decided to bring in pest control specialists from a larger, neighboring municipality to begin devising a solution.

7) These microorganisms can break down some of the rarest metal alloys, **yet** are somehow incapable of breaking down an especially common industrial metal: steel.

8) Perhaps no one community exerted as great an indirect influence on the creation of nineteenth-century sign fonts **as did** a small village located several miles from Frankfurt.

9) The new music subscription service was limited to the Pacific Northwest, was run by a novice entrepreneur, and faced significant funding difficulties during its first two years. **Nonetheless**, it grew rapidly, and soon boasted a stable of promising young artists.

10) Saving this capybara population is such a priority for environmentalists of all leanings **that** a series of video conferences was recently held, bringing together experts from across three continents.

Part 2: Identifying the Correct Transition (Answers may vary.)

11) Cindy's mature style of sculpture was the product of a painstaking process of creative evolution. **Gradually**, she began experimenting with industrial metals and slowly adapted her earlier, miniaturistic manner of working to large commissions.

12) **Although** he inspired confidence in the other miners, he nonetheless led his stalwart companions into a series of difficulties that nearly brought about their demise.

13) Among the architects who most admired Louis Sullivan was Frank Furness, who shared Sullivan's taste for ornate decoration. **However**, Furness was also interested in structural innovations, while Sullivan's buildings were mostly rectangular and, thus, mostly conservative in layout.

14) Many people mistakenly assume that tea originated in England, which is indeed famous for its citizens' consumption of the beverage. **Actually**, tea originated in China, and was imported into Europe during centuries of exploration.

15) There are thousands of different fonts available on most graphic design programs, and skilled typographers can see the small distinctions between these fonts. **Nonetheless**, most non-specialists think of fonts in terms of two simple categories: serif and sans-serif.

16) It is true that some of these measures are ethically suspect. Yet supermarkets that do not embrace such marketing tactics, **unfortunately**, may be doomed to failure in today's competitive world of commerce.

17) It may seem unlikely that two major American artists would form a harmonious student-and-mentor relationship. **However**, Edward Hopper and Robert Henri worked in a collaborative manner, with Hopper absorbing insight after insight from the older painter.

18) Newly-opened cafés often find themselves obligated to focus on serving beverages and light snacks instead of serving a full menu of warm meals. This choice, **though** necessary, can make it difficult for a new café to earn the ready loyalty of customers who are eager to settle in for gourmet dinners.

19) Captain Linnaeus Tripe created remarkable black-and-white photographs of temples in India and Southeast Asia. **Indeed**, museum-goers today are astonished by the command of atmosphere and shadow that these photographs evince.

20) The foundation has decided to bolster its efforts to raise money for science scholarships for young women, **since** it is becoming clear that gender discrimination needs to be more aggressively confronted in disciplines such as biology and engineering.

21) In his novels, Sherman Alexie depicts the enduring power of Native American tradition in a confusing modern world. **Likewise**, Leslie Marmon Silko has written about characters who find tribal tradition a healing and therapeutic influence, even in the face of twentieth-century forms of cultural disorientation.

22) **Although** she is perhaps best known as the love interest of master singer and songwriter John Lennon, Yoko Ono was an original and daring artist in her own right.

23) Sea cucumbers may be capable of surviving in extreme environments, but they can be easily injured by human touch; **consequently**, visitors to the aquarium are advised to be especially gentle if they are ever given the privilege of handling a sea cucumber.

24) Some college graduates find freelance employment such an isolating and potentially disheartening experience **that** they have begun banding together in shared workspaces.

25) A breathing exercise of this sort is designed **more as** a means of calming the nerves than as a means of imparting any measurable health benefits in terms of digestion or respiration.

Chapter Seven

Review: Wording and Punctuation

REVIEW: PUNCTUATION ERRORS

DIRECTIONS: Read the sentence and determine how to improve it by inserting new punctuation. If necessary, delete any incorrect punctuation.

Please note that there will only be ONE error in any given sentence.

Example

The rules of the game are quite clear although, some students claimed otherwise.

⬇

The rules of the game are quite **clear, although some** students claimed otherwise.

---

1) The creators of the statistical model were forced to face a difficult truth, that few of their main assumptions about the composition of the voting public were in any way accurate.

NOTES: _____

2) To create an effective college application essay, you need to use a fairly traditional structure—strong hook, lucid body paragraphs, and a single unifying theme and simultaneously demonstrate your ability to craft a compelling, revealing narrative.

NOTES: _____

3) Each member of the hockey team practiced relentlessly; each of those young women believed that her efforts would help build a victorious season only to see those hopes crushed by an unbroken series of defeats.

NOTES: _____

4) Although marine life flourished in the prehistoric era, paleontologists and laypersons alike remain most captivated by two massive aquatic animals the ichthyosaur and the plesiosaur.

NOTES: _____

5) There is actually a good reason for the "timid" corporate strategy that Gilead Sciences is following, the company would rather bide its time and spend its resources wisely than make a hasty, unwise acquisition.

NOTES: _____

6) As drawn by cartoonists, the original versions of some corporate mascots including Ronald McDonald, Mr. Peanut, and the Goodyear Tire Man—feature photo-realistic textures that have disappeared from more recent incarnations of these characters.

NOTES: _____

7) Kleptocracy a word that means ("government by those who steal") is a concept that Professor Hulton has explored in her recent articles on police states and black markets.

NOTES: _____

8) This company is a leader in a branch of the technology industry which is called Software as a Service, SaaS for short, and which has grown dramatically in the past five years.

NOTES: _____

9) John Cheever was a man of contradictions, although he was an author capable of projecting profound optimism and resounding appreciation for natural beauty, he spent much of his life struggling with a variety of personal demons.

NOTES: _____

10) I had been spending the better part of two months trying, in vain, to think of new employment options when suddenly a brilliant idea popped into my head.

NOTES: _____

11) She was universally esteemed for her business acumen; though her abrasive political opinions garnered a very different reception.

NOTES: _____

12) This fifth-grade class learned about basic economic principles by creating its own rudimentary system of currency: under this scheme, a red button re-named a "rutton" for convenience was worth twice as much as a blue button (re-named a "blutton").

NOTES: _____

13) These rock formations were shaped by wind eroding away small deposits, of sediment in a process that took thousands of years.

NOTES: _____

14) After much rumination, Socrates discovered a line of argument that foiled his harshest accusers death, in the opinion of Socrates himself, would be superior to exile from Athens.

NOTES: _____

15) In the 1950s, a young boy named Rennie Drew became a local celebrity for creating an abstract painting: reminiscent of the work of Jackson Pollock.

NOTES: _____

16) The members of the expedition were convinced that further efforts would be fatal, the available water supplies, after all, were running perilously low.

NOTES: _____

17) A 3D printer is a device that can generate a variety of different, practically important precision objects from computer images, prosthetic limbs, topographic models, and mock-ups of industrial designs.

NOTES: _____

18) There was some dispute, among the senior management about which social media platform would be best for publicizing the new product line.

NOTES: _____

19) A high school drama teacher who expects students to perform *The Threepenny Opera* or any work by Bertolt Brecht, for that matter automatically does those students an immense disservice.

NOTES: _____

20) I find it difficult to believe that her dance company, which excelled in conservative yet elegant ballet for the better part of two decades would perform the work of an unproven, upstart choreographer unless somehow pressured.

NOTES: _____

21) For years, he taught brief elective seminars on the science behind everyday phenomena; how leaves change color, for instance, or why people crave specific types of food.

NOTES: _____

22) This management textbook which is by no means the first of its kind, has been praised for how well it works in tandem with an online database that the publishers have made available to students.

NOTES: _____

23) Though some may find "dressage" (a sport in which a horse performs complicated movements under the guidance) of a trainer borderline ridiculous, dressage competitions are in fact gaining both popularity and prestige.

NOTES: _____

24) It would be surprising but, of course, by no means unbelievable for any of the specialists who so harshly criticized Dr. Hawker to ultimately wind up working with the Hawker Foundation.

NOTES: _____

25) Before they were introduced into human diets by George Washington Carver, peanuts were popular as feed for one type of animal the hog.

NOTES: _____

REVIEW: WORDING AND PHRASING ERRORS

DIRECTIONS: Read the sentence or sentences and underline the error in phrasing or wording. Then, write the word or phrase that would make the content logically and grammatically correct.

Please note that there will only be ONE error in any given sentence.

Example

The rules of the game are quite clear, and some students claimed otherwise.

↓

The rules of the game are quite **clear, although some** students claimed otherwise.

26) Eventually, the soda company began producing such unusual and unrecognizably complex flavors which its product line became almost impossible to market.

NOTES: _____

27) Despite the route may become difficult, we must press on, convinced that these difficulties are only temporary.

NOTES: _____

28) New York socialites and first-time visitors to the city regardless flocked to Sanford White's original Madison Square Garden, an opulent structure that first opened its doors to the public in 1890.

Notes: _____

29) It was quickly becoming clear that the clinical trials had not gone as hoped, and that the company was set to lose a number of its highest-ranking executives. Without these setbacks, key investors remained confident that the entire firm would thrive over the long term.

Notes: _____

30) With so many different options available, it is possible, furthermore, that a competent freelancer will feel overwhelmed rather than exhilarated by seemingly endless job opportunities.

Notes: _____

31) The popularity of high-speed (25 miles per hour, or more) bicycle racing has skyrocketed, when the sport itself carries clear liabilities. After all, some uproar arose last year when a cyclist (who at the time was going roughly 30 miles per hour) collided with a pedestrian in Manhattan's Central Park.

Notes: _____

32) Reformers may prefer numerous petitions and vehement editorials than other methods of effecting social change, but history has shown that picking only a few strategic fights is the best approach.

Notes: _____

33) It is unlikely that Black Friday "deals," contrasted to the publicity they receive, will actually save you more than discount deals that occur at other times of the year.

Notes: _____

34) The sport of soccer has grown in popularity in the United States, for a few reasons: today, more Americans gravitate to soccer games even though they are lured by accessible, state-of-the-art soccer stadiums.

Notes: _____

35) Before recent funding cuts to English as a Second Language programs, graduate students in English language teaching may have more difficulty finding employment after they graduate.

Notes: _____

36) Revealing air strike targets is as much a humanitarian measure (since citizens can be given notice to evacuate) than a piece of psychological warfare (since hostile forces cannot be fully sure that the strike will take place or that the information is accurate).

Notes: _____

37) I have found my work as a florist to be profitable and, from a marketing standpoint, low-risk. In contrast, the very work that allows me to pay my bills also allows me to exercise my sense of color, proportion, and aesthetics generally.

NOTES: _____

38) The Middle Ages will be remembered as a period of human history, which architecture, though not formally studied, reached new heights of decorative intricacy.

NOTES: _____

39) This petting zoo offers internships to high school students that want to pursue a variety of disciplines: current interns are interested in studying everything from marketing to biology at the college level.

NOTES: _____

40) Paul Gauguin found life in Paris to be both stimulating and emotionally draining; nonetheless, he departed for Tahiti in a search for solace, and for new artistic inspirations.

NOTES: _____

41) There was no greater expression of John D. Rockefeller's business acumen except his ability to save money and resources by making small refinements to industrial processes.

NOTES: _____

42) She may seem confident in public, but she has privately expressed uncertainty, which handling the endowment funds in this manner is a wise choice.

NOTES: _____

43) Directly opposing ape communities, which are typically dominated by adult males, the social groups formed by elephants are exclusively matriarchal.

NOTES: _____

44) Today's clothing industry is affected by factors other than passing fashions and new trend reports. A rise of a few cents per pound in the price of denim, in contrast, can sharply disrupt the production of blue jeans and other denim goods.

NOTES: _____

45) I have begun reading a book called *Algebra in Ten Easy Steps*. For me at least, the title of this book is ironic, although I am not finding the steps easy at all.

NOTES: _____

46) This school district is an excellent choice for parents, which would rather see their children develop social skills than see their children fixate on technology. After-school activities abound, and few of these activities require the use of a laptop.

NOTES: _____

47) It can be difficult to arrange a parade in a small town. Participating vendors and organizations may cancel at the last minute; nonetheless, the parade itself can disrupt traffic and cause noise that irritates residents.

NOTES: _____

48) These goose-down quilts are among the presents, which are most popular this holiday season; most of the other must-have items are both less useful and more reliant on strange marketing gimmicks to attain recognition.

NOTES: _____

49) Nobody, believe me, wants to be the person at a party, which has a reputation for making snide comments that offend the other guests.

NOTES: _____

50) The health benefits of walking continue to be underestimated. Indeed, multiple studies have shown that walking at least one mile each day is an excellent way to boost your metabolism, fitness devotees continue to favor biking and sprinting as their methods of choice.

NOTES: _____

ANSWERS ON THE NEXT PAGE

ANSWERS: PUNCTUATION ERRORS

1) The creators of the statistical model were forced to face a **difficult truth: that few** of their main assumptions about the composition of the voting public were in any way accurate.

2) To create an effective college application essay, you need to use a fairly traditional structure—strong hook, lucid body paragraphs, and a single unifying **theme—and** simultaneously demonstrate your ability to craft a compelling, revealing narrative.

3) Each member of the hockey team practiced relentlessly; each of those young women believed that her efforts would help build a **victorious season—only to see** those hopes crushed by an unbroken series of defeats.

4) Although marine life flourished in the prehistoric era, paleontologists and laypersons alike remain most captivated by two massive aquatic **animals: the ichthyosaur** and the plesiosaur.

5) There is actually a good reason for the "timid" corporate strategy that Gilead Sciences **is following: the company** would rather bide its time and spend its resources wisely than make a hasty, unwise acquisition.

6) As drawn by cartoonists, the original versions of some corporate **mascots—including** Ronald McDonald, Mr. Peanut, and the Goodyear Tire Man—feature photo-realistic textures that have disappeared from more recent incarnations of these characters.

7) **Kleptocracy (a word that means "government** by those who steal") is a concept that Professor Hulton has explored in her recent articles on police states and black markets.

8) This company is a leader in a branch of the technology industry which is called Software as a **Service (SaaS for short) and** which has grown dramatically in the past five years.

9) John Cheever was a man of **contradictions: although** he was an author capable of projecting profound optimism and resounding appreciation for natural beauty, he spent much of his life struggling with a variety of personal demons.

10) I had been spending the better part of two months trying, in vain, to think of new employment **options—when** suddenly a brilliant idea popped into my head.

11) She was universally esteemed for her business **acumen—though** her abrasive political opinions garnered a very different reception.

12) This fifth-grade class learned about basic economic principles by creating its own rudimentary system of currency: under this scheme, a red **button (re-named a "rutton" for convenience) was** worth twice as much as a blue button (re-named a "blutton").

13) These rock formations were formed by wind eroding away small **deposits of sediment** in a process that took thousands of years.

14) After much rumination, Socrates discovered a line of argument that foiled his harshest **accusers: death**, in the opinion of Socrates himself, would be superior to exile from Athens.

15) In the 1950s, a young boy named Rennie Drew became a local celebrity for creating an abstract **painting reminiscent of** the work of Jackson Pollock.

16) The members of the expedition were convinced that further efforts would **be fatal: the available** water supplies, after all, were running perilously low.

17) A 3D printer is a device that can generate a variety of different, practically important precision objects from **computer images: prosthetic limbs**, topographic models, and mock-ups of industrial designs.

18) There was some **dispute among the** senior management about which social media platform would be best for publicizing the new product line.

19) A high school drama teacher who expects students to perform ***The Threepenny Opera* (or any work by Bertolt Brecht, for that matter) automatically** does those students an immense disservice.

20) I find it difficult to believe that her dance company, which excelled in conservative yet elegant ballet for the better part of **two decades, would perform** the work of an unproven, upstart choreographer unless somehow pressured.

21) For years, he taught brief elective seminars on the science behind **everyday phenomena: how leaves** change color, for instance, or why people crave specific types of food.

22) This management **textbook, which is** by no means the first of its kind, has been praised for how well it works in tandem with an online database that the publishers have made available to students.

23) Though some may find "dressage" (a sport in which a horse performs complicated movements under the **guidance of a trainer) borderline** ridiculous, dressage competitions are in fact gaining both popularity and prestige.

24) It would be **surprising—but, of course, by no means unbelievable—for any** of the specialists who so harshly criticized Dr. Hawker to ultimately wind up working with the Hawker Foundation.

25) Before they were introduced into human diets by George Washington Carver, peanuts were popular as feed for one type of **animal: the hog**.

ANSWERS: WORDING AND PHRASING ERRORS

26) Eventually, the soda company began producing such unusual and unrecognizably complex flavors **that** its product line became almost impossible to market.

27) **Although** the route may become difficult, we must press on, convinced that these difficulties are only temporary.

28) New York socialites and first-time visitors to **the city alike flocked to** Sanford White's original Madison Square Garden, an opulent structure that first opened its doors to the public in 1890.

29) It was quickly becoming clear that the clinical trials had not gone as hoped, and that the company was set to lose a number of its highest-ranking executives. **Despite** these setbacks, key investors remained confident that the entire firm would thrive over the long term.

30) With so many different options available, **it is possible, indeed, that** a competent freelancer will feel overwhelmed rather than exhilarated by seemingly endless job opportunities.

31) The popularity of high-speed (25 miles per hour, or more) bicycle racing has skyrocketed, **even though** the sport itself carries clear liabilities. After all, some uproar arose last year when a cyclist (who at the time was going roughly 30 miles per hour) collided with a pedestrian in Manhattan's Central Park.

32) Reformers may prefer numerous petitions and vehement **editorials to other** methods of effecting social change, but history has shown that picking only a few strategic fights is the best approach.

33) It is unlikely that Black Friday **"deals," despite the publicity** they receive, will actually save you more than discount deals that occur at other times of the year.

34) The sport of soccer has grown in popularity in the United States, for a few reasons: today, more Americans gravitate to soccer **games because they are** lured by accessible, state-of-the-art soccer stadiums.

35) **On account of** recent funding cuts to English as a Second Language programs, graduate students in English language teaching may have more difficulty finding employment after they graduate.

36) Revealing air strike targets is as much a humanitarian measure (since citizens can be given notice to evacuate) **as a piece** of psychological warfare (since hostile forces cannot be fully sure that the strike will take place or that the information is accurate).

37) I have found my work as a florist to be profitable and, from a marketing standpoint, low-risk. **Moreover,** the very work that allows me to pay my bills also allows me to exercise my sense of color, proportion, and aesthetics generally.

38) The Middle Ages will be remembered as a period of **human history when architecture**, though not formally studied, reached new heights of decorative intricacy.

39) This petting zoo offers internships **to high school students who want** to pursue a variety of disciplines: current interns are interested in studying everything from marketing to biology at the college level.

40) Paul Gauguin found life in Paris to be both stimulating and emotionally **draining; consequently, he** departed for Tahiti in a search for solace, and for new artistic inspirations.

41) There was no greater expression of John D. Rockefeller's business **acumen than his ability** to save money and resources by making small refinements to industrial processes.

42) She may seem confident in public, but she has privately **expressed uncertainty that handling** the endowment funds in this manner is a wise choice.

43) **Unlike ape communities**, which are typically dominated by adult males, the social groups formed by elephants are exclusively matriarchal.

44) Today's clothing industry is affected by factors other than passing fashions and new trend reports. A rise of a few cents per pound in the price of denim, **for example**, can sharply disrupt the production of blue jeans and other denim goods.

45) I have begun reading a book called *Algebra in Ten Easy Steps*. For me at least, the title of this book is ironic, **because** I am not finding the steps easy at all.

46) This school district is an excellent choice for **parents who would rather** see their children develop social skills than see their children fixate on technology. After-school activities abound, and few of these activities require the use of a laptop.

47) It can be difficult to arrange a parade in a small town. Participating vendors and organizations may cancel at the **last minute, and the parade** itself can disrupt traffic and cause noise that irritates residents.

48) These goose-down quilts are among **the presents that are most** popular this holiday season; most of the other must-have items are both less useful and more reliant on strange marketing gimmicks to attain recognition.

49) Nobody, believe me, wants to be the person at **a party who has** a reputation for making snide comments that offend the other guests.

50) The health benefits of walking continue to be underestimated. **Although** multiple studies have shown that walking at least one mile each day is an excellent way to boost your metabolism, fitness devotees continue to favor biking and sprinting as their methods of choice.

Chapter Eight

Sentence Placement

SENTENCE PLACEMENT

ESSENTIALS OF SENTENCE PLACEMENT

The SAT Writing and Language section will not simply challenge your skills in grammar and word choice. At times, this portion of the test will require you to re-order the ideas in a paragraph in the most logical order possible. Often, you will be presented with questions that are formatted in the following manner.

[1] Have you ever seen an old map sporting fantastical monsters and mythical beasts? [2] This practice, born as early as some of the first maps, has a basis in the typical fears of a constantly shifting world. [3] When man began to climb, fearsome yetis and massive flying beasts appeared, and when man began to sail, sirens and sea monsters filled the waters. [4] When man began to walk, great snakes and beasts appeared. [5] The images on a map changed with cultural confidence, too: in the mid 1600s, humans were seafarers, fearlessly exploring the waters, and the monsters turned to ships, sitting square between Europe and the Americas.

To make the paragraph most logical, sentence 4 should be placed

A) where it is now.
B) before sentence 2.
C) before sentence 3.
D) after sentence 5.

Your task, for questions such as this, will be to handle a relatively large amount of information quickly and precisely. Fortunately, determining the best placement for a given sentence is not difficult. You simply need to know what information to prioritize, and on the SAT, that information will always take the form of a set of clues that must be detected and coordinated.

LOGIC, KEYWORDS, AND CONTINUITY

When you are given a sentence placement question on the SAT, you should NOT attempt to solve the question by simply plugging in each new placement (trying out "before sentence 1", "before sentence 2", etc.). Such an approach is time-consuming, and may lead to answers that "sound correct" but are not LOGICAL in the manner that the question requires.

Instead, each paragraph for a sentence placement question will feature an extremely logical, extremely orderly progression from idea to idea. You must identify what primary ideas appear in each sentence, then identify whether the ideas in the paragraph properly lead from one into the other.

To see exactly how this process plays out, return to the example given above. Temporarily disregard the options given in the question itself, and determine the topic and function of each sentence.

[1] Have you ever seen an old map sporting fantastical monsters and mythical beasts? ⟶ introduces maps and creatures

[2] This practice, born as early as some of the first maps, has ⟶ map features, changing world
a basis in the typical fears of a constantly shifting world.

[3] When man began to climb, fearsome yetis and massive
flying beasts appeared, and when man began to sail, sirens ⟶ land creatures to sea creatures
and sea monsters filled the waters.

[4] When man began to walk, great snakes and beasts ⟶ land creatures
appeared.

[5] The images on a map changed with cultural confidence, ⟶ humans at sea
too: in the mid 1600s, humans were seafarers, fearlessly
exploring the waters, and the monsters turned to ships, sitting
square between Europe and the Americas.

Do you see where the first version of the paragraph is problematic? While the first two sentences involve the same KEYWORD (maps) and an effective progression of LOGIC (question into motive), the final three sentences are jumbled in terms of both logic and keywords. Sentence 3 describes land creatures and then sea creatures, sentence 4 describes only land creatures, and sentence 5 describes only sea creatures.

Moreover, the sentences are designed to indicate that humans progressively moved AWAY FROM the land. For this reason, the best placement for sentence 4 is C, before sentence 3, so that the passage describes land creatures, then sea creatures, then ships in an orderly fashion.

1

To make the paragraph most logical, sentence 4 should be placed

A) where it is now.
B) before sentence 2.
C) before sentence 3.
D) after sentence 5.

Keep in mind that keywords and logic can be used to eliminate faulty answers. B would disrupt the logical progression from question to explanation in sentences 1 and 2; D would wrongly return to land creatures at the end of the paragraph, rather than CONSOLIDATING this topic and its keywords near sentence 3.

In essence, all of the sentence placement questions that you will find on the SAT can be solved using the methods outlined above. There are, however, a few sentence placement situations that can prove especially tricky for test-takers. The next step is to guide you through these; fortunately, these rather challenging questions can be simplified using a few special tricks and tactics.

GROUPED TONES

As you have already seen, it is possible to move through sentence placement questions with great efficiency by grouping keywords. Sometimes, you will need to group the TONES that these passages involve.

Identifying sentences with similar tones may initially seem difficult if you are dealing with a passage that presents a strong, single main topic. Yet the rules that you have learned elsewhere on the SAT are the same: think of tone primarily in terms of POSITIVE and NEGATIVE, and make sure that the transitions from one tone or one portion into the next are LOGICAL. To see how some of these challenges can be addressed, consider the example below.

[1] The TV channels are full of the death of Nelson Mandela. [2] Mandela was much admired by the Angolan pupils I taught. [3] In fact, he was second on their list of great African leaders only to Agostinho Neto, who had been Angola's own version of Mandela. [4] I so vividly remember watching him walk out of Robben Island (where he had been imprisoned for a long stretch of his life) and embarking upon a mission of national unification that would present new struggles, for all its inspiring power. [5] Some of the best essays my students wrote were about what these two men meant to the future of all of Africa.

2

To make the paragraph most logical, sentence 4 should be placed

A) where it is now.
B) after sentence 1.
C) after sentence 2.
D) after sentence 5.

It may be difficult to see the best placement for sentence 4, since the entire paragraph has a single strong subject: the life and reception of Nelson Mandela. However, if you consider the predominant tones in each sentence, you will be able to see the best placement with little trouble.

[1] The TV channels are full of the death of Nelson Mandela.  Mandela's death (Negative)

[2] Mandela was much admired by the Angolan pupils I taught. → Admiration for Mandela (Positive)

[3] In fact, he was second on their list of great African leaders only to Agostinho Neto, who had been Angola's own version of Mandela. → Mandela's and Neto's reputations (Positive)

[4] I so vividly remember watching him walk out of Robben Island (where he had been imprisoned for a long stretch of his life) and embarking upon a mission of national unification that would present new struggles, for all its inspiring power. → Mandela's imprisonment and struggle (Some Positive, some Negative)

[5] Some of the best essays my students wrote were about what these two men meant to the future of all of Africa. → Mandela's reputation among the students (Positive)

Note that sentence 4 contains some positive and some negative elements: it would thus effectively transition from sentence 1 (negative) to the other three sentences in the paragraph (which are completely positive). But keep in mind the importance of grouped topics as well, including grouped topics that may not be entirely obvious at first. In its current placement, the discussion of Mandela's life interrupts the discussion of the writer's "pupils," who are described in sentences 2, 3, and 5. Sentence 4 makes no reference to the pupils and should be repositioned in order not to interrupt this discussion.

2

To make the paragraph most logical, sentence 4 should be placed

~~A)~~ where it is now.
B) after sentence 1.
~~C)~~ after sentence 2.
~~D)~~ after sentence 5.

INTRODUCING EXAMPLES AND ACCOUNTING FOR REFERENCES

 Even SAT test-takers who know how to group keywords and tones may create sentence placements that, in more subtle ways, do not have proper logical movement. Of particular interest, here, is the question of how to coordinate examples. In order to organize examples and evidence properly, simply begin with one of the main rules of essay writing: when discussing a topic, always move from a general statement of the issue or idea at hand into more detailed information about that issue.

In these respects, consider the following example.

[1] Readers past and present have been preoccupied with these crazed characters, and if recent entertainment is any indication, mad scientists aren't going anywhere. [2] After all, the most acclaimed television series of recent times, *Breaking Bad*, features a main character who is both a brilliant chemist and a violent sociopath. [3] Perhaps mad scientists so captivate us because they are villains of the most sophisticated and dramatic kind. [4] Or perhaps these devious inquirers evoke something different in us: the awareness that every discovery, every benefit science brings, also brings the potential for distortion and destruction. [5] What is it that explains the staying power of mad scientists?

3

To make the paragraph most logical, sentence 5 should be placed

A) where it is now.
B) before sentence 1.
C) after sentence 1.
D) after sentence 4.

Notice that sentence 5 poses a question about "mad scientists", while sentences 1 and 2 explain the issue and sentences 3 and 4 provide possible reasons that mad scientists are so alluring. Sentence 5 could, perhaps, be placed before sentence 3, though this option is not included among the answer choices. Instead, sentence 5 could effectively introduce the ENTIRE topic, since its discussion of the "staying power of mad scientists" leads into the idea of readers being "preoccupied" (sentence 1) with mad scientists. In light of this logic and information, B is the best answer.

However, there is a further rationale behind placing sentence 5 before sentence 1: keep in mind that sentence 1 refers to "these crazed characters". What crazed characters, exactly? There is not a preceding sentence that names any "characters", and thus the entire structure of the paragraph (at least in its initial form) is illogical.

When working with SAT Writing and Language paragraphs, you must make sure that ANY pronoun or other stand-in phrase clearly refers to some item from the passage itself. Placing sentence 5 at the beginning of the paragraph addresses this deficiency in the above example by enabling "these crazed characters" to refer immediately and logically back to "mad scientists".

EXERCISES: Sentence Placement

DIRECTIONS: Read each excerpt and decide which of the three sentence choices is the misplaced sentence. Then, provide the correct position for the misplaced sentence (*example: before 1*).

---

1. [1] The availability of larger homes with more private yards around them attracts parents with young children. [2] Such an environment is conducive to a more family-oriented lifestyle, with better schools and more efficient public services. [3] Parents can rear their children at a comfortable pace, introducing them to the less desirable realities of life when they decide the time is right. [4] The decision to move from a densely populated city to the wide-open suburbs is a natural one for a growing family. [5] Most importantly, young parents have numerous options for the type of community they want to settle in.

Misplaced Sentence: 1, 3, or 4

Correct Position: _____

---

2. [1] The label of "feminist" has gotten a bad rap in recent years. [2] Whether such ways of viewing the world are successes or failures for the feminists of the last century, of course, depends on how these viewpoints play out in the future. [3] Radical feminists of the '60s and '70s, although moderately successful in changing the way we assign gender roles, have given the citizens of the millennial era a distasteful image when they look back into the past. [4] Young women today have not experienced the oppressive roles and attitudes that women of the '50s faced, so they see little need for equal employment initiatives, women's colleges, and other organizations that promote gender equality (sometimes at the expense of men's power). [5] Young men also seem perplexed with the existence of a modern feminist movement since they have grown up with working mothers and female supervisors.

Misplaced Sentence: 2, 4, or 5

Correct Position: _____

3.

[1] Just the other day I was cleaning my son's Lego blocks and he responded with such ardent venom that I forgot we were arguing over toys! [2] It hadn't occurred to me—all the worlds he had built, the friendships he had made among his tiny people. [3] Now I let my son decide when to tear down his worlds, when to end his friendships. [4] In the words of the child psychologist Albert Emmington, "Give the children toys. What are all things that matter to us in life but toys?" [5] Toys represent more than playthings to their child owners, a situation which results in the child's infuriation at the flippant attitudes most adults have towards toys.

Misplaced Sentence: 2, 3, or 5

Correct Position: _____

4.

[1] While it's fairly easy to disprove an idea through a single counterexample, how can we prove that something will always be true? [2] We can certainly assume that, since there's a number after nine (namely, ten), there is most likely a number after ten (indeed, eleven). [3] This is where the creativity of math comes in. [4] We cannot, however, use examples to keep proving "the next number exists" forever (a process that would be very boring). [5] Eventually, we must move beyond rote examples and tap into the sweeping resources of the imagination.

Misplaced Sentence: 1, 2, or 3

Correct Position: _____

5.

[1] Whenever I hear an announcer proclaim that such-and-such a play has only happened five times in Major League Baseball history, I am impressed. [2] But how can the word "history" properly denote a record that has only existed for little more than a century? [3] Egypt has a cultural history that spans millennia of recorded facts. [4] Speak to a paleontologist or a geologist, and you'll be regaled with a "history" in which a million years are treated as an instant. [5] Even American history, if we include the Colonial period, is barely more than four hundred years old.

Misplaced Sentence: 1, 2, or 5

Correct Position: _____

6. [1] Japanese Internment was the systematic relocation of Japanese Americans to secluded camps within the U.S. in 1942. [2] After Internment was declared unjust 40 years later, the U.S. paid a paltry twenty thousand dollars in reparation funds to each internment camp survivor. [3] As the result of Roosevelt's Executive Order 9066, local military commanders were given power to designate "exclusion zones," thereby banning those of Japanese ancestry from the Pacific coast. [4] Consequently, lawful Japanese-American citizens were displaced from their homes, many of which were lucrative farms. [5] However, there was no compensation for the lost farms.

Misplaced Sentence: 2, 3, or 5

Correct Position: _____

7. [1] The possibility of a new supercontinent, commonly referred to as "Amasia," is a prospect that fires the imagination. [2] Even so, we can speculate about where such geological upheaval will leave the species and civilizations that are here hundreds and millions of years on. [3] Perhaps all intelligent life will fuse together in a single super-civilization. [4] Naturally, none of us will live to see this new landmass. [5] But I am most intrigued by the prospect of a new super-ocean on the other side of the globe. [6] What unforeseen new forms of life will emerge to claim this giant world of water as their own?

Misplaced Sentence: 1, 3, or 4

Correct Position: _____

8. [1] I am an English teacher, but I still hear nothing wrong when my uncles pronounce "three" without the "h." [2] "Growing up Italian-American" is not a topic that seems to warrant TV specials or critical theory bestsellers. [3] Socially, it is just not a big deal. [4] But behind this face that seems to meld into any ethnic group, I am tainted by my Italian ancestry. [5] That isn't all, quirk-wise: I do quick translations in my head before ordering "gravy" or "manicot" and I use funeral prayer cards to mark pages the way most people would use a normal bookmark.

Misplaced Sentence: 1, 3, or 5

Correct Position: _____

9. [1] Bran Castle, located in the Carpathian Mountains in Romania, stands high above the surrounding farmland. [2] This edifice was originally built as a bulwark against Ottoman conquest. [3] Yet popular myth, spurred on by Bram Stoker's vampire novel, transformed Bran Castle into Dracula's home. [4] It is said that the residents of nearby Bran village had until recently been completely oblivious to Dracula. [5] However fallacious, this new status has sparked a recent wave of tourism. [6] But as new tourists have flocked in, bringing the prospect of new income, the collective memory has changed.

Misplaced Sentence: 2, 4, 6

Correct Position: _____

10. [1] Despite body types, athleticism will always be defined as personal perseverance and triumph over obstacles both mental and physical. [2] Olympic figure skating is a sport unlike any other, a sport in which months of training all boil down to a single performance. [3] In these few minutes, the athlete must prove himself through strength, control, grace, and finesse. [4] Overall, figure skating rewards those with a balance of these aspects as opposed to those with the most power. [5] Since the inception of the Olympics in 1924, the average figure skater has decreased in height by five inches; smaller, lighter bodies are optimal for the jumping, spinning, and landing required by the sport. [6] Does this mean that all figure skaters must be small? [7] Of course it doesn't.

Misplaced Sentence: 1, 3, or 7

Correct Position: _____

11. [1] For want of a better phrase or an appropriate euphemism, I must openly state that "I hate musicals." [2] In what universe does someone start singing mid-sentence or even mid-rant? [3] Both are melodramatic, cloying, irritating forms of entertainment. [4] Yet where pop culture is concerned, I'll always take a gratuitous car chase over a high-pitched melody of regret or greeting. [5] I don't like reality television either; in essence, reality television shows are just musicals without the singing.

Misplaced Sentence: 1, 2, or 5

Correct Position: _____

---

12. [1] To excel in their military endeavors, the ancient Romans did not rely on physical prowess alone, important though this was. [2] Yet should sheer strength and agility fail these soldiers, siege engines and heavy artillery could still turn the tide of battle. [3] Roman warriors would regularly perform training exercises with weapons weighing twice as much as the swords and spears that they carried into war. [4] The "foot and horse" warriors of the Roman legions were supported by battering rams, stone-throwing catapults, and devices known as scorpions, which launched blades and javelins into enemy ranks. [5] For the enemies of Rome, the best battle strategy was often a quick and unconditional surrender.

Misplaced Sentence: 3, 4, or 5

Correct Position: _____

13. [1] The Humboldt squid, which normally lives deep in the ocean off the western coasts of Central and South America, has recently been seen close to the shore as far north as Canada. [2] Although the Humboldt squid isn't nearly as giant as the giant squid, it still grows to the length of an adult human. [3] Instead of legs, though, this reclusive animal has tentacles with razor-sharp teeth on its suckers, which can flay flesh from bone in seconds. [4] Some people blame the overfishing of the squid's natural predators, while others blame climate change for this unusual spread. [5] Either way, this ruthless killer is getting farther from its own habitat—and closer to ours.

Misplaced Sentence: 1, 2, or 4

Correct Position: _____

14. [1] One of the principal characters in Henry James's novel *The Wings of the Dove* is a young woman named Milly Theale, who suffers from a chronic disease that James, for whatever reason, decided to leave unnamed. [2] Modern critics have labored to figure out what Milly's malady is. [3] They have devised possibilities as different as tuberculosis, leukemia, diabetes, and pancreatic cancer. [4] To eliminate ambiguity at every turn is to turn a novel into a dead, gray thing, a tiny medical case study instead of a teeming imagined world. [5] My own possibility is that James didn't know or care what Milly's exact affliction was, and that neither should we.

Misplaced Sentence: 2, 3, or 4

Correct Position: _____

15. [1] In 1915, Marcel Duchamp bought a snow shovel, suspended it from the ceiling of his studio, and declared it a full-fledged work of art. [2] As I see it, he was acting out a desire to make us look more closely at everyday life and find moments of artistic beauty where we least expect them. [3] He even gave this work a title, *In Advance of the Broken Arm*. [4] Duchamp's creation of this and other "readymade" artworks has been rightly viewed by most critics as a subversive gesture; after all, if a snow shovel or a hat rack or a bicycle tire can be held up as "art," where does the realm of "art" begin and the realm of "non-art" end?
[5] But I like to think that there was a second, more positive side of Duchamp's agenda.

Misplaced Sentence: 2, 3, or 5

Correct Position: _____

16. [1] Many will contend that video games have replaced reading, particularly the reading of fiction. [2] In some cases, the video game hero is faced with a calling to embark on a journey that can change his world for the better. [3] Then, he meets a mentor who guides him along the way. [4] The climax occurs when the hero faces his deepest fear, often embodied by a central antagonist. [5] While video games may have dispensed with actual bound pages, video games carry within them the kind of stories and episodes that are present in all literature.

Misplaced Sentence: 3, 4, or 5

Correct Position: _____

17. [1] "Facebook is so yesterday," my niece said with a smirk that only a fifteen year-old could pull off: one part innocence and one part arrogance. [2] There is Twitter, with its desperate 140-character bids for attention. [3] There is Instagram, with its legions of narcissistic "selfies." [4] And then, as if to prove her point and her prowess, she proceeded to list the social media sites that are "so not yesterday." [5] I felt a longing for the time before smart phones, when whether you had call-waiting or three-way calling determined your level of cool.

Misplaced Sentence: 1, 4, or 5

Correct Position: _____

18. [1] The visible part of the ear, the auricle, acts as a conical amplifier, picking up sounds and funneling them into the deeper reaches of the organ. [2] In terms of structure, the ear functions in much the same way that a seashell does. [3] If a shell were to have an opening at its pinnacle, and if the pinnacle were to be placed gently into the ear, then such an arrangement would greatly amplify the surrounding sounds. [4] The human ear is an amazing mechanism. [5] But that's not all when it comes to the workings of the ear. [6] Hearing is actually the ear's ancillary purpose: keeping the body in equilibrium is this versatile organ's more difficult, but more essential, task.

Misplaced Sentence: 3, 4, or 6

Correct Position: _____

19. [1] To most, familiarity with "theatre" means familiarity with playwrights such as Shakespeare, Arthur Miller, and maybe David Mamet or Harold Pinter. [2] And why is this so? [3] In contrast, most would not consider or think of Eastern theatrical conventions such as kabuki, the Beijing Opera, or Sanskrit drama when questioned about the proverbial stage. [4] The best explanation is that Western hegemony has pervaded most conventional understandings of art in general. [5] Unfortunately, this means that Eastern dramatic theories and practices are cast to the wayside—often belittled for departing from "standard" theatrical criteria and almost always relegated to the position of theatre that "celebrates culture," when in reality the theatre of the East has often guided the theatre of the West.

Misplaced Sentence: 1, 3, or 5

Correct Position: _____

20. [1] Despite picking up a few tidbits of information while taking my kids to planetariums and science fairs, I understand nothing about astrophysics. [2] Ask a research scientist what exactly he or she does on a daily basis, and you will probably get an answer so complicated that only another scientist in the same field could understand it. [3] It is easy to forget that the mass of obscure terms and intricate calculations that a scientist calls "work" often has poignantly human roots. [4] But it is possible that one of the children sitting next to me will look up at those same artificial constellations and someday dedicate a lifetime to studying the real universe. [5] This must be where inspiration begins.

Misplaced Sentence: 1, 2, or 3

Correct Position: _____

21. [1] A debate has raged in recent years as to whether we should apply business practices to government entities. [2] The government's job is not to produce goods, but to protect and serve its citizens. [3] Proponents of such measures believe that the public's best interests are served by limiting spending and slashing budgets. [4] Somehow, these partisans seem to have forgotten what the proper purpose of government is. [5] It is impossible to focus on the health and safety of the populace when an organization is constantly worried about whether its funding will be, like the proverbial rug, pulled out from under its feet.

Misplaced Sentence: 1, 2, or 4

Correct Position: _____

22. [1] In June of 1967, Air Force pilot Robert Henry Lawrence became the first African-American astronaut. [2] Sadly, he would never see a full space mission. [3] Americans would have to wait another 15 years before an African American was actually launched into space (an honor that went to Guion "Guy" Bluford, Jr., a participant in the 1983 Challenger space shuttle explorations). [4] Lawrence's career was cut short in December of the same year, when he lost his life in a jet crash at Edwards Air Force Base in California. [5] Since then, America has been graced with African-American astrophysicists, African-American NASA administrators, and an African-American director of the Hayden Planetarium.
[6] Such diversity came gradually; let us hope that it remains in place permanently.

Misplaced Sentence: 2, 3, or 6

Correct Position: _____

23. [1] Immigration has been and will always be a point of contention in American society. [2] During the California Gold Rush of 1848 to 1855, Chinese men, seeking work in the gold mines, immigrated to America. [3] Without any other employment prospects, these immigrants often found low-end positions in restaurants and laundry facilities, and unknowingly gave rise to the unjust theory that Chinese immigration depressed wage levels. [4] But as the initial fervor dwindled and gold extraction became highly competitive, animosity toward Chinese laborers rose dramatically. [5] Most were banished from mine work and forced to settle in enclaves on the outskirts of major cities such as San Francisco.

Misplaced Sentence: 1, 3, or 5

Correct Position: _____

24. [1] Like any normal person, I could not wait to travel to Europe, the faraway land of magic and mystical fables, castles, and languages of love. [2] Unfortunately, all of my expectations were delusions. [3] As I entered each country, I could not help but notice how alike everything looked. [4] My itinerary read like the route of a modern-day gypsy—Paris, Venice, Florence, and Prague. [5] Yes, old buildings and castles have different façades, but the differences no longer stand out when the people surrounding these structures are dressed in similar clothing and clutch identical phones. [6] Famed edifices are no longer breathtaking when each one has the kind of gift shop you are likely to find in the United States, or Canada, or probably anywhere in the world.

Misplaced Sentence: 1, 3, or 4

Correct Position: _____

25. [1] The rule of the animal world, it seems, is to follow the herd, the flock, the school, or the swarm: greater numbers mean greater cooperation, and ensure survival. [2] Yet there are animals of all types that thrive in solitude. [3] Some of these are small and self-sufficient (the sturdy desert grasshopper, the aptly-named hermit crab), but others are huge in size (the rhinoceros) or high on the food chain (the jaguar). [4] A male anteater will wander alone, crushing ant colony after ant colony, while a female will carry a child or two on its back until these offspring, too, go their singular ways. [5] Family groups for such antisocial animals seldom grow beyond a single mother and the most recent set of offspring; this is certainly the case with the giant anteater.

Misplaced Sentence: 1, 2, or 4

Correct Position: _____

ANSWERS ON THE NEXT PAGE

ANSWERS: SENTENCE PLACEMENT

1. Misplaced: Sentence 4   Correct Position: Before Sentence 1

2. Misplaced: Sentence 2   Correct Position: After Sentence 5

3. Misplaced: Sentence 5   Correct Position: Before Sentence 1

4. Misplaced: Sentence 3   Correct Position: After Sentence 4/Before Sentence 5

5. Misplaced: Sentence 5   Correct Position: After Sentence 3/Before Sentence 4

6. Misplaced: Sentence 2   Correct Position: After Sentence 4/Before Sentence 5

7. Misplaced: Sentence 4   Correct Position: After Sentence 1/Before Sentence 2

8. Misplaced: Sentence 1   Correct Position: After Sentence 4/Before Sentence 5

9. Misplaced: Sentence 4   Correct Position: After Sentence 5/Before Sentence 6

10. Misplaced: Sentence 1   Correct Position: After Sentence 7

11. Misplaced: Sentence 5   Correct Position: After Sentence 2/Before Sentence 3

12. Misplaced: Sentence 3   Correct Position: After Sentence 1/Before Sentence 2

13. Misplaced: Sentence 1   Correct Position: After Sentence 3/Before Sentence 4

14. Misplaced: Sentence 4   Correct Position: After Sentence 5

15. Misplaced: Sentence 2   Correct Position: After Sentence 5

16. Misplaced: Sentence 5   Correct Position: After Sentence 1/Before Sentence 2

17. Misplaced: Sentence 4   Correct Position: After Sentence 1/Before Sentence 2

18. Misplaced: Sentence 4   Correct Position: Before Sentence 1

19. Misplaced: Sentence 3   Correct Position: After Sentence 1/Before Sentence 2

20. Misplaced: Sentence 1   Correct Position: After Sentence 3/Before Sentence 4

21. Misplaced: Sentence 2   Correct Position: After Sentence 4/Before Sentence 5

22. Misplaced: Sentence 3   Correct Position: After Sentence 4, Before Sentence 5

23. Misplaced: Sentence 3   Correct Position: After Sentence 5

24. Misplaced: Sentence 4   Correct Position: After Sentence 1/Before Sentence 2

25. Misplaced: Sentence 4   Correct Position: After Sentence 5

Chapter Nine

Sentence Addition and Deletion

SENTENCE ADDITION AND DELETION

ESSENTIALS OF ADDING AND DELETING SENTENCES

On each SAT Writing and Language test, you will need to address a few questions that ask you to determine whether a specific sentence is an appropriate element for the passage at hand. You will have the option of accepting or rejecting the content. You will also need to determine, beyond simple acceptance and rejection, the best REASONING behind how the content should be handled.

Content questions of this sort can be presented in one of two ways. You may be asked to KEEP or DELETE a sentence that is already situated within the passage, as in the example below.

Example 1

Have you ever seen an old map sporting fantastical monsters and mythical beasts? This practice, born as early as some of the first maps, has a basis in the typical fears of a constantly shifting world. When man began to walk, great snakes and beasts appeared. **1** <u>When man began to climb, fearsome yetis and massive flying beasts appeared, and when man began to sail, sirens and sea monsters filled the waters.</u> The images on a map changed with cultural confidence, too: in the mid 1600s, humans were seafarers, fearlessly exploring the waters, and the monsters turned to ships, sitting square between Europe and the Americas.

1

The writer is considering deleting the underlined sentence to improve the paragraph. Should the sentence be kept or deleted?

A) Kept, because the sentence effectively shows how map decorations evolved to reflect human activity.

B) Kept, because the sentence reinforces the writer's criticisms of early seafarers.

C) Deleted, because the sentence simply rephrases information that is presented elsewhere in the paragraph.

D) Deleted, because the sentence would be more effectively placed at the beginning of the paragraph.

 Keep in mind that questions of this sort are NOT actually grammar questions. A flaw in grammar or basic construction will never be presented as a reason for deleting a sentence. Instead, you must determine whether the underlined sentence 1) is properly placed and 2) adds meaningful, non-redundant content to the passage in its current placement.

In other cases, an SAT question may present a new sentence that could be added at specific point. Your challenge will be to determine whether the sentence should be inserted or not.

Example 2

The TV channels are full of the death of Nelson Mandela. I so vividly remember watching him walk out of Robben Island (where he had been imprisoned for a long stretch of his life) and embarking upon a mission of national unification that would present new struggles, for all its inspiring power. Mandela was much admired by the Angolan pupils I taught. In fact, he was second on their list of great African leaders only to Agostinho Neto, who had been Angola's own version of Mandela. Some of the best essays my students wrote were about what these two men meant to the future of all of Africa.

2

At this point, the writer is considering adding the following sentence.

> I remember what it was like when I first arrived in Angola, twenty-three years ago, on a sweltering day that even then seemed so full of promise.

Should the writer make this addition here?

A) Yes, because it explains why the writer decided to pursue a career as a teacher.
B) Yes, because it explains why the writer admires Nelson Mandela.
C) No, because it distracts from the writer's discussion of important political figures.
D) No, because it distracts from the writer's discussion of his own education.

Fortunately, both variations on this type of question (KEEP/DELETE for an existing sentence, YES/NO for a new sentence) follow exactly the same strategy. The steps that you will need in order to work with these questions with ease and precision are outlined below.

DETERMINING THE APPROPRIATE CONTENT

The first step to solving any question about adding or deleting a sentence is to determine, on a basic level, whether or not the content is appropriate. On your own, you must address the basic issue (KEEP/DELETE or YES/NO) that the question presents. To do so, you must use CLUES from the paragraph, and ideally from the sentences SURROUNDING the placement, to formulate your ideas.

 Return to Example 1, and consider the sentences BEFORE and AFTER the new sentence. Determine what each sentence is about on a basic level.

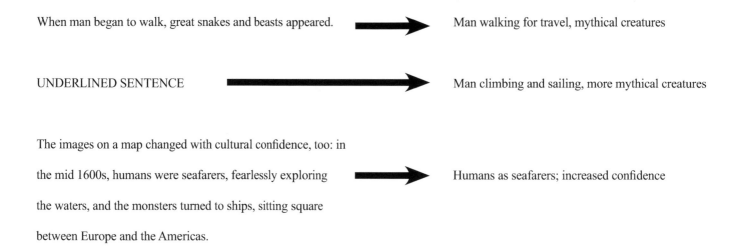

When man began to walk, great snakes and beasts appeared. → Man walking for travel, mythical creatures

UNDERLINED SENTENCE → Man climbing and sailing, more mythical creatures

The images on a map changed with cultural confidence, too: in the mid 1600s, humans were seafarers, fearlessly exploring the waters, and the monsters turned to ships, sitting square between Europe and the Americas. → Humans as seafarers; increased confidence

It should be clear, from this reading of the clues provided by each sentence, that the underlined sentence is connected to the major topic of the paragraph (humans traveling and creating maps). Moreover, the sentence provides a bridge between the idea of land travel (previous sentence) and sea travel (following sentence).

Thus, the sentence should be KEPT, and C and D can be automatically ELIMINATED.

Now, consider the same process for Example 2: this time, however, you will need to mentally place the new sentence in its proposed position.

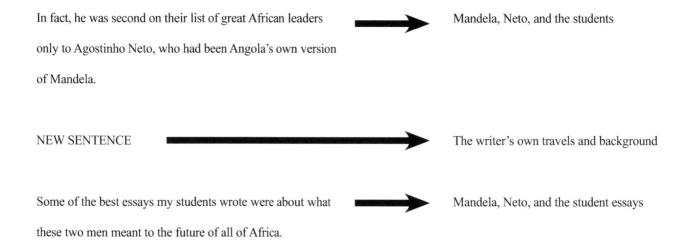

In fact, he was second on their list of great African leaders only to Agostinho Neto, who had been Angola's own version of Mandela. → Mandela, Neto, and the students

NEW SENTENCE → The writer's own travels and background

Some of the best essays my students wrote were about what these two men meant to the future of all of Africa. → Mandela, Neto, and the student essays

The two sentences that surround the new sentence address almost exactly the same keywords and key topics: Mandela, Neto, and the writer's students, who wrote essays about these two men. However, the new sentence shifts emphasis away from this group of topics and onto an EARLIER stage of the writer's life.

Thus, the sentence should NOT be inserted, and A and B can be automatically ELIMINATED

DETERMINING THE APPROPRIATE LOGIC

After you have determined whether or not a sentence fits its proposed position in a paragraph, you must determine the best REASONING for your content choice. Fortunately, if you perform the first step correctly, you will automatically have some of the information that you need for this second step.

 Return to Example 1. You have already eliminated two answers and formulated a reason for adding the sentence.

Example 1

Have you ever seen an old map sporting fantastical monsters and mythical beasts? This practice, born as early as some of the first maps, has a basis in the typical fears of a constantly shifting world. When man began to walk, great snakes and beasts appeared. When man began to climb, fearsome yetis and massive flying beasts appeared, and when man began to sail, sirens and sea monsters filled the waters. The images on a map changed with cultural confidence, too: in the mid 1600s, humans were seafarers, fearlessly exploring the waters, and the monsters turned to ships, sitting square between Europe and the Americas.

1

The writer is considering deleting the underlined sentence to improve the paragraph. Should the sentence be kept or deleted?

A) Kept, because the sentence effectively shows how map decorations evolved to reflect human activity.
B) Kept, because the sentence reinforces the writer's criticisms of early seafarers.
~~C)~~ Deleted, because the sentence simply rephrases information that is presented elsewhere in the paragraph.
~~D)~~ Deleted, because the sentence would be more effectively placed at the beginning of the paragraph.

Topic of humans and maps, connects land and sea travel

The new sentence performs a few functions: it offers a transition, and it offers a further example of how human activities influenced the work of mapmakers. Pair this reasoning against the two "Kept" options: the sentence does link maps and exploration, but does NOT criticize seafarers. The only negative that it contains ("fearsome") is used to describe "yetis" and other beasts.

Thus, ELIMINATE B and choose A as the best answer.

 Keep in mind that the reasoning provided in the answer choices may not perfectly fit your prediction. For instance, the correct answer above does not mention a transition. However, by forming a predicted answer, you will give yourself resources for seeing why false answers are completely inaccurate and will have better grounds for performing Process of Elimination.

Now, return to Example 2 and consider how the same strategy can help you arrive at the correct reasoning for deleting the sentence.

Example 2

The TV channels are full of the death of Nelson Mandela. I so vividly remember watching him walk out of Robben Island (where he had been imprisoned for a long stretch of his life) and embarking upon a mission of national unification that would present new struggles, for all its inspiring power. Mandela was much admired by the Angolan pupils I taught. In fact, he was second on their list of great African leaders only to Agostinho Neto, who had been Angola's own version of Mandela. **2** Some of the best essays my students wrote were about what these two men meant to the future of all of Africa.

2

At this point, the writer is considering adding the following sentence.

> I remember what it was like when I first arrived in Angola, twenty-three years ago, on a sweltering day that even then seemed so full of promise.

Should the writer make this addition here?

~~A)~~ Yes, because it explains why the writer decided to pursue a career as a teacher.

~~B)~~ Yes, because it explains why the writer admires Nelson Mandela.

C) No, because it distracts from the writer's discussion of important political figures.

D) No, because it distracts from the writer's discussion of his own education.

Not about Mandela, Neto, or the Writer's students

It is already clear that the important topics in this portion of the paragraph are Mandela, Neto, and the writer's students. The writer's education (in contrast to the education of the students) is not mentioned at all: bringing in this topic would be a complete distraction from the main focus of the paragraph at this point.

Thus, ELIMINATE D and choose C as the best answer.

Keep in mind that you may be led to choose the wrong reasoning if you read too quickly. For instance, it would be easy to MISREAD the reasoning presented in D as "distracts from the writer's discussion <u>by referencing</u> his own education". This misreading yields an answer that seems extremely plausible, but is actually the OPPOSITE of what D states. Here, the difference involves only a few words.

EXERCISES:
SENTENCE ADDITION

DIRECTIONS: Read each excerpt and select the best answer to the multiple-choice question that follows.

1.

[1] The decision to move from a densely populated city to the wide-open suburbs is a natural one for a growing family. The availability of larger homes with more private yards around them attracts parents with young children. Such an environment is conducive to a more family-oriented lifestyle, with better schools and more efficient public services. Parents can rear their children at a comfortable pace, introducing them to the less desirable realities of life when they decide the time is right. Most importantly, young parents have numerous options for the type of community they want to settle in.

1

At this point, the writer is considering adding the following sentence.

> At present, more Americans live in the suburbs than in major metropolitan centers.

Should the writer make this addition here?

A) Yes, because it demonstrates why Americans are moving to the suburbs.

B) Yes, because it demonstrates why cities are undesirable environments for children.

C) No, because it does not reflect the writer's interest in self-expression.

D) No, because it does not reflect the writer's interest in family life.

2.

The label of "feminist" has gotten a bad rap in recent years. Radical feminists of the '60s and '70s, although moderately successful in changing the way we assign gender roles, have given the citizens of the millennial era a distasteful image when they look back into the past. Young women today have not experienced the oppressive roles and attitudes that women of the '50s faced, so they see little need for equal employment initiatives, women's colleges, and other organizations that promote gender equality (sometimes at the expense of men's power). Young men also seem perplexed with the existence of a modern feminist movement since they have grown up with working mothers and female supervisors. [2] Whether such ways of viewing the world are successes or failures for the feminists of the last century, of course, depends on how these viewpoints play out in the future.

2

At this point, the writer is considering adding the following sentence.

> Indeed, the idea of patriarchal "oppression" can seem far-fetched now that nobody is fazed by a female CEO with legions of male subordinates.

Should the writer make this addition here?

A) Yes, because it describes a scenario that validates one of the writer's main points.

B) Yes, because it offers further background information on the main principles of radical feminism.

C) No, because it digresses from information that was presented earlier in the paragraph.

D) No, because it introduces a tone of sarcasm into a straightforward argument.

3. Toys represent more than playthings to their child owners, a situation which results in the child's infuriation at the flippant attitudes most adults have towards toys. Just the other day I was cleaning my son's Lego blocks and he responded with such ardent venom that I forgot we were arguing over toys! It hadn't occurred to me—all the worlds he had built, the friendships he had made among his tiny people. **3** Now I let my son decide when to tear down his worlds, when to end his friendships. In the words of the child psychologist Albert Emmington, "Give the children toys. What are all things that matter to us in life but toys?"

3

At this point, the writer is considering adding the following sentence.

> Indeed, adults like me can become hopelessly addicted to the fabricated and inconsequential "worlds" presented by video games and social media.

Should the writer make this addition here?

A) Yes, because it serves as an effective transition within the paragraph.
B) Yes, because it tempers the writer's earlier criticisms of adults.
C) No, because it detracts from the topic of childhood.
D) No, because it makes the writer seem uninformed.

4. While it's fairly easy to disprove an idea through a single counterexample, how can we prove that something will always be true? We can certainly assume that, since there's a number after nine (namely, ten), there is most likely a number after ten (indeed, eleven). We cannot, however, use examples to keep proving that "the next number exists" forever (a process that would be very boring). This is where the creativity of math comes in. Eventually, we must move beyond rote examples and tap into the sweeping resources of the imagination. **4**

4

At this point, the writer is considering adding the following sentence.

> There is no reason, indeed, for us to question whether eleven million is in fact an extant number: knowing and envisioning what we already do, we can take its existence on faith.

Should the writer make this addition here?

A) Yes, because it defines the "creativity of math."
B) Yes, because shows how one of the writer's assumptions can be applied.
C) No, because it calls attention to a weakness in the writer's primary argument.
D) No, because it repeats information presented earlier.

5. Whenever I hear an announcer proclaim that such-and-such a play has only happened five times in Major League Baseball history, I am impressed. But how can the word "history" properly denote a record that has only existed for little more than a century? **5** Egypt has a cultural history that spans millennia of recorded facts. Even American history, if we include the Colonial period, is barely more than four hundred years old. Speak to a paleontologist or a geologist, and you'll be regaled with a "history" in which a million years are treated as an instant.

5

At this point, the writer is considering adding the following sentence.

> The different stages of natural history that have been formulated by zoologists encompass hundreds of millions of years each.

Should the writer make this addition here?

A) Yes, because it is a logical addition to a series of examples.
B) Yes, because it establishes a premise that structures the paragraph.
C) No, because the writer does not name the different stages of natural history.
D) No, because the writer does not appear to be a zoologist.

6. Japanese Internment was the systematic relocation of Japanese Americans to secluded camps within the U.S. in 1942. As the result of Roosevelt's Executive Order 9066, local military commanders were given power to designate "exclusion zones," thereby banning those of Japanese ancestry from the Pacific coast. Consequently, lawful Japanese-American citizens were displaced from their homes, many of which were lucrative farms. **6** After Internment was declared unjust 40 years later, the U.S. paid a paltry twenty thousand dollars in reparation funds to each internment camp survivor. However, there was no compensation for the lost farms.

6

At this point, the writer is considering adding the following sentence.

> These farms were taken from their Japanese-American owners, who would never receive any directly related sort of remuneration.

Should the writer make this addition here?

A) Yes, because it offers the main reason for the writer's disdain for Japanese Internment.
B) Yes, because the sentence creates an effective transition from a negative to a positive tone.
C) No, because the paragraph focuses mainly on the military reasoning behind Japanese Internment.
D) No, because it simply re-phrases information that the writer considers elsewhere in the paragraph.

7. The possibility of a new supercontinent, commonly referred to as "Amasia," is a prospect that fires the imagination. Naturally, none of us will live to see this new landmass. Even so, we can speculate about where such geological upheaval will leave the species and civilizations that are here hundreds and millions of years on. **7** Perhaps all intelligent life will fuse together in a single super-civilization. But I am most intrigued by the prospect of a new super-ocean on the other side of the globe. What unforeseen new forms of life will emerge to claim this giant world of water as their own?

7

At this point, the writer is considering adding the following sentence.

> Perhaps a new set of adaptations will be set off among birds and large mammals.

Should the writer make this addition here?

A) Yes, because it offers a new and relevant reason for the writer's fascination.
B) Yes, because it provides new information about Amasia's geographical features.
C) No, because it repeats information from elsewhere in the paragraph.
D) No, because it distracts from the writer's main focus on cultural change.

8. "Growing up Italian-American" is not a topic that seems to warrant TV specials or critical theory bestsellers. Socially, it is just not a big deal. But behind this face that seems to meld into any ethnic group, I am tainted by my Italian ancestry. I am an English teacher, but I still hear nothing wrong when my uncles pronounce "three" without the "h." **8** That isn't all, quirk-wise: I do quick translations in my head before ordering "gravy" or "manicot" and I use funeral prayer cards to mark pages the way most people would use a normal bookmark.

8

At this point, the writer is considering adding the following sentence.

> I have never attempted to point this out to them, since they might be insulted by such an intrusion.

Should the writer make this addition here?

A) Yes, because it defines respect for elders as an important part of Italian-American culture.
B) Yes, because it shows why the writer doesn't find Italian-American life exciting.
C) No, because it distracts from the writer's listing of several Italian-American quirks.
D) No, because it is incompatible with the writer's outspokenness elsewhere in the passage.

9. Bran Castle, located in the Carpathian Mountains in Romania, stands high above the surrounding farmland. This edifice was originally built as a bulwark against Ottoman conquest. Yet popular myth, spurred on by Bram Stoker's vampire novel, transformed Bran Castle into Dracula's home. However fallacious, this new status has sparked a recent wave of tourism. It is said that the residents of nearby Bran village had until recently been completely oblivious to Dracula. But as new tourists have flocked in, bringing the prospect of new income, the collective memory has changed. **9**

9

At this point, the writer is considering adding the following sentence.

> Today, it is not uncommon to see a local shopkeeper hawking wooden talismans that were once believed to ward off "Dracula and all his evil consorts."

Should the writer make this addition here?
- A) Yes, because it alludes to an important moment from Bram Stoker's original novel.
- B) Yes, because it offers a specific response to the publicity surrounding Dracula.
- C) No, because it introduces a tone of humor that is inappropriate to the passage.
- D) No, because it does not explain whether or not selling the talismans is profitable.

10. Olympic figure skating is a sport unlike any other, a sport in which months of training all boil down to a single performance. In these few minutes, the athlete must prove himself through strength, control, grace, and finesse. Overall, figure skating rewards those with a balance of these aspects as opposed to those with the most power. **10** Since the inception of the Olympics in 1924, the average figure skater has decreased in height by five inches; smaller, lighter bodies are optimal for the jumping, spinning, and landing required by the sport. Does this mean that all figure skaters must be small? Of course it doesn't. Despite body types, athleticism will always be defined as personal perseverance and triumph over obstacles both mental and physical.

10

At this point, the writer is considering adding the following sentence.

> Both training and competition can be merciless, but figure skaters themselves can triumph by conforming to a certain "ideal" body type.

Should the writer make this addition here?
- A) Yes, because it offers an effective transition from the discussion of aptitudes to the discussion of body type.
- B) Yes, because it anticipates the writer's argument that questions of body type are irrelevant in competitive sports.
- C) No, because it wrongly indicates that figure skaters cannot effectively deal with pressure.
- D) No, because it undermines the writer's argument that athleticism is about more than body type.

11. For want of a better phrase or an appropriate euphemism, I must openly state that "I hate musicals." In what universe does someone start singing mid-sentence or even mid-rant? I don't like reality television either; in essence, reality television shows are just musicals without the singing. Both are melodramatic, cloying, irritating forms of entertainment. **11** Yet where pop culture is concerned, I'll always take a gratuitous car chase over a high-pitched melody of regret or greeting.

11

At this point, the writer is considering adding the following sentence.

> Neither is driven by psychological or social insight of any appreciable sort.

Should the writer make this addition here?

A) Yes, because it explains why the writer finds car chases enjoyable.

B) Yes, because it further explains the writer's aversion to musicals.

C) No, because it should be placed later in the paragraph.

D) No, because it introduces a topic that is irrelevant.

---

12. To excel in their military endeavors, the ancient Romans did not rely on physical prowess alone, important though this was. **12** Roman warriors would regularly perform training exercises with weapons weighing twice as much as the swords and spears that they carried into war. Yet should sheer strength and agility fail these soldiers, siege engines and heavy artillery could still turn the tide of battle. The "foot and horse" warriors of the Roman legions were supported by battering rams, stone-throwing catapults, and devices known as scorpions, which launched blades and javelins into enemy ranks. For the enemies of Rome, the best battle strategy was often a quick and unconditional surrender.

12

At this point, the writer is considering adding the following sentence.

> This approach may explain why the Romans never engaged in particularly extensive nautical campaigns, in sharp contrast to the ancient Greeks.

Should the writer make this addition here?

A) Yes, because it indicates an important limitation of Roman military strategy.

B) Yes, because it indicates an important source of Roman weapons technology.

C) No, because it distracts from the topic of military devices invented by the Romans.

D) No, because it distracts from the topic of Roman military training.

13. Although the Humboldt squid isn't nearly as giant as the giant squid, it still grows to the length of an adult human. Instead of legs, though, this reclusive animal has tentacles with razor-sharp teeth on its suckers, which can flay flesh from bone in seconds. **13** The Humboldt squid, which normally lives deep in the ocean off the western coasts of Central and South America, has recently been seen close to the shore as far north as Canada. Some people blame the overfishing of the squid's natural predators, while others blame climate change for this unusual spread. Either way, this ruthless killer is getting farther from its own habitat—and closer to ours.

13

At this point, the writer is considering adding the following sentence.

> Although clearly adapted to survive in extreme environments, both the Humboldt squid and the giant squid have natural lifespans of only a few years.

Should the writer make this addition here?

A) Yes, because it supports the characterization of the Humboldt squid as reclusive.

B) Yes, because it indicates why the Humboldt squid is spreading into new territory.

C) No, because it undermines the idea that the Humboldt squid is dangerous.

D) No, because it reintroduces the minor topic of the giant squid.

14. One of the principal characters in Henry James's novel *The Wings of the Dove* is a young woman named Milly Theale, who suffers from a chronic disease that James, for whatever reason, decided to leave unnamed. Modern critics have labored to figure out what Milly's malady is. They have devised possibilities as different as tuberculosis, leukemia, diabetes, and pancreatic cancer. **14** My own possibility is that James didn't know or care what Milly's exact affliction was, and that neither should we. To eliminate ambiguity at every turn is to turn a novel into a dead, gray thing, a tiny medical case study instead of a teeming imagined world.

14

At this point, the writer is considering adding the following sentence.

> Some daring scholars have even claimed that Milly was afflicted by the bubonic plague.

Should the writer make this addition here?

A) Yes, because it offers information relevant to why Henry James wrote *The Wings of the Dove*.

B) Yes, because it offers information relevant to the discussion of the possibilities for Milly's affliction.

C) No, because its tone is inappropriate to the rest of the writer's discussion

D) No, because it undermines the writer's primary argument.

15. In 1915, Marcel Duchamp bought a snow shovel, suspended it from the ceiling of his studio, and declared it a full-fledged work of art. He even gave this work a title, *In Advance of the Broken Arm*. Duchamp's creation of this and other "readymade" artworks has been rightly viewed by most critics as a subversive gesture; after all, if a snow shovel or a hat rack or a bicycle tire can be held up as "art," where does the realm of "art" begin and the realm of "non-art" end? **15** But I like to think that there was a second, more positive side of Duchamp's agenda. As I see it, he was acting out a desire to make us look more closely at everyday life and find moments of artistic beauty where we least expect them.

15

At this point, the writer is considering adding the following sentence.

> What better way to rebel against "elite culture" than to try to pass off a flipped over urinal (another Duchamp readymade) as an "elite culture" museum piece?

Should the writer make this addition here?

A) Yes, because it provides further evidence for the possibility that Duchamp's work was subversive.

B) Yes, because alludes to the possibility that Duchamp's work was artistically beautiful.

C) No, because it should be positioned earlier in the paragraph.

D) No, because it should be positioned later in the paragraph.

16. **16** Many will contend that video games have replaced reading, particularly the reading of fiction. While video games may have dispensed with actual bound pages, video games carry within them the kind of stories and episodes that are present in all literature. In some cases, the video game hero is faced with a calling to embark on a journey that can change his world for the better. Then, he meets a mentor who guides him along the way. The climax occurs when the hero faces his deepest fear, often embodied by a central antagonist.

16

At this point, the writer is considering adding the following sentence.

> It is commonly believed that new forms of entertainment aggressively displace more traditional media.

Should the writer make this addition here?

A) Yes, because it sets a tone of strong criticism towards those who dislike video games.

B) Yes, because it establishes an assumption that is relevant to the example that follows.

C) No, because it repeats information from elsewhere in the paragraph.

D) No, because it wrongly suggests that the writer dislikes video games.

17. "Facebook is so yesterday," my niece said with a smirk that only a fifteen year-old could pull off: one part innocence and one part arrogance. And then, as if to prove her point and her prowess, she proceeded to list the social media sites that are "so not yesterday." There is Twitter, with its desperate 140-character bids for attention. There is Instagram, with its legions of narcissistic "selfies." **17** I felt a longing for the time before smart phones, when whether you had call-waiting or three-way calling determined your level of cool.

17

At this point, the writer is considering adding the following sentence.

> There are noise-canceling headphones, which teenagers have taken to wearing virtually everywhere.

Should the writer make this addition here?
A) Yes, because it introduces the idea that the writer is nostalgic.
B) Yes, because it implies that the writer is comfortable with some new forms of technology.
C) No, because it undermines the writer's idea that new technologies are detrimental to society.
D) No, because the writer is focusing on forms of connection and communication.

---

18. **18** The human ear is an amazing mechanism. The visible part of the ear, the auricle, acts as a conical amplifier, picking up sounds and funneling them into the deeper reaches of the organ. In terms of structure, the ear functions in much the same way that a seashell does. If a shell were to have an opening at its pinnacle, and if the pinnacle were to be placed gently into the ear, then such an arrangement would greatly amplify the surrounding sounds. But that's not all when it comes to the workings of the ear. Hearing is actually the ear's ancillary purpose: keeping the body in equilibrium is this versatile organ's more difficult, but more essential, task.

18

At this point, the writer is considering adding the following sentence.

> Many of the workings of the human body can, in fact, be understood through analogy to other parts of the natural universe.

Should the writer make this addition here?
A) Yes, because it establishes a tone of fascination with the workings of the human body.
B) Yes, because the writer later compares the ear to other body parts.
C) No, because it presents an idea that would probably be familiar to most readers.
D) No, because it introduces a topic that is much broader than the paragraph's emphasis.

19. To most, familiarity with "theatre" means familiarity with playwrights such as Shakespeare, Arthur Miller, and maybe David Mamet or Harold Pinter. In contrast, most would not consider or think of Eastern theatrical conventions such as kabuki, the Beijing Opera, or Sanskrit drama when questioned about the proverbial stage. And why is this so? The best explanation is that Western hegemony has pervaded most conventional understandings of art in general. [19] Unfortunately, this means that Eastern dramatic theories and practices are cast to the wayside—often belittled for departing from "standard" theatrical criteria and almost always relegated to the position of theatre that "celebrates culture," when in reality the theatre of the East has often guided the theatre of the West.

[19]

At this point, the writer is considering adding the following sentence.

> Shakespeare and Miller are fixtures on high school and college syllabi; Kabuki and Sanskrit drama certainly are not.

Should the writer make this addition here?

A) Yes, because it supports the writer's argument that Western drama is less complex than Eastern drama.
B) Yes, because it offers meaningful analysis of information introduced earlier.
C) No, because it is incompatible with the writer's respect for Eastern drama.
D) No, because it repeats a series of facts that the writer introduced earlier.

20. Ask a research scientist what exactly he or she does on a daily basis, and you will probably get an answer so complicated that only another scientist in the same field could understand it. [20] It is easy to forget that the mass of obscure terms and intricate calculations that a scientist calls "work" often has poignantly human roots. Despite picking up a few tidbits of information while taking my kids to planetariums and science fairs, I understand nothing about astrophysics. But it is possible that one of the children sitting next to me will look up at those same artificial constellations and someday dedicate a lifetime to studying the real universe. This must be where inspiration begins.

[20]

At this point, the writer is considering adding the following sentence.

> My wife, for instance, is a molecular biologist, and regularly publishes articles in a campus magazine at the university where she works.

Should the writer make this addition here?

A) Yes, because it transitions into the writer's discussion of his own family life.
B) Yes, because it supports the writer's idea that everyday activity can inspire scientific insight.
C) No, because it detracts from the writer's discussion of the difficulty of explaining scientific concepts.
D) No, because it would be better placed as the first sentence of the paragraph.

21. A debate has raged in recent years as to whether we should apply business practices to government entities. Proponents of such measures believe that the public's best interests are served by limiting spending and slashing budgets. **21** Somehow, these partisans seem to have forgotten what the proper purpose of government is. The government's job is not to produce goods, but to protect and serve its citizens. It is impossible to focus on the health and safety of the populace when an organization is constantly worried about whether its funding will be, like the proverbial rug, pulled out from under its feet.

21

At this point, the writer is considering adding the following sentence.

> After all, if cost-efficiency creates world-class companies in technology and finance, why can't the same principle create geopolitical superpowers?

Should the writer make this addition here?

A) Yes, because it helps to explain the reasoning behind an idea discussed by the writer.
B) Yes, because it singles out specific industries that the writer views with disdain.
C) No, because it would be more effectively placed earlier in the paragraph.
D) No, because it makes the writer seem confused and indecisive.

---

22. In June of 1967, Air Force pilot Robert Henry Lawrence became the first African-American astronaut. Sadly, he would never see a full space mission. Lawrence's career was cut short in December of the same year, when he lost his life in a jet crash at Edwards Air Force Base in California. **22** Americans would have to wait another 15 years before an African American was actually launched into space (an honor that went to Guion "Guy" Bluford, Jr., a participant in the 1983 Challenger space shuttle explorations). Since then, America has been graced with African-American astrophysicists, African-American NASA administrators, and an African-American director of the Hayden Planetarium. Such diversity came gradually; let us hope that it remains in place permanently.

22

At this point, the writer is considering adding the following sentence.

> Nor would he be the last African-American space pioneer to lose his life in pursuing new horizons.

Should the writer make this addition here?

A) Yes, because it indicates a sociological difficulty that African Americans faced.
B) Yes, because it shows why Lawrence is respected by later African-American aerospace experts.
C) No, because the paragraph does not discuss any other fatalities involving African Americans.
D) No, because the sentence wrongly indicates that the writer is critical of the American space program.

23. Immigration has been and will always be a point of contention in American society. **[23]** During the California Gold Rush of 1848 to 1855, Chinese men, seeking work in the gold mines, immigrated to America. But as the initial fervor dwindled and gold extraction became highly competitive, animosity toward Chinese laborers rose dramatically. Most were banished from mine work and forced to settle in enclaves on the outskirts of major cities such as San Francisco. Without any other employment prospects, these immigrants often found low-end positions in restaurants and laundry facilities, and unknowingly gave rise to the unjust theory that Chinese immigration depressed wage levels.

[23]

At this point, the writer is considering adding the following sentence.

> Even today, political debates rage over whether United States automakers should manufacture their cars domestically or build new factories abroad.

Should the writer make this addition here?

A) Yes, because it substantiates the point introduced in the first sentence of the paragraph.

B) Yes, because it anticipates the point made in the last sentences of the paragraph.

C) No, because it does not directly relate to the topic of immigration.

D) No, because it contradicts the writer's ideas on immigration.

24. Like any normal person, I could not wait to travel to Europe, the faraway land of magic and mystical fables, castles, and languages of love. My itinerary read like the route of a modern-day gypsy—Paris, Venice, Florence, and Prague. **[24]** Unfortunately, all of my expectations were delusions. As I entered each country, I could not help but notice how alike everything looked. Yes, old buildings and castles have different façades, but the differences no longer stand out when the people surrounding these structures are dressed in similar clothing and clutch identical phones. Famed edifices are no longer breathtaking when each one has the kind of gift shop you are likely to find in the United States, or Canada, or probably anywhere in the world.

[24]

At this point, the writer is considering adding the following sentence.

> Every new city would transport me to an adventure like none I had ever before seen.

Should the writer make this addition here?

A) Yes, because it presents a negative stance that the writer develops later in the passage.

B) Yes, because it helps to establish the writer's specific misconceptions about foreign travel.

C) No, because it would be better placed later in the passage.

D) No, because it does not name the specific cities that the writer visited.

25. The rule of the animal world, it seems, is to follow the herd, the flock, the school, or the swarm; greater numbers mean greater cooperation, and ensure survival. **25** Yet there are animals of all types that thrive in solitude. Some of these are small and self-sufficient (the sturdy desert grasshopper, the aptly-named hermit crab), but others are huge in size (the rhinoceros) or high on the food chain (the jaguar). Family groups for such antisocial animals seldom grow beyond a single mother and the most recent set of offspring; this is certainly the case with the giant anteater. A male anteater will wander alone, crushing ant colony after ant colony, while a female will carry a child or two on its back until these offspring, too, go their singular ways.

25

At this point, the writer is considering adding the following sentence.

> Moreover, zoologists find large animal groups such as these relatively easy to study, providing as they do large population samples with clear patterns of behavior.

Should the writer make this addition here?

A) Yes, because it offers direct support for the general point made in the first sentence.

B) Yes, because it indicates the source of the writer's information about large animals.

C) No, because it introduces a point that is contradicted elsewhere in the paragraph.

D) No, because it introduces a topic that is not addressed elsewhere in the paragraph.

CONTINUE TO THE NEXT PAGE FOR SENTENCE DELETION EXERCISES

EXERCISES:
SENTENCE DELETION

DIRECTIONS: Read each excerpt and select the best answer to the multiple-choice question that follows.

---

26. At some point in your life, you have probably put together a chair, table, or set of bookshelves from IKEA. **26** But you may not be familiar with the intriguing history of this now-widespread brand of build-it-yourself furniture. It turns out that the founder of IKEA, Sweden's Ingvar Kamprad, did not even conceive IKEA primarily as a furniture business; instead, he began his business career selling small household items through the mail. The IKEA brand itself appeared in 1943, but IKEA began selling furniture five years later.

26

The writer is considering deleting the underlined sentence to improve the paragraph. Should the sentence be kept or deleted?

A) Kept, because it responds to an objection raised in the first sentence.

B) Kept, because it offers an effective transition to the content that follows.

C) Deleted, because it blurs the paragraph's focus by alluding to brands other than IKEA.

D) Deleted, because it contradicts the claim made in the first sentence of the paragraph.

---

27. Each day at the bird hospital presents Leonard with a series of new challenges. He may begin the morning improvising a splint for the leg of a wounded blackbird, and finish his duties by mending the wing of a red-tailed hawk. But each day of work at the Raptor Trust Bird Sanctuary also offers Leonard stability and repose. "You become very close to some of the birds over time," he explains. "After a while, some of the owls, ravens, and other majestic birds that we keep on premises while they recover begin to seem like co-workers." **27** A few years ago, Leonard worked in a small arts and crafts store, but thought that this employment was too uneventful day-to-day.

27

The writer is considering deleting the underlined sentence to improve the paragraph. Should the sentence be kept or deleted?

A) Kept, because it explains Leonard's desire for human co-workers.

B) Kept, because it explains why Leonard is attracted to nature.

C) Deleted, because the paragraph deals entirely with Leonard's idealistic values system.

D) Deleted, because the paragraph deals entirely with Leonard's present activities.

28. Murasaki Shikibu was born into the Japanese aristocracy at some point in the late tenth century A.D. While the exact dates of her birth and death are open to dispute, what few would question is that "Lady Murasaki" (as she is now known) created one of the great psychological novels of world literature. That novel, *The Tale of Genji*, portrays in great detail the elite world that Murasaki knew so well. [28] This narrative is no mere social drama, and is rich in observations of the universals of human nature. Murasaki's creation serves as a meditation on forces such as proper conduct and personal affection, themes that transcend class and time.

[28]

The writer is considering deleting the underlined sentence to improve the paragraph. Should the sentence be kept or deleted?

A) Kept, because it introduces an idea that is analyzed at greater length in the sentence that follows.

B) Kept, because it explains why Murasaki was widely respected by other members of the Japanese elite.

C) Deleted, because it simply re-states content from earlier in the passage.

D) Deleted, because it detracts from the writer's focus on the debate surrounding Murasaki's birth and death.

29. Last autumn, I received the surprise of my life: the company that had employed me for the past sixteen years decided, without the slightest indication, to terminate my job. I was granted a respectable severance package, of course, and I did have some savings. However, I knew that these funds would not be sufficient to cover all my living expenses while I looked for a new job. It was up to me to economize, and I did so partially by relying on my own cleverness and partially by relying on websites. [29] It turns out that the Internet is a treasure trove of advice for those of us who want (or in my case need) to save a few dollars. The first gem that I found was ThePennyHoarder.com, a site that offers short point-by-point articles on how to find part-time work, how to eliminate debt, and how to put your existing money to the best possible uses.

[29]

The writer is considering deleting the underlined sentence to improve the paragraph. Should the sentence be kept or deleted?

A) Kept, because it helps to shift the focus from the writer's dilemma to the writer's solution.

B) Kept, because it helps to shift the focus from the writer's past job to the writer's new career.

C) Deleted, because it undermines the idea that the termination of the writer's job was surprising.

D) Deleted, because it undermines the idea that the writer's savings were insufficient.

30. Ants are capable of carrying several times their body weight and of building complex underground networks of tunnels. **30** Most people have encountered these facts so often that they no longer find them remotely interesting. Yet did you know that ants can also walk backwards? A recent study, conducted by researchers from the University of Edinburgh and the Research Centre on Animal Cognition, has demonstrated that "ants can get their bearings whatever the orientation of their body," as reported in Science Daily. This finding overturns earlier beliefs about ant navigation, particularly the idea that ants navigated solely by memorizing predictable sequences of visual clues—sequences that ants, presumably, could not process in reverse.

30

The writer is considering deleting the underlined sentence to improve the paragraph. Should the sentence be kept or deleted?

A) Kept, because it anticipates a possible objection to the writer's main argument.

B) Kept, because it suggests a reason that the research described later on is especially valuable.

C) Deleted, because it presents a viewpoint that the writer goes on to firmly reject.

D) Deleted, because it introduces commentary that detracts from the writer's main topic.

31. J.K. Rowling frequented her local coffee shop while conceiving and writing the *Harry Potter* series. It was there that she imagined and envisioned her magical world, possibly pulling inspiration from the daily operations of the café and the coffee lovers walking in and sitting near her. The people at the café were not people at all, but prototypes of the characters that she would eventually bring to life on the page. **31** While some may argue that writing today has become merely a means of appropriating a stranger's life, who really cares? Writing is not the espousal of another's experiences; it is the dramatization and reimagining of that life as a story so specific that it inadvertently becomes universal.

31

The writer is considering deleting the underlined sentence to improve the paragraph. Should the sentence be kept or deleted?

A) Kept, because it effectively sums up a perspective that J.K. Rowling criticizes in some of her own writings.

B) Kept, because it effectively sums up a perspective that the writer challenges in the following sentence.

C) Deleted, because it does not take into account the difficulty of creating realistic characters.

D) Deleted, because it does not take into account important differences between J.K. Rowling and other café-based writers.

32. Anthropologists have long noted that all human cultures possess some level of superstition or magical thinking. Recently, a new theory has attempted to explain the benefits that such seemingly irrational beliefs can yield. Since our brains are finite organs, a bit of magic keeps our attention spans from spreading too thin; a supernatural explanation can provide focus and comfort. If we were to worry all day about the why and the how of the past and the future, we could never prioritize the present for long enough to survive. **32** After all, superstitious thought of some form or other is a truly universal human trait. Furthermore, now that survival isn't as difficult for all of us, we can seek new explanations of matters that extend beyond the present moment.

32

The writer is considering deleting the underlined sentence to improve the paragraph. Should the sentence be kept or deleted?

A) Kept, because it further explains how superstitions can ensure survival.

B) Kept, because it relates specific superstitions to the reader's own culture.

C) Deleted, because it merely reformulates content from elsewhere in the paragraph.

D) Deleted, because it would be better situated as the final sentence of the paragraph.

33. Everybody in my town—if you could call acres upon acres of western Maryland farmland a town—belonged to one of the clubs offered by the community center. The girls mostly raised rabbits or rode horses, while the boys opted mostly for remote-control planes and model rockets. I chose rockets. **33** Actually, "chose" would be a bit of an understatement: I threw myself into the task, body and mind, heart and soul. I would spend hours putting together pre-designed models, then hours more figuring out my own fin and nose cone combinations. I would launch my rockets early in the morning, on a nearby football field. I would stand there wondering what it would be like to create a rocket that could reach past the clouds, past the atmosphere.

33

The writer is considering deleting the underlined sentence to improve the paragraph. Should the sentence be kept or deleted?

A) Kept, because it helps the writer to explain why he was first drawn to rocketry.

B) Kept, because it plays an important role in clarifying the writer's attitude.

C) Deleted, because the writer's passion for rocketry is made apparent earlier.

D) Deleted, because it does not take into account the writer's place in his community.

34. [34] The writing of art history and the writing of criticism melded as never before in the early years of the twentieth century. Before, it had been fashionable for philosophers to dabble in art criticism, as Denis Diderot did in the late eighteenth century; it had also been common for art critics to tinge their tracts and essays with philosophical theory, as nineteenth-century writers such as John Ruskin and Charles Baudelaire did. Yet it was a historian of the modernist era, Clement Greenberg, who truly brought these two disciplines together. Greenberg and his followers applied the same deft precision to classic philosophical distinctions that they applied to the canvases of Picasso and Matisse. And in so doing, they forever changed the way we think about art.

[34]

The writer is considering deleting the underlined sentence to improve the paragraph. Should the sentence be kept or deleted?

A) Kept, because it introduces an idea directly relevant to the writer's main idea.

B) Kept, because it introduces an idea directly relevant to Denis Diderot.

C) Deleted, because it wrongly implies that Greenberg was not an influential figure.

D) Deleted, because it wrongly implies that Ruskin and Baudelaire lived in the twentieth century.

35. In 1956, Gordon Moore, one of the co-founders of the technology giant Intel, formulated an idea that has guided our conception of technological advancement in the decades since. [35] Curiously, however, Moore's idea would play only a limited role in Intel's business development and investor relations strategies, remarkable though his conception was. According to "Moore's Law," the power and efficiency of computer processing technology will increase considerably over time. Simultaneously, the cost of producing information technology essentials, such as semiconductors, will decrease over time. These developments work together to yield exponential increases in the speed and efficiency of technology over time.

[35]

The writer is considering deleting the underlined sentence to improve the paragraph. Should the sentence be kept or deleted?

A) Kept, because it clarifies Moore's role at Intel.

B) Kept, because it addresses a common misinterpretation of Moore's Law.

C) Deleted, because it detracts from the discussion of how Moore's Law operates.

D) Deleted, because it contradicts the claim that Moore's Law was an influential idea.

36. It is commonplace for people to offhandedly describe the foods that they love as "addictive." Recent chemistry has proven that there is a genuinely addictive side to one supremely common food: cheese. [36] Among the most abundant components of cheese is Casein. When Casein is digested, fragments known as "casomorphins" are released. These casomorphins react with the body in a manner that recalls the impact of dangerous habit-forming drugs, such as opiates. Of course, cheese "addiction" isn't life-threatening, but the "addictive" effects of cheese are real.

[36]

The writer is considering deleting the underlined sentence to improve the paragraph. Should the sentence be kept or deleted?

A) Kept, because it explains a term that is important to the content that follows.

B) Kept, because it explains why cheese can be accurately regarded as addictive.

C) Deleted, because it places too much emphasis on a relatively unimportant idea.

D) Deleted, because it detracts from the writer's ironic and conversational tone.

37. Walrus tusks are central to forms of competition and displays of dominance within walrus social groups. Male walruses use their tusks in combat with one another as they vie for power; in many cases, the leader of a group of walruses will be the male who possesses the largest tusks. [37] Such large tusks are prized by ivory poachers, who can profit handsomely from tusks that are at least one meter long. However, individual walruses also know how to put their tusks to an important practical use. If a walrus ever has trouble climbing out of the water and onto an ice ledge, it can sink its tusks into the ice and pull itself up.

[37]

The writer is considering deleting the underlined sentence to improve the paragraph. Should the sentence be kept or deleted?

A) Kept, because it suggests an important difference between male and female walruses.

B) Kept, because it indicates a source of new information about walrus tusks.

C) Deleted, because how walruses compete and cooperate is the writer's main focus.

D) Deleted, because how walruses employ their tusks is the writer's main focus.

38. As a professional psychiatrist, I have to make a conscious effort to remind myself that not everybody is my patient. This applies even to the characters that I find on the page. Recently I have been reading *Anna Karenina*, and I have been laboring mightily to figure out why exactly the title character acts the way she does. Does Anna suffer from a form of obsessive compulsive disorder? Does she languish under a repressed trauma? [38] Does she have an Electra Complex or some other psychological problem derived from Greek myth? Or is it undiagnosed and untreated paranoid schizophrenia? Does any of this matter? It probably doesn't matter as much as my basic enjoyment of the book matters, but enjoyment is difficult when all this professional apparatus gets in the way.

38

The writer is considering deleting the underlined sentence to improve the paragraph. Should the sentence be kept or deleted?

A) Kept, because it establishes the writer's ironic and amused tone.

B) Kept, because it continues a series of ideas important to the writer's stance.

C) Deleted, because it uses inappropriately advanced vocabulary.

D) Deleted, because it undermines the writer's central argument.

39. [39] It has been said that all historical events happen twice, first as tragedy and then as farce. In the 1950s and 1960s, Americans who feared that nuclear warfare would obliterate humanity began building elaborate bomb shelters, stocking them with battery-powered devices and canned goods. Today, virtually identical measures are being taken by civilians known as "preppers" and "survivalists." These Americans believe that catastrophe may be imminent, and learn the skills of resource conservation that will be necessary should environmental upheaval or (yes) nuclear war destroy civilization. True to form, they also have a tendency to buy up and store away canned goods.

39

The writer is considering deleting the underlined sentence to improve the paragraph. Should the sentence be kept or deleted?

A) Kept, because it explains how the writer first became interested in unusual political events.

B) Kept, because it offers a clear explanation for such irrational possibilities as nuclear war.

C) Deleted, because it does not accurately reflect the ideas that the writer sets forward later.

D) Deleted, because it sets forward an idea that "preppers" and "survivalists" would dispute.

40. As humankind explores more and more of the known universe, a new question will become increasingly important: how does spending time in space impact the human body? [40] Indeed, can space travel actually accelerate the body's normal healing processes? The effect of low- to zero-gravity environments on the human anatomy has yet to be comprehensively understood. Nonetheless, some intriguing early work in this line of inquiry has been performed by researchers from the University of Michigan, who have found that astronauts' brain compositions can be altered during space missions. Twelve astronauts from a shuttle crew and fourteen from the International Space Station offered brain imaging data to the Michigan study. As it turns out, the absence of gravity can re-wire a brain's pathways in much the same way that learning a new skill shifts the brain's organization.

[40]

The writer is considering deleting the underlined sentence to improve the paragraph. Should the sentence be kept or deleted?

A) Kept, because it corrects a popular misconception about the effects of space travel.

B) Kept, because it explains one of the central premises of the University of Michigan study.

C) Deleted, because it subtly undermines a claim that the writer goes on to make.

D) Deleted, because it raises a topic that the writer does not discuss.

ANSWERS ON THE NEXT PAGE

ANSWERS:
SENTENCE ADDITION AND DELETION

1. D

2. A

3. C

4. B

5. A

6. D

7. A

8. C

9. B

10. A

11. B

12. D

13. D

14. B

15. A

16. B

17. D

18. D

19. B

20. C

21. A

22. C

23. C

24. B

25. D

26. B

27. D

28. A

29. A

30. D

31. B

32. C

33. B

34. A

35. C

36. A

37. D

38. B

39. C

40. D

Chapter Ten

Content Choice

MOST APPROPRIATE CONTENT CHOICE

FULFILLING PROMPT REQUIREMENTS

You have already seen how the SAT will ask you to determine where to place sentences of content, and whether specific sentences are relevant. However, the SAT questions that ask you to evaluate passage content present one final challenge. In some cases, it will be up to you to determine what content best fulfills a specific objective, or is the best fit for a theme, idea, or structural technique within a passage.

Compared to questions that simply ask you to reposition, add, or delete a sentence, questions such as these—which ask you to determine the best or most appropriate content—can appear much more complex. Yet appearances are not wholly accurate here, since questions about the best possible content often include helpful clues that can guide your entire answering process.

In these respects, consider the following content question.

Example 1

Have you ever seen an old map sporting fantastical monsters and mythical beasts? This practice, born as early as some of the first maps, has a basis in the typical fears of a constantly shifting world. When man began to walk, great snakes and beasts appeared. When man began to climb, fearsome yetis and massive flying beasts appeared, and when man began to sail, sirens and sea monsters filled the waters. The images on a map changed with cultural confidence, too: in the mid 1600s, humans were seafarers, fearlessly exploring the waters, and the monsters turned to ships, sitting square between Europe and the Americas. **1** Humankind thus began to prioritize maps that were more accurate in measurement, if less artistically pleasing.

1

Which choice provides a statement that accurately sums up the progression of ideas in the paragraph?

A) NO CHANGE
B) Humankind thus entered an era in which science took the place of unthinking superstition.
C) Humankind thus crafted a technology that would, eventually, render merchant caravans and overland trade irrelevant.
D) Humankind thus expressed mastery of an element that, in earlier eras, had been a source of dread.

To answer this question and others like it, you should follow a few essential steps.

1) **Determine** what the question prompt is asking

2) **Provide** an approximate yet useful answer of your own

3) **Pair** your predicted answer against the answer choices, and use Process of Elimination to arrive at the best multiple-choice answer

Move through these steps systematically, and you will answer the question with ease.

Step 1

Through a reading of the prompt, you DETERMINE that you need to sum up the ideas in the paragraph as they progress from one to the next.

1

Which choice provides a statement that accurately sums up the progression of ideas in the paragraph?

A) NO CHANGE
B) Humankind thus entered an era in which science took the place of unthinking superstition.
C) Humankind thus crafted a technology that would, eventually, render merchant caravans and overland trade irrelevant.
D) Humankind thus expressed mastery of an element that, in earlier eras, had been a source of dread.

Step 2

As required by the prompt, you re-read the paragraph. You will see that the paragraph discusses map images over time; these images initially reflected "fears of a constantly shifting world" but eventually registered "cultural confidence."

You should PROVIDE an answer of your own to reflect this information: for instance, "changing map images, monsters to ships, negative to positive" are all useful ideas here.

Changing map images, monsters to ships, negative to positive

Step 3

Now, PAIR your answer against the choices.

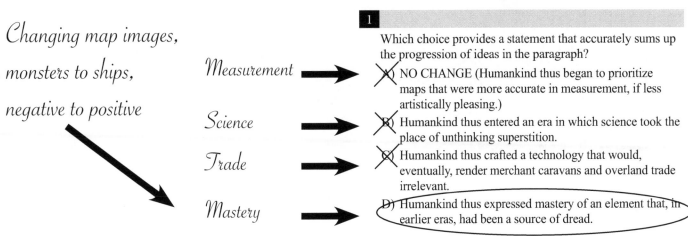

Changing map images, monsters to ships, negative to positive

Measurement →
Science →
Trade →
Mastery →

1

Which choice provides a statement that accurately sums up the progression of ideas in the paragraph?

A) NO CHANGE (Humankind thus began to prioritize maps that were more accurate in measurement, if less artistically pleasing.)
B) Humankind thus entered an era in which science took the place of unthinking superstition.
C) Humankind thus crafted a technology that would, eventually, render merchant caravans and overland trade irrelevant.
D) Humankind thus expressed mastery of an element that, in earlier eras, had been a source of dread.

As you can see, the incorrect answers raise topics such as "measurement" (A), "science" (B), and "trade" (C) that are not major concerns of the passage. Only D, which refers back to the major issue of "mastery" or "confidence," is an appropriate choice.

Keep in mind that you CANNOT solve content questions such as these by using first impressions. All four of the answers follow correct grammar, and any of the four may "sound correct" if slotted in and read quickly. The real trap is that A, B, and C do not fulfill the CONDITIONS OF THE PROMPT.

WORKING WITH BROADER "LOGIC" QUESTIONS

While some SAT content choice questions feature extremely clear prompt requirements, others may seem less precise on a first read. Questions that fall into the second category will simply ask you which content choice "most logically" or "most effectively" works with specific content that is already in the passage. Consider, in this regard, the following example.

The TV channels are full of the death of Nelson Mandela. I so vividly remember watching him walk out of Robben Island (where he had been imprisoned for a long stretch of his life) and embarking upon a mission of national unification that would present new struggles, for all its inspiring power. Mandela was much admired by the Angolan pupils I taught **2** during my years as a composition instructor. In fact, he was second on their list of great African leaders only to Agostinho Neto, who had been Angola's own version of Mandela. Some of the best essays my students wrote were about what these two men meant to the future of all of Africa.

2

Which choice most logically sets up the content that follows?

A) NO CHANGE
B) when I was much younger and much more idealistic.
C) in the course of a temporary appointment in South Africa.
D) as a result of my disillusionment with other global political movements.

This question will challenge you to provide a strong reading of the passage on your own. Fortunately, a modified version of the three steps that you have already seen will prove useful.

Step 1

You need to DETERMINE which content logically leads into the later sentences of the paragraph. Be aware that some of the answers may be ILLOGICAL or IRRELEVANT, and can thus be eliminated on these grounds.

Step 2

PROVIDE a good working summary of the content that occurs in the later portions of the passage. Here, the writer discusses Nelson Mandela, Agostinho Neto, his Angolan students, and his teaching. A logical choice would lead away from the discussion of Mandela alone and into one of these topics.

Step 3

Now, DETERMINE which of the possible pieces of content logically lead into the ideas that you have located within the passage, and eliminate any that do not.

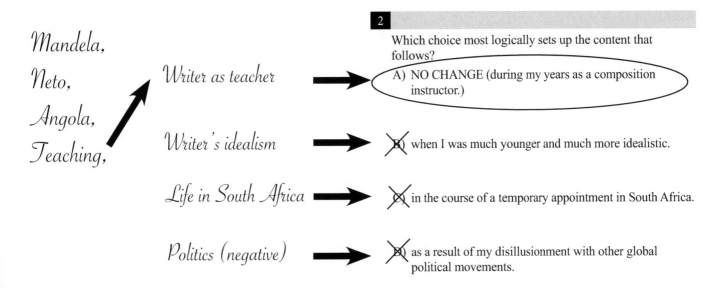

Again, all of the choices are grammatically correct, but all choices EXCEPT A commit noticeable errors in terms of tone, focus, and logic. B raises the topics of youth and idealism, which are out of context. C wrongly states that the writer was in South Africa, when in fact the Angolan pupils would most logically have lived in Angola itself; D wrongly introduces a negative tone, when in fact the writer is mostly positive about political figures (Mandela and Neto).

You should see that A is an excellent choice because it refers back to the writer's role as a teacher. Moreover, this answer enhances the discussion by logically explaining WHY the writer's students were writing "essays": as a "composition instructor," the writer would be reading student essays as part of his natural and expected job duties.

EXERCISES BEGIN ON THE NEXT PAGE

EXERCISES:
MOST APPROPRIATE CONTENT CHOICE

DIRECTIONS: Read each excerpt and select the best answer to the multiple-choice question that follows.

1. The decision to move from a densely populated city to the wide-open suburbs is a natural one for a growing family. The availability of larger homes with more private yards around them attracts parents with young children. Such an environment is conducive to a more family-oriented lifestyle, with better schools, **1** recreational opportunities appropriate for all ages, and more efficient public services. Parents can rear their children at a comfortable pace, introducing them to the less desirable realities of life when they decide the time is right. Most importantly, young parents have numerous options for the type of community they want to settle in.

1

Which further example most effectively supports the main idea of the sentence?

A) NO CHANGE
B) funding for innovative small businesses,
C) public presentations on the dangers of income inequality,
D) efforts to replace carpooling and ride-sharing with new forms of public transportation,

2. The label of "feminist" has gotten a bad rap in recent years. Radical feminists of the '60s and '70s, although moderately successful in changing the way we assign gender roles, have given the citizens of the millennial era a distasteful image when they look back into the past. Young women today have not experienced the oppressive roles and attitudes that women of the '50s faced, so they see little need for equal employment initiatives, women's colleges, and other organizations that promote gender equality (sometimes at the expense of men's power). **2** Consequently, scholars of women's studies have attempted a more accommodating approach that bridges contemporary and "radical" feminism. Young men also seem perplexed with the existence of a modern feminist movement since they have grown up with working mothers and female supervisors.

2

Which choice most effectively sets up the information that follows?

A) NO CHANGE
B) At one time, feminists such as Judy Brady were eager to subject gender limitations to a type of vicious satire that is disappearing from feminist discourse.
C) Nor are such qualms about the usefulness and relevance of "radical feminist" ideas limited to today's women.
D) The disappearance of some trappings of "radical feminism," however, has not entirely robbed the movement of its influence.

129

3. Toys represent more than playthings to their child owners, a situation which results in the child's infuriation at the flippant attitudes most adults have towards toys. Just the other day I was cleaning my son's Lego blocks and he responded with such ardent venom that I forgot we were arguing over toys! It hadn't occurred to me—all the worlds he had built, the friendships he had made among his tiny people. Now I let my son decide when to tear down his worlds, when to end his friendships. In the words of the child psychologist Albert Emmington, "Give the children toys. What are all things that matter to us in life but toys?" **3**

3

Which choice most clearly ends the paragraph with a restatement of the writer's primary claim?

A) The design and marketing of children's toys is by no means child's play.

B) The process of growing up, in truth, can be a process of dumbing down.

C) The imaginary friendships a child forms can be more real than any real-world bond.

D) The world of playthings contains a world of significance.

4. While it's fairly easy to disprove an idea through a single counterexample, how can we prove that something will always be true? We can certainly assume that, since there's a number after nine (namely, ten), there is most likely a number after ten (indeed, eleven). We cannot, however, use examples to keep proving "the next number exists" forever (a process that would be very boring). This is where the creativity of math comes in **4** and elevates our understanding of numbers beyond mere drudgery. Eventually, we must move beyond rote examples and tap into the sweeping resources of the imagination.

4

Which choice most logically and accurately reflects the writer's reasoning?

A) NO CHANGE

B) and raises a series of parallels between higher mathematics and the creation of fine art.

C) and reminds us that mathematical genius is not as rare as we might suspect.

D) and shows how comical the idea of infinite counting really is.

5. Whenever I hear an announcer proclaim that such-and-such a play has only happened five times in Major League Baseball history, I am impressed. But how can the word "history" properly denote a record that has only existed for little more than a century? Egypt has a cultural history that spans millennia of recorded facts; **5** such information has reached us through the hieroglyphic "writings" carved on temple walls. Even American history, if we include the Colonial period, is barely more than four hundred years old. Speak to a paleontologist or a geologist, and you'll be regaled with a "history" in which a million years are treated as an instant.

5

Which choice provides the most relevant detail?

A) NO CHANGE

B) the Middle Ages, by some measures, lasted approximately one thousand years.

C) its political life and agricultural practices changed relatively little during all this time.

D) nonetheless, Egypt has exerted less of an influence on Western thought than ancient Greece or imperial Rome has.

6. Japanese Internment was the systematic relocation of Japanese Americans to secluded camps within the U.S. in 1942. As the result of Roosevelt's Executive Order 9066, local military commanders were given power to designate "exclusion zones," thereby banning those of Japanese ancestry from the Pacific coast. Consequently, lawful Japanese-American citizens were displaced from their homes, many of which were lucrative farms. After Internment was declared unjust 40 years later, the U.S. paid a paltry twenty thousand dollars **6** (an amount to be put to virtually any suitable use) in reparation funds to each internment camp survivor. However, there was no compensation for the lost farms.

6

Which choice provides the most useful and logical context for the writer's discussion?

A) NO CHANGE

B) (an amount that was arrived at by a bipartisan Congressional committee)

C) (an amount much greater than any reparations ever paid to the descendants of slaves)

D) (an amount that is barely more than one year of salary at the U.S. poverty line)

7. The possibility of a new supercontinent, commonly referred to as "Amasia," is a prospect that fires the imagination. Naturally, none of us will live to see this new landmass. Even so, we can speculate about where such geological upheaval will leave the species and civilizations that are here hundreds and millions of years on, **7** wondering why our predictions were so different from their reality. Perhaps all intelligent life will fuse together in a single super-civilization. But I am most intrigued by the prospect of a new super-ocean on the other side of the globe. What unforeseen new forms of life will emerge to claim this giant world of water as their own?

7

The writer wishes to project a tone of interest without departing from the primary topic of the paragraph. Which choice best accomplishes this goal?

A) NO CHANGE

B) privileged to see whatever stark transformations might manifest themselves.

C) equipped with technology considerably more advanced than ours.

D) eager to re-discover the societies and cultures that exist today.

8. "Growing up Italian-American" is not a topic that seems to warrant TV specials or critical theory bestsellers. **8** Socially, it is just not a big deal. But behind this face that seems to meld into any ethnic group, I am tainted by my Italian ancestry. I am an English teacher, but I still hear nothing wrong when my uncles pronounce "three" without the "h." That isn't all, quirk-wise: I do quick translations in my head before ordering "gravy" or "manicot" and I use funeral prayer cards to mark pages the way most people would use a normal bookmark.

8

Which choice effectively anticipates and addresses the writer's idea that "Growing up Italian-American" is not a topic that receives exceptional attention?

A) There are indeed musicals and novels about Italian-American communities, but the legion of narratives about "Growing up African-American" or "Growing up Hispanic-American" overwhelm them.

B) Although we Italian Americans avidly consume all forms of entertainment, I must admit that I am most drawn to stories that have nothing to do with the Italian-American experience.

C) Perhaps this neglect is for the best; in the past, popular culture has stereotyped Italian Americans as criminals, sentimentalists, or both at once.

D) Of course, the neglect that surrounds the topic of "Growing up Italian-American" does not dampen American interest in Italian-American cuisine.

9. Bran Castle, located in the Carpathian Mountains in Romania, stands high above the surrounding farmland. This edifice was originally built as a bulwark against Ottoman conquest. Yet popular myth, spurred on by Bram Stoker's vampire novel, transformed Bran Castle into Dracula's home. However fallacious, this new status has sparked a recent wave of tourism. It is said that the residents of nearby Bran village had until recently been completely oblivious to Dracula. But as new tourists have flocked in, bringing the prospect of new income, the collective memory has changed. **9** The incentives behind such a revenue-generation scheme are many, and are understandable; without the money generated by Dracula-based tourism, Bran village would lack the basic resources to make basic infrastructure and public works improvements.

9

Which choice most effectively concludes the paragraph?

A) NO CHANGE

B) Now, it is not uncommon to find shopkeepers who had been all but ignorant of Dracula a few years before showing off sanctified crosses that had once warded off "the sinister Count Dracula himself."

C) The new Dracula-related publicity has been assisted by the fact that the depiction of Bran Castle in Stoker's novel is remarkably true to life, even though Stoker's knowledge of Romanian culture was fragmentary at best.

D) Perhaps the influx of money can be attributed to the sensational nature of Stoker's narrative; after all, attempts to profit from the more staid Victorian novels of George Eliot and Thomas Hardy have proven unsuccessful.

10. Olympic figure skating is a sport unlike any other, a sport in which months of training all boil down to a single performance. In these few minutes, the athlete must prove himself through strength, control, grace, and finesse. Overall, figure skating rewards those with a balance of these aspects as opposed to those with the most power. Since the inception of the Olympics in 1924, the average figure skater has decreased in height by five inches, **10** while the average weight has increased over time to 110 pounds; smaller, lighter bodies are optimal for the jumping, spinning, and landing required by the sport. Does this mean that all figure skaters must be small? Of course it doesn't. Despite body types, athleticism will always be defined as personal perseverance and triumph over obstacles both mental and physical.

10

Which choice provides the most appropriate and logically consistent detail at this point?

A) NO CHANGE

B) while the average weight has fluctuated considerably but never broken 110 pounds.

C) while the average weight has diminished over time to roughly 110 pounds.

D) while the average weight has remained constant at 110 pounds.

11. For want of a better phrase or an appropriate euphemism, I must openly state that "I hate musicals." In what universe does someone start singing mid-sentence or even mid-rant? **11** Are we, indeed, living in a universe where the most discerning critics find such displays disarming? I don't like reality television either; in essence, reality television shows are just musicals without the singing. Both are melodramatic, cloying, irritating forms of entertainment. Yet where pop culture is concerned, I'll always take a gratuitous car chase over a high-pitched melody of regret or greeting.

11

Which choice gives a second and related supporting statement that continues the writer's discussion?

A) NO CHANGE

B) Has any random group of strangers really ever broken into perfectly choreographed tap dancing?

C) Could any production cost or marketing plan remotely justify such a blatant departure from realism?

D) Have the demarcations between such debased "pop culture" and actual art ever proven so unclear?

12. To excel in their military endeavors, the ancient Romans did not rely on physical prowess alone, important though this was. [12] Roman warriors would regularly perform training exercises with weapons weighing twice as much as the swords and spears that they carried into war. Yet should sheer strength and agility fail these soldiers, siege engines and heavy artillery could still turn the tide of battle. The "foot and horse" warriors of the Roman legions were supported by battering rams, stone-throwing catapults, and devices known as scorpions, which launched blades and javelins into enemy ranks. For the enemies of Rome, the best battle strategy was often a quick and unconditional surrender.

12

Which choice provides the most logical explanation for why Roman warriors trained using exceptionally heavy weapons?

A) To daunt and dispirit their enemies, Roman warriors

B) In keeping with a well-established religious tradition, Roman warriors

C) To build both endurance and dexterity, Roman warriors,

D) In order to stress the difference between themselves and their opponents, Roman warriors

13. Although the Humboldt squid isn't nearly as giant as the giant squid, it still grows to the length of an adult human. Instead of legs, though, this reclusive animal has tentacles with razor-sharp teeth on its suckers, which can flay flesh from bone in seconds. The Humboldt squid, which normally lives deep in the ocean off the western coasts of Central and South America, has recently been seen close to the shore as far north as Canada. Some people blame the overfishing of the squid's [13] natural predators, while others blame climate change for this unusual spread. Either way, this ruthless killer is getting farther from its own habitat—and closer to ours.

13

Which choice adds the most appropriate and specific supporting information to the paragraph?

A) natural predators, particularly the large toothed whales that roam Arctic waters,

B) natural predators, particularly the swordfish and marlins that can be found off the South American coast,

C) natural predators, which normally consume Humboldt Squids as part of their diet,

D) natural predators, which have been discovered with deep wounds inflicted by the "teeth" of adult Humboldt squids,

14. One of the principal characters in Henry James's novel *The Wings of the Dove* is a young woman named Milly Theale, who suffers from a chronic disease that James, for whatever reason, decided to leave unnamed. Modern critics have labored to figure out what Milly's malady is. [14] Treating this literary issue exactly like a medical case study, they have devised possibilities as different as tuberculosis, leukemia, diabetes, and pancreatic cancer. My own possibility is that James didn't know or care what Milly's exact affliction was, and that neither should we. To eliminate ambiguity at every turn is to turn a novel into a dead, gray thing, a tiny medical case study instead of a teeming imagined world.

14

Which choice most provides the most logical introduction to the sentence?

A) NO CHANGE

B) Expending a truly absurd amount of time and energy,

C) Hoping raise the status of literary criticism among actual doctors,

D) Inspired by James's own example as a uniquely meticulous author,

15. In 1915, Marcel Duchamp bought a snow shovel, suspended it from the ceiling of his studio, and declared it a full-fledged work of art. He even gave this work a [15] title that displayed intentionally poor grammar, *In Advance of the Broken Arm*. Duchamp's creation of this and other "readymade" artworks has been rightly viewed by most critics as a subversive gesture; after all, if a snow shovel or a hat rack or a bicycle tire can be held up as "art," where does the realm of "art" begin and the realm of "non-art" end? But I like to think that there was a second, more positive side of Duchamp's agenda. As I see it, he was acting out a desire to make us look more closely at everyday life and find moments of artistic beauty where we least expect them.

15

Which choice provides the most relevant and contextually appropriate explanation of what made the Duchamp artwork so subversive?

A) NO CHANGE

B) title that had little direct link to the work's appearance,

C) title that not even he fully understood at the time,

D) title that he personally found meaningful and dignified,

16. Many will contend that video games have replaced reading, particularly the reading of fiction. While video games may have dispensed with actual bound pages, video games carry within them the kind of stories and episodes that are present in all literature. In some cases, the video game hero is faced with a calling to embark on a journey that can change his world for the better. Then, he meets a mentor who guides him along the way. The climax occurs when the hero faces his deepest fear, often embodied by a central antagonist. **16** Whether or not other elements of the narrative (such as the mentor) re-appear at this climax is left to the discretion of the game's design team.

16

Which choice most logically continues and concludes the writer's discussion of the structure of video games?

A) NO CHANGE
B) This climax is the supreme test of the video game player's skill, and may also (since it may take half an hour or more to reach) test the player's endurance.
C) With the defeat of this antagonist, the hero returns to his home community, much as a hero in folklore or even the hero of a novel would.
D) But the creative power of such a climax is arguably undermined by the fact that a few clever gaming "tricks" can promise easy victory

17. "Facebook is so yesterday," my niece said with a smirk that only a fifteen year-old could pull off: one part innocence and one part arrogance. And then, as if to prove her point and her prowess, she proceeded to list the social media sites that are "so not yesterday." There is Twitter, with its desperate 140-character bids for attention. There is Instagram, with its legions of narcissistic "selfies." **17** Her words left me both amused and somewhat annoyed. I felt a longing for the time before smart phones, when whether you had call-waiting or three-way calling determined your level of cool.

17

Which choice most effectively sets up the writer's statement in the following sentence?

A) NO CHANGE
B) Her words left me both saddened and somewhat optimistic.
C) Her words left me both despondent and somewhat compassionate.
D) Her words left me both nostalgic and somewhat disconnected.

18. The human ear is an amazing mechanism. The visible part of the ear, the auricle, acts as a conical amplifier, picking up sounds and funneling them into the deeper reaches of the organ. [18] To understand this organ's workings, we can resort to a straightforward everyday comparison. In terms of structure, the ear functions in much the same way that a seashell does. If a shell were to have an opening at its pinnacle, and if the pinnacle were to be placed gently into the ear, then such an arrangement would greatly amplify the surrounding sounds. But that's not all when it comes to the workings of the ear. Hearing is actually the ear's ancillary purpose: keeping the body in equilibrium is this versatile organ's more difficult, but more essential, task.

18

Which choice most effectively introduces the discussion that immediately follows?

A) NO CHANGE

B) Unlike some other elements of the body, the ear suggests rough analogies to common objects.

C) Recent research has clarified how the ear channels sound, and has underscored this organ's remarkable efficiency.

D) The manner in which the ear captures sound and transmits it to the brain was once a source of mystery.

19. [19] The perspective of the typical modern theatre-goer is sadly limited. To most, familiarity with "theatre" means familiarity with playwrights such as Shakespeare, Arthur Miller, and maybe David Mamet or Harold Pinter. In contrast, most would not consider or think of Eastern theatrical conventions such as kabuki, the Beijing Opera, or Sanskrit drama when questioned about the proverbial stage. And why is this so? The best explanation is that Western hegemony has pervaded most conventional understandings of art in general. Unfortunately, this means that Eastern dramatic theories and practices are cast to the wayside—often belittled for departing from "standard" theatrical criteria and almost always relegated to the position of theatre that "celebrates culture," when in reality the theatre of the East has often guided the theatre of the West.

19

Which opening sentence best captures the overall focus and tone of the writer's discussion of Eastern and Western theatre?

A) NO CHANGE

B) It is extremely difficult to determine the main reason that Eastern theatre is so often neglected.

C) New efforts are underway to correct the past slights that have been dealt to Eastern theatre.

D) Though many of them have respected Eastern theatre, few Western playwrights have engaged Eastern genres head-on.

20. Ask a research scientist what exactly he or she does on a daily basis, and you will probably get an answer so complicated that only another scientist in the same field could understand it. It is easy to forget that the mass of obscure terms and intricate calculations that a scientist calls "work" often has poignantly **[20]** human roots. Despite picking up a few tidbits of information while taking my kids to planetariums and science fairs, I understand nothing about astrophysics. But it is possible that one of the children sitting next to me will look up at those same artificial constellations and someday dedicate a lifetime to studying the real universe. This must be where inspiration begins.

[20]

Which choice best continues the writer's discussion by anticipating the content that follows?

A) human roots in activities that offer a wealth of knowledge to the most discerning experts.

B) human roots in activities that are designed to promote lifelong careers in the sciences.

C) human roots in activities that may seem like little more than leisurely enrichment.

D) human roots in activities that are deeply entertaining but questionable in their educational content.

21. A debate has raged in recent years as to whether we should apply business practices to government entities. Proponents of such measures believe that the public's best interests are served by limiting spending and slashing budgets. Somehow, these partisans seem to have forgotten what the proper purpose of government is. The government's job is not to produce goods, but to protect and serve its citizens **[21]** through judicious investments in infrastructure. It is impossible to focus on the health and safety of the populace when an organization is constantly worried about whether its funding will be, like the proverbial rug, pulled out from under its feet.

[21]

Which choice adds the most relevant and appropriate example at this point in the paragraph?

A) NO CHANGE

B) through respectful, public debate that welcomes a variety of perspectives.

C) by maintaining an efficient national security apparatus.

D) by appointing officials who seek consensus rather than partisan power.

22. In June of 1967, Air Force pilot Robert Henry Lawrence became the first African-American astronaut. Sadly, he would never see a full space mission. Lawrence's career was cut short in December of the same year, when he lost his life in a jet crash at Edwards Air Force Base in California. [22] NASA and other government agencies had just begun to emphasize ethnic diversity, and Americans would have to wait another 15 years before an African American was actually launched into space (an honor that went to Guion "Guy" Bluford, Jr., a participant in the 1983 Challenger space shuttle explorations). Since then, America has been graced with African-American astrophysicists, African-American NASA administrators, and an African-American director of the Hayden Planetarium. Such diversity came gradually; let us hope that it remains in place permanently.

[22] Which choice presents the most logically valid reason for the content that immediately follows?

A) NO CHANGE

B) This catastrophe could not be traced to any failure of either protocol or expertise,

C) Such events did not deter African Americans from seeking prominent positions in scientific agencies,

D) Relatively few African Americans were active in the aeronautics industry at the time,

---

23. Immigration has been and will always be a point of contention in American society. During the California Gold Rush of 1848 to 1855, Chinese men, seeking work in the gold mines, immigrated to America. But as the initial fervor dwindled and gold extraction became highly competitive, animosity toward Chinese laborers rose dramatically. Most were banished from mine work and forced to settle in enclaves on the outskirts of major cities such as San Francisco. Without any other employment prospects, these immigrants often found low-end positions in restaurants and laundry facilities, and unknowingly gave rise to the unjust theory that Chinese immigration depressed wage levels. [23]

[23] Which choice most effectively concludes the writer's entire discussion of the economics of immigration?

A) Only in the twentieth century would protections against workplace abuses make such low-end labor a means of securing a living wage.

B) Today we once again face controversy in this area; labor advocates see temporary non-contract jobs and a stagnant minimum wage as throwbacks to the problems that the Chinese immigrants encountered.

C) Yet, in a possible correspondence to today, such immigrants may simply have been taking over jobs that longer-established civilians had no interest in working.

D) Reassuringly, discrimination of this sort did not tempt Chinese-Americans to engage in the desperate and ultimately self-destructive speculation that had fueled the Gold Rush itself.

24. Like any normal person, I could not wait to travel to Europe, the faraway land of magic and mystical fables, castles, and languages of love. My itinerary read like the route of a modern-day gypsy—Paris, Venice, Florence, and Prague. Unfortunately, all of my expectations were delusions, **24** the end results of a lifetime of education that emphasized self-expression over practicality. As I entered each country, I could not help but notice how alike everything looked. Yes, old buildings and castles have different façades, but the differences no longer stand out when the people surrounding these structures are dressed in similar clothing and clutch identical phones. Famed edifices are no longer breathtaking when each one has the kind of gift shop you are likely to find in the United States, or Canada, or probably anywhere in the world.

24

In context, which continuation of the sentence provides the most effective and appropriate explanation for the writer's "delusions"?

A) NO CHANGE

B) the outcomes of an ill-designed scholarly attempt to document the modern expatriate experience.

C) the hopes and dreams of someone who had recently been faced with a series of personal setbacks.

D) the products of images gleaned from idealistic old fables and romantic black-and-white movies.

25. The rule of the animal world, it seems, is to follow the herd, the flock, the school, or the swarm; greater numbers mean greater cooperation, and ensure survival. **25** There are animals of all types that thrive in solitude. Some of these are small and self-sufficient (the sturdy desert grasshopper, the aptly-named hermit crab), but others are huge in size (the rhinoceros) or high on the food chain (the jaguar). Family groups for such antisocial animals seldom grow beyond a single mother and the most recent set of offspring; this is certainly the case with the giant anteater. A male anteater will wander alone, crushing ant colony after ant colony, while a female will carry a child or two on its back until these offspring, too, go their singular ways.

25

Which choice, if inserted here, most logically builds on the preceding discussion of animals?

A) Of course, without a certain amount of healthy "infighting," an animal group may produce weaker and weaker offspring over time.

B) Yet greater numbers can impede mobility if "stragglers" begin to burden the group.

C) It is tempting to link such species-based solitude to the absence of natural predators.

D) Nonetheless, only a few of the world's large mammals exhibit this tendency.

26. At some point in your life, you have probably put together a chair, table, or set of bookshelves from IKEA. But you may not be familiar with the intriguing history of this now-widespread brand of build-it-yourself furniture. It turns out that the founder of IKEA, Sweden's Ingvar Kamprad, did not even conceive IKEA primarily as a furniture business; instead, he began his business career selling small household items through the mail. [26] A customer could buy paper, pencils, and erasers first from Kamprad and then from the nascent IKEA. The IKEA brand itself appeared in 1943, but IKEA began selling furniture five years later.

26

Which of the following would provide the most appropriate supporting example at this point in the paragraph?

A) NO CHANGE

B) Eventually, Kamprad realized that a mail order business specializing in odds-and-ends would have limited growth potential.

C) It is impossible to say whether Kamprad at this time envisioned IKEA's rise to international prominence.

D) The growing popularity of build-it-yourself furniture kits, however, actually followed the rise of IKEA.

27. Each day at the bird hospital presents Leonard with a series of new challenges. He may begin the morning improvising a splint for the leg of a wounded blackbird, and finish his duties by mending the wing of a red-tailed hawk. [27] But each day of work at the Raptor Trust Bird Sanctuary also offers Leonard stability and repose. "You become very close to some of the birds over time," he explains. "After a while, some of the owls, ravens, and other majestic birds that we keep on premises while they recover begin to seem like co-workers."

27

Which choice provides the most relevant additional scenario at this point in the paragraph?

A) He has never, fortunately, needed to keep a single injured bird on premises for more than seven months.

B) Only in rare instances will he be called away to help out at a nearby wetlands museum.

C) Alternately, he may start the day prepping a golden eagle for release back into the wild, and finish by assigning a newly-arrived owl to its recovery pen.

D) Normally, he prefers to work on minute surgery and bandaging tasks early in the day when his mind is sharpest, and saves administrative work for later.

28. Murasaki Shikibu was born into the Japanese aristocracy at some point in the late tenth century A.D. While the exact dates of her birth and death **28** are up to dispute, what few would question is that "Lady Murasaki" (as she is now known) created one of the great psychological novels of world literature. That novel, *The Tale of Genji*, portrays in great detail the elite world that Murasaki knew so well. This narrative is no mere social drama, and is rich in observations of the universals of human nature. Murasaki's creation serves as a meditation on forces such as proper conduct and personal affection, themes that transcend class and time.

28
The writer wishes to add information that preserves the tone and meaning of the discussion as a whole. Which change to the original version best accomplishes this objective?

A) tend to be dismissed by many of her readers as irrelevant,

B) have been considered, but not definitively determined, by some of her admiring readers,

C) were once widely known and well publicized,

D) were never at any point carefully recorded,

29. **29** Sometimes, the grass really is greener at another job. Last autumn, I received the surprise of my life: the company that had employed me for the past sixteen years decided, without the slightest indication, to terminate my job. I was granted a respectable severance package, of course, and I did have some savings. However, I knew that these funds would not be sufficient to cover all my living expenses while I looked for a new job. It was up to me to economize, and I did so partially by relying on my own cleverness and partially by relying on websites. It turns out that the Internet is a treasure trove of advice for those of us who want (or in my case need) to save a few dollars. The first gem that I found was ThePennyHoarder.com, a site that offers short point-by-point articles on how to find part-time work, how to eliminate debt, and how to put your existing money to the best possible uses.

29
Which choice most effectively anticipates the discussion that follows?

A) NO CHANGE

B) Sometimes, necessity is the mother of thriftiness.

C) Sometimes, you can't make lemonade no matter how many lemons life gives you.

D) Sometimes, your worst fears come true.

30. Ants are capable of carrying several times their body weight and of building complex underground networks of tunnels. Yet did you know that ants can also walk backwards? A recent study, conducted by researchers from the University of Edinburgh and the Research Centre on Animal Cognition, has demonstrated that "ants can get their bearings whatever the orientation of their body," as reported in Science Daily. This finding overturns earlier beliefs about ant navigation, particularly the idea that ants navigated solely by memorizing predictable sequences of visual clues—sequences that ants, presumably, could not process in reverse. **30** <u>The same abilities that help them build matrices of tunnels also aid individual navigation.</u>

30

Which choice best articulates the main point of the paragraph?

A) NO CHANGE

B) Their processes of cognition are more complex and adaptive than was once thought.

C) Debate is likely to arise from a research result that contradicts the common knowledge about ants and their habits.

D) Such findings have initiated a larger scientific re-thinking of how insects perceive their surroundings.

---

31. J.K. Rowling frequented her local coffee shop while conceiving and writing the *Harry Potter* series. It was there that she imagined and envisioned her magical world, possibly pulling inspiration from the daily operations of the café and the coffee lovers walking in and sitting near her. The people at the café were not people at all, but prototypes of the characters that she would eventually bring to life on the page. **31** <u>Nor was Rowling the first female author to profit from such inspirations; Agatha Christie crafted her mystery novel characters, for instance, by borrowing features from eccentric passersby.</u> While some may argue that writing today has become merely a means of appropriating a stranger's life, who really cares? Writing is not the espousal of another's experiences; it is the dramatization and reimagining of that life as a story so specific that it inadvertently becomes universal.

31

Which choice best supports the writer's argument at this point in the paragraph?

A) NO CHANGE

B) This transmutation of life into literature is all the more remarkable when one considers how easily the *Harry Potter* books translate into media such as film and even theater.

C) The famous Hogwarts Academy of the *Harry Potter* franchise, for instance, is based in part on a group of stone towers that Rowling observed from a coffee shop window.

D) Students from George Heriot's school, which was near Rowling's coffee shop of choice, undoubtedly contributed features and mannerisms to the fictional students of the *Harry Potter* books.

32. Anthropologists have long noted that all human cultures possess some level of superstition or magical thinking. [32] The benefits of such thought are dubious, since superstitions can become time consuming and simply bizarre; consequently, eccentrics and amateurs are among the few who have pursued superstition as a scholarly topic. Recently, a new theory has attempted to explain the benefits that such seemingly irrational beliefs can yield. Since our brains are finite organs, a bit of magic keeps our attention spans from spreading too thin; a supernatural explanation can provide focus and comfort. If we were to worry all day about the why and the how of the past and the future, we could never prioritize the present for long enough to survive. Furthermore, now that survival isn't as difficult for all of us, we can seek new explanations of matters that extend beyond the present moment.

[32]

Which choice offers an example that clarifies and substantiates the writer's claims?

A) NO CHANGE

B) Indeed, anthropologists have found that, in explaining such superstition, extensive fieldwork is less useful than canny analysis of everyday events.

C) Even a "culture" as small as a sports team may develop personalized chants or gestures that serve as good luck superstitions.

D) For some theorists, this idea represents a new and fascinating fusion of classic anthropological thought and modern neurology.

---

33. Everybody in my town—if you could call acres upon acres of western Maryland farmland a town—belonged to one of the clubs offered by the community center. The girls mostly raised rabbits or rode horses, while the boys opted mostly for remote-control planes and model rockets. [33] Unwilling to conform, I chose rockets. Actually, "chose" would be a bit of an understatement: I threw myself into the task, body and mind, heart and soul. I would spend hours putting together pre-designed models, then hours more figuring out my own fin and nose cone combinations. I would launch my rockets early in the morning, on a nearby football field. I would stand there wondering what it would be like to create a rocket that could reach past the clouds, past the atmosphere.

[33]

Which choice best preserves the tone and purpose of the paragraph?

A) NO CHANGE

B) Allowing chance to intervene,

C) Mystified by the prospect of exploring space,

D) Hoping to discover a world of sophistication beyond my community,

34. The writing of art history and the writing of criticism melded as never before in the early years of the twentieth century. Before, it had been fashionable for philosophers to dabble in art criticism, as Denis Diderot did in the late eighteenth century; it had also been common for art critics to tinge their tracts and essays with philosophical theory, as nineteenth-century writers such as John Ruskin and Charles Baudelaire did. Yet it was a historian of the modernist era, Clement Greenberg, who truly brought these two disciplines together. Greenberg and his followers applied the same deft precision to **34** the classic literary and narrative distinctions explored by Impressionist painters that they applied to the canvases of Picasso and Matisse. And in so doing, they forever changed the way we think about art.

34

Which choice is most consistent both with the writer's entire discussion and with the examples provided later in the sentence?

A) NO CHANGE

B) the classic distinctions that are implicit in experimental novels such as *Mrs. Dalloway* and *Ulysses*

C) the classic distinctions drawn by famed philosophers such as Descartes and Hume

D) the classic distinctions that modern painters had previously neglected

35. In 1956, Gordon Moore, one of the co-founders of the technology giant Intel, formulated an idea that has guided our conception of technological advancement in the decades since. According to "Moore's Law," the power and efficiency of computer processing technology will increase considerably over time. Simultaneously, the cost of producing information technology essentials, such as semiconductors, will decrease over time. **35** Technological advances of this sort, moreover, harmonize in potent ways. These developments work together to yield exponential increases in the speed and efficiency of technology over time.

35

Which choice most effectively sets up the main idea of the following sentence?

A) NO CHANGE

B) No other facets of technology obey similar principles; practices premised on Moore's Law, naturally, have benefited software developers.

C) Yet Moore's Law alone cannot explain the factors that have helped today's technology companies to profit.

D) Despite the fame of Moore's Law, similar theories of synergy are evident in other industries.

36. It is commonplace for people to offhandedly describe the foods that they love as "addictive." Recent chemistry has proven that there is a genuinely addictive side to one supremely common food: cheese. Among the most abundant components of cheese is Casein. When Casein is digested, fragments known as "casomorphins" are released. These casomorphins react with the body in a manner that recalls the impact of dangerous habit-forming drugs, such as opiates. Of course, cheese "addiction" isn't life-threatening, but the "addictive" effects of cheese are real. **36** It remains uncertain whether such "addiction"-inducing substances can be found in other dairy products.

36

Which choice most effectively and definitively concludes this paragraph as a whole?

A) NO CHANGE

B) Curiously enough, Casein does not seem to serve any practical nutritional use, despite its potency as an "addictive" agent.

C) Sometimes there really is considerable amount of truth embedded in casual speech.

D) This science may (to some extent) explain the prevalence of cheese in mass-marketed cuisine.

37. Walrus tusks are central to forms of competition and displays of dominance within walrus social groups. Male walruses use their tusks in combat with one another as they vie for power; in many cases, the leader of a group of walruses will be the male who possesses the largest tusks. However, individual walruses also know how to put their tusks to an important practical use. If a walrus **37** that is especially large and exhausted ever has trouble climbing out of the water and onto an ice ledge, it can sink its tusks into the ice and pull itself up.

37

Which piece of information, if true, best presents and underscores a difference between the two uses of tusks discussed in the paragraph?

A) NO CHANGE

B) which has recently been ostracized

C) in the pursuit of its prey

D) of any size or gender

38. As a professional psychiatrist, I have to make a conscious effort to remind myself that not everybody is my patient. [38] It is a danger that I have observed in my colleagues, and that sometimes I fear I will (by some insidious means) transmit to my patients. This applies even to the characters that I find on the page. Recently I have been reading *Anna Karenina*, and I have been laboring mightily to figure out why exactly the title character acts the way she does. Does Anna suffer from a form of obsessive compulsive disorder? Does she languish under a repressed trauma? Does she have an Electra Complex or some other psychological problem derived from Greek myth? Or is it undiagnosed and untreated paranoid schizophrenia? Does any of this matter? It probably doesn't matter as much as my basic enjoyment of the book matters, but enjoyment is difficult when all this professional apparatus gets in the way.

[38] Which choice provides the most logical continuation of the writer's discussion at this point?

A) NO CHANGE

B) Whether I am at the supermarket, a little league game, or a cocktail party, I must fight the temptation to "psycho-analyze" those around me.

C) Such a tendency is so absurdly intriguing that, at one point, I wrote an article about it for a news magazine.

D) Habits such as these, explainable though they are, remind me how open we psychologists are to stereotyping and satire.

39. In the 1950s and 1960s, Americans who feared that nuclear warfare would obliterate humanity began building elaborate bomb shelters, stocking them with battery-powered devices and canned goods. Today, virtually identical measures are being taken by civilians known as "preppers" and "survivalists." These Americans believe that catastrophe may be imminent, and learn the skills of resource conservation that will be necessary should environmental upheaval or (yes) nuclear war destroy civilization. True to form, they also have a tendency to buy up and store away canned goods. [39] A select few of these Americans have been profiled sympathetically by the media; the vast majority, though, have been subjected to condescension and ridicule.

[39] Which choice most logically reflects the writer's ideas as presented in this passage?

A) NO CHANGE

B) Unlike their 1950s and 1960s predecessors, "preppers" and "survivalists" can be remarkably optimistic: some even maintain upbeat blogs that preach the possibility of a better, though post-apocalyptic, world.

C) Ironically, the actual upheavals of the past decade (such as freak snowstorms and hurricanes) were not successfully predicted by any avowed "preppers."

D) Some of the most dogged of these Americans have also built fortified sheds in remote locations, or subterranean bunkers in their own backyards.

40. As humankind explores more and more of the known universe, a new question will become increasingly important: how does spending time in space impact the human body? [40] Although gravity-free environments can be easily and accurately simulated in laboratory settings, the effect of low- to zero-gravity environments on the human anatomy has yet to be comprehensively understood. Nonetheless, some intriguing early work in this line of inquiry has been performed by researchers from the University of Michigan, who have found that astronauts' brain compositions can be altered during space missions. Twelve astronauts from a shuttle crew and fourteen from the International Space Station offered brain imaging data to the Michigan study. As it turns out, the absence of gravity can re-wire a brain's pathways in much the same way that learning a new skill shifts the brain's organization.

40

The writer wishes to add content that renders the conclusion of the sentence somewhat surprising. Which choice best accomplishes this goal?

A) NO CHANGE

B) Although funding for manned space missions has increased steadily over the past fifteen years,

C) Although few contemporary scientists would claim that aerospace and medicine are mutually exclusive disciplines,

D) Although astrophysicists continue to discover everything from new galaxies to remote, Earth-like "exoplanets,"

ANSWERS ON THE NEXT PAGE

ANSWERS:
MOST APPROPRIATE CONTENT CHOICE

1. A

2. C

3. D

4. A

5. B

6. D

7. B

8. A

9. B

10. C

11. B

12. C

13. B

14. A

15. B

16. C

17. D

18. A

19. A

20. C

21. C

22. D

23. C

24. D

25. B

26. A

27. C

28. B

29. B

30. B

31. D

32. C

33. C

34. C

35. A

36. C

37. D

38. B

39. D

40. A

Practice Tests

Note: the following practice sections are designed to test the most challenging SAT Writing questions as discussed in this practice book. For more SAT Writing practice, please see the IES New SAT Grammar Practice Book of the Advanced Practice Series!

Test One

Writing Test
35 MINUTES, 44 QUESTIONS

Turn to Section 2 of your answer sheet to answer the questions in this section.

DIRECTIONS

Each passage below is accompanied by a number of questions. For some questions, you will consider how the passage might be revised to improve the expression of ideas. For other questions, you will consider how the passage might be edited to correct errors in sentence structure, usage, or punctuation. A passage or a question may be accompanied by one or more graphics (such as a table or graph) that you will consider as you make revising and editing decisions.

Some questions will direct you to an underlined portion of a passage. Other questions will direct you to a location in a passage or ask you to think about the passage as a whole.

After reading each passage, choose the answer to each question that most effectively improves the quality of writing in the passage or that makes the passage conform to the conventions of standard written English. Many questions include a "NO CHANGE" option. Choose that option if you think the best choice is to leave the relevant portion of the passage as it is.

Questions 1-11 are based on the following passage.

Less Is a Bore: The Architecture of Robert Venturi and Denise Scott Brown

In the middle decades of the 20th century, European and American architecture was dominated by an aesthetic of austerity and predictability. The skyscrapers of this era, for instance, presented stately surfaces of steel and glass; these structures tended to be box-like in shape and **1** much more cost-efficient than the stone and terracotta buildings of the previous century. However, this situation began to change as the result of the work of two pioneering American architects: Robert Venturi and Denise Scott Brown.

The partnership between Venturi and Scott Brown began with a strong personal connection. Their first meeting took place **2** around 1960. The two young architects were both teaching

1

Which choice is the most logical addition to the writer's discussion?

A) NO CHANGE
B) were often planned out according to the much-cited principle that "form follows function."
C) tended to alienate the very American officeworkers who routinely spent time in them.
D) normally did not feature any prominent exterior carvings or other decorations.

2

Which choice best combines to two sentences at the underlined portion?

A) around 1960, when the two young architects were both
B) around 1960, whereas the two young architects were both
C) around 1960—and the two young architects were both
D) around 1960: the two young architects both

CONTINUE

at the University of Pennsylvania. Venturi and Scott Brown were married in 1967, and in 1969 Scott Brown joined **3** Venturi's firm, Venturi and Rauch: which operates today under the name Venturi, Scott Brown, and Associates (commonly abbreviated as VSBA).

Today, VSBA is a celebrated company. But in the 1960s, Venturi and Scott Brown embarked on an architectural mission that was both radical and rebellious. **4** By designing buildings that were austere and predictable, the duo devised structures that incorporated unexpected arcs, sharp angles, and pop culture allusions. For instance, with its wide, slanting roof, the Vanna Venturi House—**5** which was designed for Venturi's mother— looks **6** as much like a quirky cardboard cutout. Another 1960s structure—Fire Station #4 in Columbus, Indiana, which sports a blocky central tower—looks as though it is made of red and white Lego pieces.

3

A) NO CHANGE
B) Venturi's firm (Venturi and Rauch, which operates today): under the name Venturi,
C) Venturi's firm, Venturi and Rauch which operates today, under the name Venturi,
D) Venturi's firm Venturi and Rauch, which operates today under the name Venturi,

4

A) NO CHANGE
B) Upon
C) Beyond
D) Rather than

5

The writer is considering deleting the underlined information. Should the writer make this deletion?

A) Yes, because Venturi's mother is not mentioned elsewhere in the passage.
B) Yes, because it is not evident that Venturi's mother was interested in architecture.
C) No, because it specifies the identity of the Vanna Venturi House.
D) No, because it clarifies the aesthetics of the Vanna Venturi House.

6

A) NO CHANGE
B) so much
C) very much
D) too much

CONTINUE

Though the Vanna Venturi House and the fire station were rather small commissions, Venturi and Scott Brown's lively style **7** caught on; it was popularized by books such as *Complexity and Contradiction in Architecture* (which Venturi wrote alone) and *Learning from Las Vegas* (which the couple co-authored). **8** As the shift to joint authorship suggests, early tensions generally disappeared from their partnership. Among the important buildings that these two architects have designed are Princeton University's Gordon Wu Hall and the premises of the Seattle Art Museum.

[1] However, the style that Venturi and Scott Brown championed was not completely new to **9** corporation-sponsored architecture. [2] One of the buildings that both of these architects worked to protect during their early days was the Furness Library at the University of Pennsylvania: [3] Scott Brown was instrumental in the preservation of this structure. [4] This opinion is no surprise: **10** the Furness Library being a massive, ornate, asymmetrical structure crafted in stark red. [5] Venturi, for his part, regarded it as an exemplary case of dynamic, picturesque architecture. [6] With such a memorable form, it is the proud ancestor of Venturi and Scott Brown's own fanciful designs. **11**

7
A) NO CHANGE
B) caught on; popularized by books
C) caught on; with books
D) caught on: in books

8
Which choice effectively transitions between the topics present in this paragraph?
A) NO CHANGE
B) Eventually, even the most stately institutions saw the appeal of Venturi and Scott Brown's ideas.
C) These books were premised on the idea that architecture and modern advertising could serve similar functions.
D) Venturi and Scott Brown, by some accounts, wanted to elevate architecture to the level of painting or sculpture within artistic discourse.

9
Which choice most effectively and directly anticipates the discussion that follows?
A) NO CHANGE
B) architecture in academic settings.
C) architecture that rebelled against European principles.
D) their own architectural practice.

10
A) NO CHANGE
B) the Furness Library is
C) the Furness Library, situated as
D) DELETE the underlined portion.

11
To make the order of ideas in the paragraph most logical, sentence 4 should be placed
A) where it is now.
B) after sentence 2.
C) after sentence 5.
D) after sentence 6.

CONTINUE

Questions 12-22 are based on the following passage.

Networking for Inventors

A couple years ago, I devised an idea for a useful culinary product: a cooking spray that is infused with gourmet [12] spices and that if offered (in several different flavors) could render an extensive in-home spice and seasoning rack unnecessary. I had created a spray can prototype, along with some advertising bullet points; I had even shared my idea with [13] a few close friends and family members, who all regarded my invention with enthusiasm. Despite this positive reception, I was uncertain about how to approach my proposed product as a long-term proposition. Should I quit my day job and devote all my energies to this one endeavor, or should I simply treat my idea as a passion project?

[14] It turns out that I went with neither of these approaches. Instead, after a little Internet research, I decided to join a local inventors' group, the Tampa Bay Inventors Council. For a budding inventor such as myself, there are multiple advantages to organizations [15] such as the Council, these can be found all

---

12

A) NO CHANGE
B) and that (if offered in several different flavors) could
C) and that (if offered) in several different flavors could
D) and that (if offered in several) different flavors could

13

A) NO CHANGE
B) a few close friends and family members who all regarded my invention, with enthusiasm.
C) a few close friends and family members: who all regarded my invention, with enthusiasm.
D) a few close friends and family members, who all regarded my invention, with enthusiasm.

14

The writer is considering deleting the underlined sentence. Should the sentence be kept or deleted?

A) Kept, because it effectively transitions from a discussion of shortcomings to an overview of the writer's future plans.
B) Kept, because it effectively transitions from a discussion of alternatives to an explanation of the writer's actions.
C) Deleted, because it introduces a tone of ambivalence into an otherwise decisive discussion.
D) Deleted, because it introduces a colloquial tone into an otherwise formal discussion.

15

A) NO CHANGE
B) such as the Council, and these can be found
C) such as the Council, which can be found
D) such as the Council, and can have found

157

across the United States. For instance, [16] with its rather unpredictable schedule, the Council keeps me consistently focused on developing my invention, but does not become an overbearing or stressful time commitment. [17]

Today, the optimal approach for an inventor is, indeed, one that balances creative thought with a steady job that is not invention-oriented. [18] Furthermore, few inventors today rely exclusively on income from their inventions. The fact that inventors have banded together—often forming networks in which seasoned inventors mentor newcomers—can be explained by these economic realities. [19] Because the word "inventor" still conjures the image of a solitary genius (Benjamin Franklin or Thomas Edison, for instance), the reality of how inventors work entails constant discussion and dialogue.

[16]

Which piece of information best develops the writer's point about the Council as a time commitment?
A) NO CHANGE
B) with its semi-monthly meetings,
C) with its mentorship program,
D) with its online forum,

[17]

At this point in the passage, the writer is considering adding the following sentence

> Some of my fellow inventors have small children at home, and would never have joined a costly program in the first place.

Should the writer make this addition here?
A) Yes, because it suggests that the writer's situation as an inventor is more common than the reader might expect.
B) Yes, because it anticipates the writer's argument about the low likelihood of profiting from an invention.
C) No, because it inaccurately implies that the writer of the passage has small children at home.
D) No, because it shifts the emphasis of the paragraph away from the writer's own involvement.

[18]

A) NO CHANGE
B) Surprisingly,
C) Nonetheless,
D) After all,

[19]

A) NO CHANGE
B) Unless
C) Although
D) As long as

CONTINUE

[1] Moreover, I have gleaned some valuable long-term tips (choose one or two industries, and specialize in inventions that target them) and learned about common inventing pitfalls [20] (always be suspicious of online courses that will teach you how to make money off inventions; too many are scams). [2] My cooking spray still isn't too far beyond the prototype stage at this point. [3] But even if this creation never becomes a runaway success, I have still gained the contacts and the industry expertise that I will need to create [21] my next device—or my next hundred devices—with efficiency and professionalism. [4] Socialization, not necessity, is really the mother of invention. [5] Within my own inventors' group, I have acquired practical knowledge of the best marketing practices and of the patent application process, all courtesy of inventors with several patents to their names. [22]

20

The writer is considering deleting the underlined parenthetical phrase. Should this content be kept or deleted?

A) Kept, because it provides a specific example of an inventing pitfall that can be logically avoided.

B) Kept, because it expands upon the recommendation for inventors provided in the sentence's earlier parenthetical phrase.

C) Deleted, because the writer has not mentioned or analyzed online scams elsewhere in the passage.

D) Deleted, because it presents information that is unrelated to the writer's expertise.

21

A) NO CHANGE

B) my next device or—my next hundred devices—with efficiency and professionalism.

C) my next device—or my next hundred devices with efficiency—and professionalism.

D) my next device or—my next hundred devices with efficiency—and professionalism.

22

To make the order of ideas within the paragraph most logical, sentence 5 should be placed

A) where it is now.

B) before sentence 1.

C) after sentence 1.

D) before sentence 4.

CONTINUE

Questions 23-33 are based on the following passage.

The Fountain of Youth . . . For Mice?

[1] New research confirms that by turning on or off a set of four genes known as the Yamanaka factors, which are associated with the embryonic cellular state scientists can make, somatic cells in an aged state revert to a more youthful state. [2] For many years, researchers have sought to alleviate a variety [23] of conditions, including trauma-related paralysis and, in some cases, aging itself—through the understanding and application of stem cells. [3] These are the pluripotent cells that, in the embryonic stages of growth, differentiate to become the specific cells of every tissue in the body, [24] and that persist in the bone marrow after maturity. [4] One of the mechanisms by which embryonic stem cells change into specific types of cell, known as somatic cells, is a process of marking individual [25] genes so that they do or do not have the potential to be translated into proteins within the cell. [26]

23

A) NO CHANGE
B) conditions—including trauma-related paralysis and in some cases, aging itself, through
C) conditions—including trauma-related paralysis and, in some cases, aging itself—through
D) conditions, including trauma-related paralysis and in some cases, aging itself, through

24

The writer is considering deleting the underlined portion. Should this content be kept or deleted?

A) Kept, because it adds meaningful detail to the writer's description of pluripotent cells.
B) Kept, because it adds meaningful detail to the writer's description of the embryonic stages of growth.
C) Deleted, because this information is not directly related to the Yamanaka factors experiment.
D) Deleted, because this information is relevant only to experiments involving human test subjects.

25

A) NO CHANGE
B) genes, whereas they
C) genes to preclude that they
D) genes, and they

26

To make the order of ideas in the paragraph most logical, sentence 1 should be placed

A) where it is now.
B) after sentence 2.
C) after sentence 3.
D) after sentence 4.

CONTINUE

[27] To correct a misconception about the Yamanaka factors, researchers from the Salk Institute designed a series of four experiments to observe the consequences of Yamanaka activation in three groups of mice: a group genetically engineered to age prematurely, a group injected with corrosive cobra venom, and a group whose pancreases were stripped of their insulin-producing cells. For all three groups, activation of the Yamanaka factors revealed positive changes [28] until compared with the activity of a control group. The skin and other organs of the aged mice became healthier. Their lifespans increased by a third as compared with those of other prematurely aged mice. The mice injected with cobra venom, which destroys muscle tissue, regenerated [29] less muscle tissue than mice without Yamanaka activation. Finally, Yamanaka-active mice whose insulin-producing cells had been destroyed, causing them to be unable to regulate their blood sugar levels, regenerated those cells faster than other mice.

27

Which choice best provides a logical context for the information that follows?

A) NO CHANGE
B) To build upon an earlier research endeavor in mammal genetics,
C) To determine the specific effects of the Yamanaka factors,
D) To develop new therapeutic methods that would utilize embryonic stem cells,

28

A) NO CHANGE
B) when
C) where
D) since

29

Which choice would best reflect the main point of the paragraph?

A) NO CHANGE
B) more muscle tissue than
C) the same amount of muscle tissue as
D) more muscle tissue but at a slower rate than

CONTINUE ➡

The longevity of mice and many other multicellular [30] organisms including humans, has some constraints regardless of overall health. Over a lifetime of cellular replication, despite many safeguard mechanisms, errors eventually accumulate in the DNA, and these errors can cause diseases such as cancer, as well as other phenomena, like loss of skin elasticity. However, Yamanaka factors could function to "de-age" a cell and cause these age-related diseases to occur later in life, thereby increasing longevity. Based on the wide variety of cellular damage types that Yamanaka activation countered in the Salk Institute's experiment, such genetic treatment could alleviate [31] many conditions: from muscle scarring after surgery [32] as well as diabetes, which result partially from damage or change to the genome.

For now, such a panacea is far from application in routine doctor's visits. One day, turning on or off specific genes like the Yamanaka factors could result in people living not only longer, but also in a more healthy manner. [33]

[30]
A) NO CHANGE
B) organisms, including humans has some constraints
C) organisms, including humans, has some constraints
D) organisms—including humans, has some constraints

[31]
A) NO CHANGE
B) many conditions: from muscle scarring,
C) many conditions, from muscle scarring
D) many conditions, from muscle scarring,

[32]
A) NO CHANGE
B) to diabetes, which result
C) as well as diabetes that result
D) to diabetes that result

[33]
The writer is considering concluding the passage by adding the following statement at this point.

> Until then, we can at least contemplate the ways in which society might be re-structured by what, admittedly, is futuristic possibility.

Should the writer insert this sentence here?
A) Yes, because it refers to an ongoing debate that is referenced in the introduction to the passage.
B) Yes, because it explains why a non-specialist would be most interested in Yamanaka factors.
C) No, because it does nothing more than reiterate the content of a previous sentence.
D) No, because it introduces a topic that is only tangentially related to the passage's main concerns.

CONTINUE

Questions 34-44 are based on the following passage.

A Humanitarian Purpose for GM Foods

Scientific advancement is plagued [34] by a paradox: the more we become capable of significantly altering the world around us, the more we become fearful of the consequences of those alterations. Genetically modified food offers an excellent example of this paradox: [35] over time, consumers and consumer advocates alike have discovered that costly scientific processes can result in cheaper yet relatively low-quality foodstuffs. The debate about genetically modified (GM) foods has been particularly concentrated in developed countries. In such nations, individuals most often have the purchasing power to pay extra [36] for non-GM foods. Evidence suggests that it is individuals living in developing countries who have the most to gain from genetic modification.

34
A) NO CHANGE
B) by a paradox, when the more we
C) by a paradox, because the more we
D) by a paradox; we

35
Which choice most logically and effectively substantiates the writer's main idea at this point?
A) NO CHANGE
B) organism-altering technologies that once inspired fear have now proliferated to such an extent that they barely inspire even casual reflection.
C) many anxieties come to the surface when people consider whether something that they are about to ingest has been modified by scientific means.
D) prosperous nations have led the way in this field, even as fears about genetic modification have run rampant in poorer countries.

36
Which choice best combines the two sentences at the underlined portion?
A) for non-GM foods, although evidence suggests
B) for non-GM foods, since evidence suggests
C) for non-GM foods; indeed, evidence suggests
D) for non-GM foods: evidence suggests

CONTINUE

[1] In developing countries, individuals tend to be much more limited in their diet, with a large portion of their typical food intake being comprised of a small number of staples. [2] **37** It is thus particularly important, that a diet with little diversity still meet nutritional needs and genetic modification permits this by enhancing the nutritional value of key crops. [3] Crops such as rice, sorghum, maize and wheat can be subjected to genetic alterations which function to increase the vitamins, minerals and nutrients they contain. [4] One key example of this is golden rice, a variety of genetically engineered rice that contains much higher levels of beta carotene than non GM-rice. [5] Beta carotene is an important source **38** of Vitamin A, because the latter is a nutrient that is lacking in the diets of many individuals in developing countries, especially children. [6] Vitamin A deficiency can result in blindness and other disabilities, and even death. [7] Since, in areas where Vitamin A deficiency tends to be problematic, rice constitutes a significant part of the population's diet, modifying rice so that it can function **39** in a way of this nutrient to be accessed by individuals offers a hopeful possibility for greater health and well-being. **40**

37

A) NO CHANGE
B) It is thus particularly important that a diet, with little diversity, still meet nutritional needs and genetic modification permits this, by enhancing the nutritional value of key crops.
C) It is thus particularly important that a diet with little diversity still meet nutritional needs, and genetic modification permits this by enhancing the nutritional value of key crops.
D) It is thus particularly important that a diet, with little diversity still meet nutritional needs and genetic modification, permits this by enhancing the nutritional value of key crops.

38

A) NO CHANGE
B) of Vitamin A; nonetheless, the latter is
C) of Vitamin A, the latter is
D) of Vitamin A; the latter is

39

A) NO CHANGE
B) as a way of
C) in a way for
D) as a way for

40

To make the order of ideas in the paragraph most logical, sentence 2 should be placed

A) where it is now.
B) after sentence 3.
C) after sentence 6.
D) after sentence 7.

CONTINUE

[41] The nutritional quality, of the crops consumed by individuals in developing countries, is not the only factor of great importance; obtaining sufficient quantities of food can also be difficult, especially if crops are damaged by drought, pests, or other environmental factors. [42] Moreover, researchers have altered the genetic structure of maize so that it becomes less sensitive to drought, [43] unexpectedly increasing the likelihood that the yield of crops will remain relatively stable even if environmental conditions decline. Other plants have been altered so that they become toxic to the insects that might otherwise consume them; this strategy may carry additional environmental benefits, [44] since by creating plants that are longer-lived and more physically robust, people will have less need to apply toxic chemicals. Considering the ways in which genetic modification can benefit the vulnerable populations of developing countries, it is important for people to put their fears aside and remain open to new ways of improving the food we eat.

41
A) NO CHANGE
B) The nutritional quality of the crops consumed by individuals in developing countries is not the only factor, of great importance
C) The nutritional quality of the crops, consumed by individuals in developing countries, is not the only factor of great importance
D) The nutritional quality of the crops consumed by individuals in developing countries is not the only factor of great importance

42
The writer is considering adding the following sentence at this point in the paragraph

> Genetically modifying staple crops can help to make them more resistant to an array of threats.

Should the writer make this addition here?
A) Yes, because it effectively transitions away from the topic of the drawbacks of genetically modified crops.
B) Yes, because it effectively transitions into the topic of the benefits of genetically modified crops.
C) No, because it undermines the writer's tone of ambivalence towards genetically modified crops.
D) No, because it reiterates information presented in the previous sentence.

43
A) NO CHANGE
B) in contrast
C) previously
D) thus

44
Which choice best supports the reasoning articulated by the writer?
A) NO CHANGE
B) since by outfitting plants with a kind of built-in pesticide,
C) since by taking such measures to finally stabilize the ecosystems of poorer nations,
D) since by selectively driving predatory insect species to extinction,

165

STOP

Answer Key: TEST 1

Test 1

PASSAGE 1

Less Is a Bore: The Architecture of Robert Venturi and Denise Scott Brown

1. D
2. A
3. D
4. D
5. C
6. C
7. A
8. B
9. B
10. B
11. C

PASSAGE 2

Networking for Inventors

12. B
13. A
14. B
15. C
16. B
17. D
18. D
19. C
20. A
21. A
22. B

PASSAGE 3

The Fountain of Youth . . . For Mice?

23. C
24. A
25. A
26. D
27. C
28. B
29. B
30. C
31. C
32. B
33. D

PASSAGE 4

A Humanitarian Purpose for GMO Foods

34. A
35. C
36. A
37. C
38. D
39. D
40. A
41. D
42. B
43. D
44. B

Answer Explanations

SAT Practice Test #1

Passage 1: Less Is a Bore: The Architecture of Robert Venturi and Denise Scott Brown

1) CORRECT ANSWER: D
At this point in the discussion, the writer is explaining the "aesthetic of austerity [lack of decoration] and predictability" followed by skyscrapers: buildings without "carvings" or "decorations" would fit such an aesthetic. Choose D and eliminate A (costs) and C (officeworkers) as raising issues that detract from the topic of appearance or "aesthetic". B is a trap answer: the writer is concerned with HOW the buildings look, not with the topic in this false choice, WHY they look a specific way.

2) CORRECT ANSWER: A
The underlined portion is describing the year of a meeting ("1960") or "when" the meeting took place; A combines the sentences while properly articulating this relationship. B wrongly introduces a contrast, C uses an awkward construction that indicates addition (rather than calling attention to the issue of time), and D wrongly uses a colon (which should only introduce substantiating information or a set of items) to introduce a fragment.

3) CORRECT ANSWER: D
Both A and B wrongly place a fragment (as opposed to items or an explanatory clause) after a colon and should be quickly eliminated. Keep in mind also that Venturi and Scott Brown's firm "operates today under the name" given; this information is closely connected and should not be broken by a comma as in C ("today, under"). Eliminate this answer and select D as the best choice.

4) CORRECT ANSWER: D
The sentence should contrast the design of "austere and predictable" buildings with the surprising and lively design work of Venturi and Scott Brown. D properly captures a contrast relationship. A, B, and C all indicate that Venturi and Scott Brown MAINLY or ALSO designed "austere and predictable buildings" (but may have later departed from or moved "beyond" this work) and must be eliminated as capturing the wrong primary relationship.

5) CORRECT ANSWER: C

The writer has introduced the "Vanna Venturi House" without explaining who exactly Vanna Venturi is: the underlined portion provides the needed explanation. Choose C and eliminate D, because the IDENTITY of the house (not its aesthetic or appearance) is clarified. A and B point to actual facts (that Venturi's mother is only mentioned here and that she is not clearly interested in architecture), yet such reasoning does not justify eliminating the underlined portion, which provides needed CONTEXT for the house itself.

6) CORRECT ANSWER: C

The underlined portion must help to compare the "Vanna Venturi House" to a "cardboard cutout"; the house thus looks "very much" like a cutout, so that C is the best answer. A and B would only be appropriate if the house were being compared to something OTHER than a cutout or if the sentence were being continued. (The proper constructions would be "as much . . . as" and "so much . . . that", respectively). D serves to criticize the house as excessive and is thus inappropriate to the writer's mostly positive discussion.

7) CORRECT ANSWER: A

The original version makes proper use of a semicolon, which separates the independent clauses "style . . . caught on" and "it was . . .". Choose A and eliminate B and C, each of which wrongly places a sentence fragment after a semicolon. D follows a colon with a fragment introduced by a preposition (NOT an independent clause or a set of items) and should be eliminated for improper usage.

8) CORRECT ANSWER: B

While the early stages of the paragraph discuss "rather small commissions", the final sentence discusses "important buildings"; B properly indicates that the appeal of Venturi and Scott Brown's work is expanding to important "stately institutions". Eliminate A because the paragraph does not present the architects' partnership in a negative light, and eliminate C and D because (even though they seem to EXPAND UPON Venturi and Scott Brown's ideas) they do not TRANSITION from the earlier to later content involving specific buildings.

9) CORRECT ANSWER: B

The content that follows the underlined portion discusses the "Furness Library at the University of Pennsylvania", a building in an "academic" setting. B is the best answer while A identifies the wrong kind of institution (a "corporation"). C wrongly indicates that the Furness Library rebelled against European models (when in fact its cultural influences are not clearly explained); D wrongly shifts attention back to Venturi and Scott Brown's buildings and AWAY from the topic of an older architectural work that they respected.

10) CORRECT ANSWER: B

The content after the colon must be a full sentence that explains why a specific "opinion" is no surprise: B creates a full sentence while A and C both create fragments. D presents an item (another possible colon use) but does not align with anything BEFORE the colon; the "opinion" cannot be a "structure", so that this answer must be eliminated.

11) CORRECT ANSWER: C

Sentence 4 describes a specific "opinion" that must be articulated in the sentence that precedes it; sentence 5 describes how Venturi "regarded" a specific building, so that sentence 4 could effectively follow sentence 5. C is the best answer. Sentences 3 (A) and 2 (B) describe ACTIONS taken by the architects, not explicit OPINIONS; sentence 6 (D) primarily presents the writer's opinion of Venturi and Scott Brown's work, not (as sentence 4 requires) an opinion OTHER THAN the writer's regarding the Furness Library.

Passage 2: Networking for Inventors

12) CORRECT ANSWER: B

The content in parentheses should present a single contained thought about the spices, which may be "offered in several different flavors". B properly consolidates this description between parentheses; A, C, and D break up the linked content, and D even creates a non-grammatical sentence if its version of the parenthetical content ("if offered in several") is omitted.

13) CORRECT ANSWER: A

The underlined sentence should use a single, unbroken phrase to explain the single idea of how the invention was regarded; various people "regarded my invention with enthusiasm". A is thus a proper usage; B, C, and D all wrongly use a single comma ("invention, with") to break or interrupt this idea and should thus be eliminated.

14) CORRECT ANSWER: B

The underlined sentence refers to the two "approaches" outlined in the first paragraph and indicates that the writer went with "neither"; in fact, the writer went with an approach outlined in the paragraphs that follow. B effectively refers to the sentence's useful role as a transition, while A is problematic because the writer transitions into discussing an approach that she is PRESENTLY pursuing (not a "future plan"). C ("ambivalence" or uncertainty) and D ("colloquial" or informal) both provide inaccurate characterizations of this decisive and mostly formal statement of the writer's choice.

15) CORRECT ANSWER: C

While choice A creates a comma splice ("there are", "these can"), C properly uses the word "which" to avoid this faulty construction and to refer to "organizations". B presents a needlessly awkward and wordy version of a similar construction, and D wrongly shifts the tense of the sentence from present to past.

16) CORRECT ANSWER: B

The writer characterizes the Council as a consistent but not burdensome time commitment: regular "semi-monthly" or twice-a-month meetings would be appropriate to this characterization. B is thus the best answer, while A ("unpredictable") introduces a faulty negative tone. C ("mentorship") and D ("forum") do not refer directly to the issue of "time commitment" and should be eliminated as off-topic.

17) CORRECT ANSWER: D

In the paragraph, the writer's primary focus has been why "I decided to join a local inventor's group"; mentioning "fellow inventors" with small children would actually shift focus away from the writer herself. D is the best answer, while C is incorrect because, if anything, the proposed content indicates that the writer DOESN'T have small children (since this is a circumstance faced only by "fellow inventors"). A (the reader's assumptions and other inventors) and B (profiting from an invention) both wrongly introduce topics other than the writer's own scheduling and commitment.

18) CORRECT ANSWER: D

The sentence that precedes the underlined portion explains that an inventor must normally have a "steady job" that is not invention-oriented; the reason for this arrangement is that few inventors "rely exclusively" on invention-based income. The best transition would indicate explanation, as in D. A indicates addition (NOT reasoning or consequences), while B and C wrongly signal unexpected or contrasting information.

19) CORRECT ANSWER: C

In this sentence, the writer creates a contrast between "solitary genius" and "discussion and dialogue". C properly captures a contrast relationship, while A and D both wrongly indicate cause and effect. B is a trap answer: although "Unless" may seem to designate a contrast, it in fact indicates a condition that must be fulfilled (and is thus close in meaning to the other false answers).

20) CORRECT ANSWER: A

The underlined content describes one of the "common inventing pitfalls", the presence of "online courses" that are "scams" but that can be easily identified as scams and avoided. A is the best answer: the content should be kept because it refers directly to the "pitfalls", not to the content in the "earlier" parenthetical phrase (eliminating B). Though a somewhat new side topic, the discussion of "scams" is related to the writer's main focus on how inventors work. Eliminate C as providing an irrelevant reason for deletion and D as providing faulty logic.

21) CORRECT ANSWER: A

In the original version, dashes are properly used to offset a somewhat long interrupting phrase and to create a sentence that would be properly constructed ("my next device . . . with") if the phrase were to be eliminated. A is the best choice. B ("or . . . with") and D ("or . . . and") would both result in non-grammatical sentence constructions with the omission of the phrase between dashes. C would re-coordinate the sentence to indicate that the writer is creating a device "and professionalism" and would thus introduce an illogical or awkward meaning.

22) CORRECT ANSWER: B

Sentence 5 describes the "practical knowledge" that the writer has attained in an inventors' group; sentence 1 offers examples of such practical knowledge, including "tips" and awareness of "pitfalls". B is thus the best placement, while the current placement in A would place the general statement AFTER the examples that it should introduce. C and D would also create this error, and C would have the additional drawback of interrupting the writer's discussion of her cooking spray.

Passage 3: The Fountain of Youth . . . For Mice?

23) CORRECT ANSWER: C
The underlined portion involves a long descriptive phrase ("including . . . itself") that contains commas, and that would be most effectively coordinated if placed between two dashes. C uses dashes to offset the phrase from the larger sentence. A and B wrongly use only a single dash each, while D creates confusion by using several commas (as opposed to dashes and commas) to manage the sentence's content.

24) CORRECT ANSWER: A
The underlined portion of the sentence describes the sentence's main topic, "pluripotent cells", in a manner that provides new yet relevant and appropriate information. A is the best answer, while B wrongly indicates that the content describes stages of growth (which cannot logically "persist in the bone marrow" as cells can). Keep in mind that the information is specifically related to research involving Yamanaka factors (directly contradicting and eliminating C) and that the writer has not YET differentiated human test subjects from other test subjects (and in fact suggests that mice can be used to understand human test subjects, eliminating D).

25) CORRECT ANSWER: A
The writer is describing a process of "marking" genes to create specific results, or "so that" the genes have specific potentialities. A creates the proper sentence relationship (condition or cause-and-effect), while B indicates a contrast and D simply indicates addition. C is a trap answer: to "preclude" means to "prevent", and in context this answer would mean that ALL potentialities are being prevented, not that the "marking" is being used to create specific possibilities.

26) CORRECT ANSWER: D
While sentences 2 through 4 describe the fundamental science of stem cells, sentence 1 introduces the topic of Yamanaka factors, which are discussed at length in the next paragraph. Introducing the specific Yamanaka factors after explaining the general theory is a sensible choice, so that D is the best answer and A, B, and C all position the discussion of Yamanaka factors too early to effectively transition into the paragraph that follows.

27) CORRECT ANSWER: C
According to the content that follows the underlined portion, the researchers wanted to "observe the consequences of Yamanaka activation". These researchers are thus interested in the "specific effects" of Yamanaka factors, so that C is the best answer. A introduces an irrelevant negative tone, while B ("earlier research") and D ("therapeutic methods") refer to topics that are OUTSIDE the researchers' specific focus on how exactly Yamanaka factors work.

28) CORRECT ANSWER: B
In context, the sentence should explain what a comparison between two groups revealed, or what one group's results revealed "when" compared with those of another. B properly indicates that the two groups were simultaneously compared. A and D both wrongly indicate that the comparison CAUSED changes (not that it REVEALED changes caused by other factors), while C would normally refer to place, not to time.

29) CORRECT ANSWER: B
The writer has noted that the mice with activated Yamanaka factors revealed "positive changes": regenerating more muscle tissue than did the mice in a control group would be such a change. B is the best answer, while A indicates a negative change and C indicates no change at all. D does not clearly indicate a positive change (since slowed regeneration could be disadvantageous regardless of the amount of tissue regenerated) and should thus be eliminated.

30) CORRECT ANSWER: C
The sentence should be coordinated so that the subject-verb combination ("longevity . . . has") is NOT separated by a single comma. C correctly offsets the phrase "including humans" with two commas, while A and B both introduce faulty single-comma constructions. D, by using a comma and a dash (instead of the proper two commas or two dashes for interrupting content), also breaks the coordination of the sentence and should be eliminated.

31) CORRECT ANSWER: C
The content that ends the sentence should NOT be introduced by a colon, since it takes the form of a phrase introduced by "from", not the form of a set of items. Eliminate A and B. Then, make sure that the connected ideas in the phrase "from muscle scarring after surgery" are not interrupted by punctuation. D wrongly inserts a comma, while C allows the phrase to flow together and is thus the best answer.

32) CORRECT ANSWER: B
The sentence that contains the underlined portion should use the standard phrase "from . . . to": both A and C wrongly use the phrase "as well as" in this combination and should be eliminated. Next, the underlined portion must be coordinated to properly refer to the "conditions" which "result": D wrongly uses "that" to assign the noun "diabetes" to the verb "result". C, however, properly aligns "conditions" with "result" using "which" and is thus the best answer.

33) CORRECT ANSWER: D
Throughout the passage, the writer has mostly been concerned with individual, patient-by-patient health: the proposed sentence wrongly broadens the entire discussion to consider the topic of society at large, which is not addressed earlier. D is thus the best answer, while C is incorrect because the sentence DEPARTS from earlier content. A can be eliminated using similar logic (that the sentence is a departure from the passage's concerns), while B wrongly introduces the perspective of a non-specialist (an issue that is not EXPLICITLY addressed in the proposed sentence and is thus out of scope.).

Passage 4: A Humanitarian Purpose for GMO Foods

34) CORRECT ANSWER: A
The sentence in its original form properly presents the "paradox" using a full sentence that follows a colon: A is the best answer, while B (time relationship) and C (cause-and-effect relationship) do not set up an EXPLANATION in a similar manner. D breaks the parallel construction that is properly created in A ("the more . . . the more") and should be eliminated for this reason.

35) CORRECT ANSWER: C

At this point in the passage, the writer's main focus is the idea that as people become more able to alter the world they also become "fearful of the consequences" of alterations: A does not mention the topic of fear, while C properly describes the "anxieties" surrounding modified foods. Choose this answer and eliminate B (which indicates that people are NOT fearful) and D (which wrongly indicates that people in "prosperous nations" are relatively unconcerned about alterations, when in fact these people might be the most aware of anxiety-inducing advancements).

36) CORRECT ANSWER: A

The combined sentence contrasts the situation of individuals in developed "nations" with the situation of people in "developing countries", so that A properly uses the transition "although" to link the topics. Choose this answer and eliminate B (cause-and-effect), C (intensification), and D (example) as choices that introduce incorrect relationships.

37) CORRECT ANSWER: C

To address this question, consider which ideas should NOT be broken up by commas: the phrase "It is . . . needs" describes a single condition for diets and should thus not be interrupted at any point. A, B, and D all break up this phrase using commas, while C treats the phrase as a single unit of a larger sentence and is thus the best answer.

38) CORRECT ANSWER: D

The sentence as a whole presents facts about beta carotene and Vitamin A; however, the original version is incorrect because the ABSENCE of Vitamin A in certain countries (a social fact) does not explain the PRESENCE of Vitamin A in beta carotene (a scientific fact). Eliminate the faulty cause-and-effect relationship in A and the faulty contrast in B for a sentence that simply presents facts using two independent clauses ("Beta carotene is", "the latter is"). C wrongly links two such clauses using a dash (which is closest in function to a comma), while D uses a semicolon to link the clauses and is thus the best answer.

39) CORRECT ANSWER: D

The underlined portion must describe a "rice", which enables or serves "as a way for" a nutrient ("Vitamin A") to be accessed. D is idiomatically correct and captures the context of "ability" or "enabling". A and B both wrongly indicate possession ("of"), while C wrongly indicates literal direction or placement ("in").

40) CORRECT ANSWER: A

In all of its versions, sentence 2 emphasizes the importance of "enhancing the nutritional value of key crops". Sentence 3 lists a few such crops, while the sentences that follow explain how the nutritional value of rice can be enhanced. It would thus be best to keep the sentence in its current placement: choose A and eliminate B (since the broad category of "key crops" would then be wrongly mentioned BEFORE the examples in sentence 3). C would wrongly place a general statement within an extended example, while D would wrongly place a general statement AFTER the content that it should introduce and explain.

41) CORRECT ANSWER: D

The phrases "nutritional quality of the crops . . . countries" and "only factor of great importance" are single, unified phrases that contain information essential to the meaning of the sentence. A and C wrongly treat parts of the phrase "crops . . . countries" as inessential items that can be offset by commas; B wrongly does much the same by dividing up the essential phrase "only factor of great importance". Only D rightly avoids the commas and thus properly combines the writer's important ideas.

42) CORRECT ANSWER: B

The proposed content would transition from a sentence that describes a "difficult" prospect into a sentence that describes an advantage of maize but begins with "Moreover": to justify this sentence opening, ANOTHER benefit must be listed before the "Moreover" transition. The sentence itself rightly sets up the topic of the benefits of genetically modified crops. Choose B and eliminate A (negative) and C (ambivalent), which inaccurately represent the writer's positive tone. D is problematic because the previous sentence lists a CHALLENGE that populations face, not a BENEFIT of modified "staple crops" that address the challenge.

43) CORRECT ANSWER: D

The researchers have modified the "genetic structure" of maize and, consequently, made stable crop yields more likely. The sentence calls for a cause-and-effect relationship: A (surprise), B (difference in ideas), and C (different time signatures) all introduce inappropriate transitions. D, "thus", properly designates an effect and is the correct answer.

44) CORRECT ANSWER: B

According to the writer, the plants have been made "toxic to the insects that might otherwise consume them" or function as though they have a "pesticide" that eliminates insects. B is the best answer. A wrongly refers to an enhancement that would not target and destroy insects, C refers to a sociological topic from elsewhere ("poorer nations"), and D refers to an insect-destroying measure that is too extreme for the context: the plants protect themselves but do not destroy ENTIRE insect species.

Test Two

Writing Test
35 MINUTES, 44 QUESTIONS

Turn to Section 2 of your answer sheet to answer the questions in this section.

DIRECTIONS

Each passage below is accompanied by a number of questions. For some questions, you will consider how the passage might be revised to improve the expression of ideas. For other questions, you will consider how the passage might be edited to correct errors in sentence structure, usage, or punctuation. A passage or a question may be accompanied by one or more graphics (such as a table or graph) that you will consider as you make revising and editing decisions.

Some questions will direct you to an underlined portion of a passage. Other questions will direct you to a location in a passage or ask you to think about the passage as a whole.

After reading each passage, choose the answer to each question that most effectively improves the quality of writing in the passage or that makes the passage conform to the conventions of standard written English. Many questions include a "NO CHANGE" option. Choose that option if you think the best choice is to leave the relevant portion of the passage as it is.

Questions 1-11 are based on the following passage.

Captivated by Carbon Capture

[1] Solar and wind power technologies continue to improve, and expand providing energy without the cost in carbon emissions of other sources of energy, such as coal and natural gas. However, entrepreneurial-minded engineers can take advantage of this emissions gap [2] to develop new technologies aimed at not only capturing the carbon that burning fossil fuels releases, but also using captured carbon to create chemical products useful to other industries. These novel measures would maximize the efficiency of energy production while minimizing environmental harm.

[1] A chemical plant in India has patented a chemical [3] that when sprayed into the chimney of a coal boiler, strips up to 90% of the carbon dioxide from the emissions and

1

A) NO CHANGE
B) Solar and wind power technologies continue to improve, and expand, providing energy without the cost in carbon emissions,
C) Solar and wind power technologies continue to improve and expand, providing energy without the cost in carbon emissions
D) Solar and wind power technologies continue to improve and expand, providing energy without the cost in carbon emissions,

2

Which is the most logical content choice?
A) NO CHANGE
B) to lobby for harsher anti-carbon regulations
C) to re-purpose older industrial instruments
D) to establish innovative companies

3

A) NO CHANGE
B) that, when
C) which when
D) which

CONTINUE

redirects the carbon dioxide. [2] Then, the CO2 can be gathered

and used as an ingredient in compounds like the versatile soda

ash, which is commonly known as washing soda. [3] This

compound is necessary for the production of glass, paper,

detergents, and many other materials and products. [4] Indeed,

some established companies have found inventive solutions to

carbon management. [5] While the plant's owner, Ramachandran

Gopalan, said he had no environmentalist ambitions in

developing **4** the technology—needing "a reliable stream

of CO2," his approach may become popular among energy

companies and governments looking to increase efficiency of

energy production and decrease carbon emissions. **5**

Carbon management— **6** whereas it relies on long-term

storage or on an industrial "recycling" of carbon dioxide into

other materials, as in the example of Gopalan's plant—is

a diverse field that relies on the collaboration of chemists,

geologists, and engineers to develop technologies, **7** as well as

seasoned policymakers to implement them. Some industries, like

the chemical industry, may rely heavily on chemical engineers

to research new, more efficient ways of capturing carbon in a

state useful to manufacturing. Other industries, like the fossil

fuel industry, may also focus on employing geologists and other

earth scientists to find new ways to store captured carbon deep

underground.

4

A) NO CHANGE
B) the technology, by needing
C) the technology or needed
D) the technology but rather needed

5

To make the order of ideas in the paragraph most logical,
sentence 4 should be placed

A) where it is now.
B) before sentence 1.
C) before sentence 3.
D) after sentence 5.

6

A) NO CHANGE
B) although
C) whether
D) as

7

The writer is considering deleting the underlined portion
and ending the sentence with a period after "technologies."
Should the writer make these modifications?

A) Yes, because the writer never explains why
   policymakers would be interested in carbon capture.
B) Yes, because policy makers were not involved in the
   Gopalan and NRC WA Parish projects.
C) No, because this information supports the writer's ideas
   about diversity in carbon management.
D) No, because this information adds meaningful details to
   the discussion of Gopalan's plant.

CONTINUE

Storage-oriented approaches are now in place at some coal- and gas-burning power plants, such as the NRC WA Parish generating station outside of Houston, Texas. This **8** technology, which uses a solvent to absorb carbon dioxide from chimney flues and then stores the substance in compressed tanks underground—was developed by chemical engineers **9** investigating the molecular dynamics of solvents and by geologists studying the best ways to contain carbon in the earth. By working together, these scientists have developed a solution for a major industrial problem.

Decreasing carbon emissions worldwide remains a major challenge for scientists and **10** engineers having many disciplines. However, the field of carbon capture is full of opportunities for collaboration. **11** The potential for large-scale adoption of such technologies indicates that these fields will only continue to grow.

8

A) NO CHANGE
B) technology—which uses a solvent to absorb carbon dioxide from chimney flues and then
C) technology which uses a solvent to absorb—carbon dioxide from chimney flues and then
D) technology which uses a solvent to absorb carbon dioxide—from chimney flues and then

9

Which content is most logically consistent with the rest of the writer's discussion?

A) NO CHANGE
B) eager to build off of Gopalan's innovation
C) researching the compositions of common natural gases
D) hoping to facilitate a shift away from coal-burning energy

10

A) NO CHANGE
B) engineers, and their many disciplines.
C) engineers despite their many disciplines.
D) engineers across many disciplines.

11

The writer is considering adding the following sentence at this point in the passage.

> And if carbon capture technology can be even more efficiently manufactured, the industry as a whole could become profitable in ways that not even Gopalan could envision.

Should the writer make this addition here?

A) Yes, because it indicates one likely result of the NRC WA Parish project.
B) Yes, because it presents the primary reason for the predicted growth of carbon capture employment.
C) No, because the passage establishes earlier that Gopalan is not interested in new carbon capture developments.
D) No, because the passage has shifted from the specific example of Gopalan to a broader discussion.

CONTINUE

Questions 12-22 are based on the following passage.

Children's Literature: Seen, and Definitely Heard

As any good persuasive writer knows, it is easier to convey a lesson by embedding it in an entertaining story [12] as by delivering it in the course of a long, technical lecture. This principle of the power of storytelling holds especially true in children's literature: children, in their innocence and inexperience, are uniquely in need of useful lessons. [13] What better way to transmit a moral than by weaving it into a story about knights or witches or time machines?

In some cases, the lessons that are taught by children's literature are straightforward. Classic folkloric tales such as "Snow White" and "Little Red Riding Hood," [14] moreover, can be read as cautionary narratives that warn against trusting suspicious strangers. Yet it is also possible for [15] literature, that targets young audiences, to promote entire systems of values—

12

A) NO CHANGE
B) than by delivering
C) when by delivering
D) unlike by delivering

13

The writer is considering deleting the underlined sentence. Should the sentence be kept or deleted?

A) Kept, because it substantiates the writer's argument that most children's literature is similar to folklore.
B) Kept, because it helps to support the writer's argument that adult literature and children's literature are fundamentally different.
C) Deleted, because it wrongly implies that young readers are drawn exclusively to fantasy narratives.
D) Deleted, because it primarily re-phrases an idea that the writer has already established effectively.

14

A) NO CHANGE
B) by some accounts,
C) for instance,
D) apparently,

15

A) NO CHANGE
B) literature that targets young audiences
C) literature, which targets young audiences
D) literature which targets young audiences,

CONTINUE

not simply one or two principles of conduct. The nineteenth and early twentieth centuries provide several seminal examples of this kind of worldview-oriented **16** children's writing. Louisa May Alcott's adolescent novel *Little Women* (1868) encouraged young readers to be both thoughtful and independent, while Kenneth Grahame's *The Wind in the Willows* (1908) praises the virtues of friendship and cooperation. **17**

[1] However, by the middle of the 20th century, **18** children's writing had come to be dominated by writers who directly criticized Alcott and Grahame. [2] Young readers were no longer exhorted to be polite or compliant. [3] Instead, some authors exhorted children to embrace exactly the opposite qualities: self-assertion, critical thought, and unbounded imagination. [4] Among the most famous specimens of this approach is *The Little Prince*, a celebrated and at times cuttingly humorous adventure tale by Antoine de Saint-Exupéry. [5] The narrative of this slim, whimsically illustrated children's book mirthfully defies the logical rules of everyday life. [6] However,

16

Which choice best combines the two sentences at the underlined portion?
A) children's writing, in which Louisa May Alcott's
B) children's writing, because Louisa May Alcott's
C) children's writing, Louisa May Alcott's
D) children's writing: Louisa May Alcott's

17

At this point, the writer is considering adding the following sentence.

> Ironically, Alcott's and Grahame's creations are currently more popular among adults (including scholars of literature) than among the audience of young readers that they were designed to address.

Should the writer make this addition here?
A) Yes, because it effectively balances the writer's criticisms of Alcott and Grahame.
B) Yes, because it anticipates one of the writer's main arguments about *The Little Prince*.
C) No, because it shifts focus from the two writers' values to their readership.
D) No, because it creates a false parallel between 19th- and 20th-century writers.

18

Which choice most logically anticipates the content of the paragraph that follows?
A) NO CHANGE
B) writers with more philosophical inclinations had begun to turn their talents to children's writing.
C) earlier works of children's writing had been all but forgotten by most adolescents.
D) the ideology behind children's writing had undergone significant changes.

CONTINUE

the book also comments directly on how closed-minded adults are—incapable of appreciating children's most treasured games and drawings. [7] In a purposeful manner, Saint-Exupéry urges a mentality of lively independence. [8] The "Little Prince" of the title lives mostly by himself on an asteroid and sometimes consorts with a rose [19] that is described using metaphors derived from modern poetry. [20]

Other books directed towards children (or at least relatively young readers) have continued Saint-Exupéry's project of casting a skeptical light on the wisdom of adults. From *Matilda* to *James and the Giant Peach*, the novels of Roald Dahl feature mean aunts, malevolent educators, and other figures of misplaced and misused authority. Teachers who don't seem to deserve their power also appear in Louis Sachar's popular novel *Sideways Stories from Wayside* [21] *School, which takes* the form of a series of comical, irreverent vignettes.

Does this mean that children's literature has lost its instructive power? Of course not. The lesson has [22] simply changed—as be bold, be imaginative, and be on guard against adulthood at its worst.

---

[19]

The writer wants the underlined portion to reflect one of the traits of Saint-Exupéry's writing enumerated in the paragraph. Which choice best accomplishes this goal?

A) NO CHANGE

B) that may be a veiled reference to an event from Saint-Exupéry's life.

C) that is treated exactly as though "she" is a full-fledged person.

D) that at times causes the Little Prince to feel unhappy.

[20]

To make the order of the ideas in the paragraph most logical, sentence 6 should be placed

A) where it is now.

B) after sentence 4.

C) after sentence 7.

D) after sentence 8.

[21]

A) NO CHANGE

B) *School* that takes

C) *School* to take

D) *School,*

[22]

A) NO CHANGE

B) simply changed: be bold

C) simply changed, to be bold

D) simply changed; thus, to be bold

CONTINUE

Questions 23-33 are based on the following passage.

Not So Fast, Urban Renewal!

[1] Each day, I commute to work by train; my route normally takes me through Newark, New Jersey, a city that has undergone significant changes in the two decades that I have been riding past. [2] Most of the city's apartment buildings were once low-to-the-ground and old-fashioned. [3] About fifteen years ago, the landscape of Newark was dominated by a few skyscrapers and many industrial warehouses. [4] Now, every time I look out the window of my morning train, I see sleek new condominium-style buildings, which are appearing in ever greater numbers along the Newark waterfront. [5] A walk through downtown Newark **23** (or just a passing commuter's glance) reveals that the city is succeeding in replacing some of its many diners with sit-down gourmet options. [6] Now, high-quality supermarkets, including a recently-installed Whole Foods, have even begun to appear. **24**

Newark is undergoing a process commonly described as "urban renewal." Under initiatives of this sort, older structures **25** are cleared. Dynamic new businesses and prosperous new residents will be drawn to the area. Such projects are often undertaken with the best of intentions, **26** however, are still susceptible to criticism.

23

The writer wants to add a parenthetical phrase that is appropriate to the context of the passage. Which choice best accomplishes this goal?

A) NO CHANGE
B) (or a short visit elsewhere in New Jersey)
C) (or a sit-down discussion with an urban planner)
D) (or a stay in one of the city's many landmark hotels)

24

To make the order of ideas in the paragraph most logical, sentence 2 should be placed

A) where it is now.
B) after sentence 3.
C) after sentence 4.
D) after sentence 5.

25

Which choice most effectively combines the sentences at the underlined portion?

A) are cleared after dynamic
B) are cleared so that dynamic
C) are cleared, whereas dynamic
D) are cleared; likewise, dynamic

26

A) NO CHANGE
B) furthermore,
C) yet
D) or

CONTINUE

One possible liability of urban **27** renewal—is that despite the appearance of growing prosperity—it in fact does little to address the social and economic problems of modern cities. Consider an urban renewal project in a city where many citizens live in poverty. **28** It is possible that the worst-off residents, instead of taking part in a new era of prosperity, will simply be ignored as new structures rise. Urban renewal that introduces this **29** scenario (is typically and derisively) described as "gentrification." In gentrification at its most exaggerated, an elite or "gentry" of outsiders will take over and develop a small area of prime real estate, while patterns of crime and poverty that exist in other parts of the city **30** will begin to abate.

27

A) NO CHANGE
B) renewal is that—despite the appearance of growing prosperity—it in fact does little
C) renewal is—that despite the appearance of growing prosperity it in fact does little
D) renewal is that, despite the appearance of growing prosperity it in fact does little

28

At this point in the passage, the writer is considering inserting the following sentence.

> Consider, also, that the poorest inhabitants in such a city tend to be allocated less education funding than their wealthier counterparts.

Should the writer add this content here?

A) Yes, because it anticipates and addresses a possible argument against the writer's thesis.
B) Yes, because it broadens the writer's discussion to explain the origin of urban poverty.
C) No, because it introduces a social problem that is apparently not a current priority in Newark.
D) No, because it introduces an issue that is not clearly and directly related to real estate.

29

A) NO CHANGE
B) scenario is typically (and derisively described)
C) scenario is typically (and derisively) described
D) scenario (is typically and derisively described)

30

Which choice most accurately reflects the writer's reasoning?

A) NO CHANGE
B) will prompt an exodus from poorer areas.
C) will eventually affect the "gentrified" area.
D) will continue uninterrupted.

CONTINUE

However, there is a second possible problem with urban renewal: that it can prove too successful and can consequently undermine a city's distinctive character. Much of the urban renewal in Newark, for instance, revolves around **31** restaurant choices that though in some cases high-quality, are corporation-owned. Yet a city that comes to be dominated by Starbucks and Chipotle is a city that has lost some of its personality.

"Character" of this sort is one of Newark's own strong points, **32** even though city residents are typically willing to trade such "character" for economic prosperity. Urban renewal does not simply challenge planners and politicians to make wise use of available resources. It challenges them as well to balance a commitment to public good **33** from a sensitivity to a city's unique heritage, culture, and appeal.

31

A) NO CHANGE
B) restaurant choices that, though in some cases high-quality
C) restaurant choices that, though in some cases high-quality,
D) restaurant choices: that though in some cases high-quality

32

Which additional content best supports the argument that the writer is making at this point in the passage?

A) NO CHANGE
B) no matter how much critics may point out that even Starbucks was founded with European coffee shop "character" in mind.
C) as evidenced by the vibrant independent restaurants of Newark's Ironbound District.
D) and nearby cities such as Paterson are trying, with mixed results, to replicate some of the very qualities that make Newark unique.

33

A) NO CHANGE
B) with a sensitivity
C) as a sensitivity
D) to a sensitivity

CONTINUE

Questions 34-44 are based on the following passage.

Heavy Metal, Asteroid Style

[1] The popular saying "It's what inside that counts" may hold true for celestial bodies as well as people, **34** but there is currently no feasible way to investigate the core of a celestial body for research purposes. [2] **35** This fact is what makes 16 Psyche a metallic asteroid, such a source of excitement for astronomy experts. [3] Spanning over 200 kilometers in diameter and constituting almost 1% of the total mass of the asteroid belt, 16 Psyche is not only impressive in scale but also unique in composition. [4] Most asteroids are composed of ice and rock. [5] Since metal elements make up the core of Earth itself, this key difference in composition has led scientists **36** to speculate: that 16 Psyche may actually be the exposed iron core of a protoplanet. [6] As demonstrated by radar readings, 16 Psyche, however, is composed primarily of iron and nickel. **37**

34

Which choice best leads into the discussion that follows?

A) NO CHANGE

B) but scientists have spent the past fifteen years developing new technologies that, amazingly, can be applied to both of these pursuits.

C) but scientists can often map the exact contents of planets and asteroids more precisely than they can map the unpredictable human mind.

D) but that reality has not stopped humanity from speculating about both heavenly bodies and individual psyches in great detail.

35

A) NO CHANGE

B) This fact is what makes 16 Psyche, a metallic asteroid such a source of excitement, for astronomy experts.

C) This fact is what makes 16 Psyche, a metallic asteroid, such a source of excitement for astronomy experts.

D) This fact is what makes 16 Psyche a metallic asteroid: such a source of excitement for astronomy experts.

36

A) NO CHANGE

B) to speculate; that 16 Psyche may

C) to speculate—that 16 Psyche may

D) to speculate that 16 Psyche may

37

To make the order of ideas in the paragraph most logical, sentence 5 should be placed

A) where it is now.

B) after sentence 2.

C) after sentence 3.

D) after sentence 6.

CONTINUE

[38] Protoplanets are small celestial objects (typically about the size of Earth's moon). The relationship of protoplanets to fully-fledged planets resembles that between a seed and a tree: after forming out of molecular dust and other particles pulled together by gravity, protoplanets have the potential to [39] grow in size (usually through collisions) with other objects. As protoplanets grow, heavier elements like metals sink, eventually forming a metallic inner core, while lighter elements rise.

If 16 Psyche does indeed represent the core of a protoplanet, [40] one question is obvious. What happened to the rest of it? One theory suggests that a violent collision between the protoplanet and another object led to the outer crust of the planet being peeled off, leaving the metallic core exposed. As a result, 16 Psyche [41] holds vast potential for facilitating a deeper understanding of planetary composition and structure. Dr Lindy Elkins-Tanton, of Arizona State University, spearheaded a proposal to explore 16 Psyche, explaining that, "16 Psyche is the only known object of its kind in the solar system, and this is the only way humans will ever visit a core. We learn about inner space by visiting outer space."

38

The writer is considering deleting the underlined sentence. Should the writer make this deletion?

A) Yes, because the sentence contradicts information about 16 Psyche.

B) Yes, because the sentence simply reiterates information from elsewhere.

C) No, because the sentence defines a concept central to the passage

D) No, because the sentence qualifies one of the writer's main arguments.

39

A) NO CHANGE

B) grow in size (usually through collisions with other objects).

C) grow in size, usually (through collisions with other objects).

D) grow in size, usually through collisions, with other objects.

40

The writer realizes that the two sentences should be combined at the underlined portion. Which choice offers the best logic and grammar?

A) one question is obvious, what happened

B) one question is: obviously, what happened

C) one question is obvious: what happened

D) one question is—obviously, what happened

41

Which sentence best leads into the ideas set forward by Dr. Elkins-Tanton?

A) NO CHANGE

B) exhibits properties that have not been detected in studies of other, nearby metal asteroids.

C) is ripe for scientific study, even though humans will never explore the asteroid firsthand.

D) may prompt humans to develop methods for sending unmanned space missions to planets outside the solar system.

CONTINUE

The unique opportunities for better understanding the inner workings of a planet led to the development of a plan for a robotic Psyche orbiter. [42] While this orbiter is activated, the topography, gravity, and magnetism of the asteroid will be studied, along with other characteristics. The mission is currently under development with [43] NASA targeted to launch in 2023, with a projected arrival date of 2030. The project will largely make use of previously developed technology; [44] ironically, it should be relatively affordable. The insights 16 Psyche may offer, however, could be priceless.

[42]

At this point, the writer is considering adding the following sentence to the paragraph.

This spacecraft will orbit Psyche for six months.

Should the writer make this addition here?

A) Yes, because it suggests one of the main difficulties of the space exploration mission.
B) Yes, because it adds detail to the explanation of the mission's projected timeline.
C) No, because it does not discuss the composition or movement of Psyche 16.
D) No, because it offers a prediction about an event that will probably not come to pass.

[43]

A) NO CHANGE
B) NASA that is targeted to launch in 2023,
C) NASA, which is targeted to launch in 2023,
D) NASA and is targeted to launch in 2023

[44]

A) NO CHANGE
B) nonetheless,
C) similarly,
D) consequently,

189

STOP

Answer Key: TEST 2

Test 2

PASSAGE 1
Captivated by Carbon Capture

1. C
2. A
3. B
4. D
5. B
6. C
7. C
8. B
9. A
10. D
11. D

PASSAGE 2
Children's Literature: Seen, and Definitely Heard

12. B
13. D
14. C
15. B
16. D
17. C
18. D
19. C
20. D
21. A
22. B

PASSAGE 3
Not So Fast, Urban Renewal!

23. A
24. B
25. B
26. C
27. B
28. D
29. C
30. D
31. C
32. C
33. B

PASSAGE 4
Heavy Metal, Asteroid Style

34. C
35. C
36. D
37. D
38. C
39. B
40. C
41. A
42. B
43. D
44. D

Answer Explanations

SAT Practice Test #2

Passage 1: Captivated by Carbon Capture

1) CORRECT ANSWER: C
The sentence that contains the underlined portion begins with a discussion of specific technologies ("Solar . . . expand"), then shifts to a statement of how these technologies are beneficial ("providing . . . energy"). C properly uses a comma to divide these two major segments. A and B wrongly use a comma to separate two verbs ("improve and expand") that are closely in parallel; D wrongly breaks the connected phrase "cost . . . of other" with a single comma and should thus be eliminated.

2) CORRECT ANSWER: A
The paragraph describes "entrepreneurial-minded engineers" who create new and improved products, so that A would properly describe the engineers' activity of creating "new technologies". B ("regulations") and D ("companies") wrongly focus on measures other than the technologies or products THEMSELVES. C is an inaccurate description, since the engineers "create products" instead of re-purposing existing products.

3) CORRECT ANSWER: B
The inessential phrase "when . . . boiler" should be offset using two commas: B is the only answer that provides the needed second comma and is thus the correct answer. A, C, and D would only use ONE comma in a manner that would wrongly interrupt the subject-verb combination "chemical that . . . strips".

4) CORRECT ANSWER: D
The underlined portion should create a contrast between a motive that Gopalan denied ("environmentalist ambitions") and his real motive ("a reliable stream of income). D creates the required contrast. A (which suggests similarity between the possible motives), B (which suggests cause-and-effect), and C (which places the motives as similar alternatives, NOT as a true motive and a denied motive) all create sentence relationships that are illogical in context.

5) CORRECT ANSWER: B
Sentence 4 offers a general statement about the "inventive solutions to carbon management" developed by some companies: sentence 1 and the content that follows describe how one chemical plant managed carbon dioxide. Thus, sentence 4 would effectively introduce the case described in the paragraph. Choose B and eliminate A and C, which would interrupt the writer's discussion of the "chemical plant in India" with a broad statement. D would place a statement that should INTRODUCE a case study of an established company AFTER the entire description, and should thus be eliminated.

6) CORRECT ANSWER: C

The underlined portion should lead into a discussion of alternatives, since the sentence describes carbon management that may rely on storage "or" on recycling. C, "whether", pairs effectively with "or" to describe alternatives and is the best choice. A and B would both suggest contrasts or opposites, and D indicates close similarity or analogy. While these meanings do not fit the context, the word choices themselves break the standard phrase "whether . . . or" and can be eliminated quickly for this reason.

7) CORRECT ANSWER: C

In the paragraph that contains the underlined portion and elsewhere, the writer emphasizes the element of "collaboration" across disciplines in carbon management: "policymakers" would be a group with whom scientists could collaborate. C is thus the best answer, while the fact that the Gopalan plant is only a focus of OTHER paragraphs can be used to eliminate B and D. A is contradicted by information in the previous paragraph: as the writer explains, "governments" and thus policymakers may be interested in the energy efficiency issues related to carbon capture.

8) CORRECT ANSWER: B

Two dashes must be used to separate the descriptive phrase that interrupts the subject-verb combination "technology . . . was developed"; A uses only a single dash and must thus be eliminated. Both C and D use dashes to break up the phrase "which uses . . . underground", which must be kept together as a SINGLE long description that modifies "technology". Eliminate these answers and choose B as the answer that properly coordinates the sentence.

9) CORRECT ANSWER: A

The "chemical engineers" described by the underlined portion helped to develop technology that employed a "solvent": A would thus describe a logical research focus for these chemical engineers. B wrongly describes a topic (Gopalan's plant) only considered in PREVIOUS paragraphs, C identifies the wrong research focus ("natural gases", not carbon dioxide), and D wrongly focuses on a goal of environment-conscious industries or environmentalists (not of researchers, who would naturally be most interested in experimental inquiries).

10) CORRECT ANSWER: D

In context, the underlined portion describes "scientists and engineers" who come from a variety of disciplines and work collaboratively. These specialists come from "across" disciplines, so that D is the best answer. A wrongly indicates that EACH individual scientist or engineer has many disciplines, B indicates that the disciplines themselves (NOT the people who specialize in them) face challenges, and C introduces a contrast rather than simply describing the scientists and engineers.

11) CORRECT ANSWER: D

Overall, the passage has considered the career-oriented and collaboration-based aspects of carbon capture using a variety of examples: Gopalan is simply one example, and the profitability of carbon capture is at best a minor topic. D properly indicates that the new sentence is a distraction, while C is contradicted by Gopalan's involvement in carbon capture. The issue of "profitability", the main theme of the proposed sentence, is not emphasized in the discussion of the NRC WA Parish project (eliminating A) or pointed to as a main reason for the growth of carbon capture employment (which is linked more to opportunities for collaboration and adoption of technology, eliminating B).

Passage 2: Children's Literature: Seen, and Definitely Heard

12) CORRECT ANSWER: B

The underlined portion must form the standard phrase "easier . . . than" in order to compare different storytelling methods: B is thus the best answer. A and C both break the standard phrase and suggest similarity (NOT difference), while D sets up a contrast ("unlike") yet departs completely from the needed "easier . . . than" combination.

13) CORRECT ANSWER: D

The writer has already explained that a "lesson" can be conveyed by "embedding it in an entertaining story": the underlined content mostly re-phrases this idea, so that D is the best answer. Keep in mind that the writer is concerned with children's literature ITSELF, not in relation to folklore (eliminating A) or adult literature (eliminating B). C is a misreading of the proposed content: the writer indicates that children are drawn to fantasy narratives, but never that they are not drawn to OTHER narratives.

14) CORRECT ANSWER: C

In this sentence, the writer mentions "Snow White" and "Little Red Riding Hood" as examples or "instances" of children's stories that contain lessons. C is the best answer, while A wrongly indicates that the preceding sentence contains similar or ADDITIONAL examples (not that it SETS UP the examples with a more general idea). B refers to outside perspectives and D indicates skepticism or incomplete certainty: neither of these answers captures the fact that the writer is moving from a broad idea to specific examples.

15) CORRECT ANSWER: B

In context, the writer is specifying a certain kind of literature "that targets young audiences": the information about the audience is thus essential and should not be separated from "literature" with a comma. Eliminate A and choose B as the best answer. C and D wrongly use a single comma to interrupt the unified phrase or idea "possible . . . to promote" and should thus be eliminated.

16) CORRECT ANSWER: D

While the content in the first part of the sentence refers to specific examples of "children's writing", the content in the second part explains how two books for children guided their readers. This idea and illustration relationship can be effectively coordinated using a colon: D is the best answer. A wrongly indicates placement or ownership and creates an awkward construction, B indicates cause-and-effect (NOT illustration of an idea), and C introduces a comma splice.

17) CORRECT ANSWER: C

The paragraph is primarily concerned with the "systems of values" that works of literature such as Alcott's and Grahame's promote; the proposed sentence wrongly shifts emphasis to the question of readership and should thus not be inserted. Choose C and eliminate D (which wrongly refers to broad categories of "writers", not simply to Alcott and Grahame) as using irrelevant reasoning. A is problematic because the writer never in fact criticizes Alcott and Grahame (who are only discussed objectively then subjected to analysis), while B mistakes one of the writer's ACTUAL points about *The Little Prince* (its criticisms of adults) for a very different idea (its popularity among adults).

18) CORRECT ANSWER: D

In the paragraph that contains the underlined portion, the writer explains that young readers "were no longer exhorted to be polite or compliant" as children's literature evolved. The ideology behind children's literature thus changed, so that D is the best answer. EARLIER children's literature writers are not directly discussed at length (eliminating A and C as answers that wrongly place emphasis on a side topic), while the new writers of children's literature are important because they value independence and imagination (NOT because they are "philosophical", eliminating B).

19) CORRECT ANSWER: C

The writer explains that Saint-Exupéry's writing "defiles the logical rules of everyday life": treating a flower as a "full-fledged person" would be one example of how such rules are defied. C is the best choice. Topics such as "poetry" (A), "Saint-Exupéry's own life" (B), and "unhappiness" (D) may in fact be traits of *The Little Prince* but are not traits mentioned anywhere "in the paragraph". Eliminate these answers as out of scope.

20) CORRECT ANSWER: D

While much of the paragraph describes the whimsical quality of *The Little Prince*, sentence 6 focuses on the topic of "how closed-minded adults are", a topic continued in the paragraph that follows. Sentence 6 should thus be used as a transition into the next paragraph. Choose D and eliminate A, B, and C (which would break up the writer's discussion of the POSITIVE qualities promoted by *The Little Prince*).

21) CORRECT ANSWER: A

The underlined portion should refer to Sachar's "popular novel", which takes the form of a series of vignettes. A properly uses "which" to refer to the "novel" mentioned earlier, while B flows together with the word *School* and illogically indicates that the school itself is a group of vignettes or stories. C wrongly indicates a future condition or possibility, while D lacks a coordinating transition that links back to the word "novel" and should be eliminated as an incorrect, awkward construction.

22) CORRECT ANSWER: B

The content that occurs in the later segment of the sentence should describe the ideas behind the "lesson": this idea-and-illustration structure can be set up using a colon followed by items (such as the recommendations that begin with "be"). B is the best answer. A wrongly uses a dash and indicates comparison (not illustration), C is an awkward construction that indicates that the "lesson" ITSELF is being bold, and D uses a semicolon in place of a colon and inappropriately indicates a cause-and-effect relationship.

Passage 3: Not So Fast, Urban Renewal!

23) CORRECT ANSWER: A

The passage as a whole considers the perspective of a writer who commutes "to work by train" through Newark, New Jersey. A properly refers to the perspective of such a commuter. B (locations OTHER than Newark) and C (an interview) raise topics that are not directly mentioned, while D ("hotels") raises a topic that is actually unrelated to the writer's actions. The writer simply passes through Newark and does not stay at one of the city's "landmark hotels" at any point that the passage designates.

24) CORRECT ANSWER: B

Sentence 2 describes how the apartment buildings in Newark "once" were; this detail supports the discussion of Newark "About fifteen years ago" that is introduced in sentence 3. Eliminate A and choose B, which places sentences 2 and 3 in the correct order by introducing the time period and THEN describing earlier buildings. Both C and D would interrupt a discussion of present-day Newark with a reference to how Newark once was, and should thus be eliminated.

25) CORRECT ANSWER: B

The sentences should be joined using a cause-and-effect relationship: if "older structures" are removed, new businesses and new residents will be drawn to the revitalized area. B properly captures this sequence of events, while A REVERSES the events (placing the appearance of new residents and buildings first in time). C indicates a contrast and D indicates similarity, so that neither answer provides the needed cause-and-effect transition.

26) CORRECT ANSWER: C

The sentence pairs a positive ("best of intentions") with a negative ("criticism") and should thus link these ideas with a contrast: the original version provides a contrast with "however" yet creates an awkward non-grammatical structure ("with the best of intentions are still susceptible to criticism") if the content between comma is removed. Eliminate A and choose C for the proper contrast. B wrongly indicates addition while D wrongly indicates alternatives, NOT a difference in tone.

27) CORRECT ANSWER: B

Sentences that use dashes must involve grammatical constructions if the content between dashes is factored out: A would create the phrase "renewal it in fact" if the content between dashes is temporarily removed. Eliminate this answer and choose B, which would involve the grammatically-correct phrase "that it in fact does little" in the absence of the content between dashes. C and D wrongly separate the linked phrases "is that . . . it in fact does little" with only ONE unit of punctuation (dash and comma, respectively) and should be eliminated as departing from the rules for coordinating intervening phrases.

28) CORRECT ANSWER: D

In this paragraph, the writer is most concerned with the problems that arise from gentrification in terms of real estate: "education funding" is indeed an urban problem, but is a topic that distracts from the writer's focus. Choose D and eliminate A, B, and C, which all wrongly assume that the writer discusses "education funding" elsewhere or that this topic has a clearly-articulated relationship to "gentrification" in the passage.

29) CORRECT ANSWER: C

The sentence must be coordinated to describe "Urban renewal" in such a manner that, if the content in parentheses were to be deleted, the sentence would still be properly constructed. C would yield the phrase "typically described" if the parenthetical content were to be disregarded: choose this answer and eliminate A and D (which wrongly place the verb "is" inside the parentheses and thus break the subject-verb combination "Urban renewal . . . is described"). B would create the mis-constructed phrase "typically as" without the parenthetical content and should thus be eliminated.

30) CORRECT ANSWER: D

The writer explains that poorer areas may "simply be ignored" under gentrification; the problems in these areas would continue, eliminating positive answer A and justifying negative answer D. B wrongly assumes that the non-developed area will be de-populated (not be "ignored" and continue to worsen), while C wrongly indicates that the residents of a "small area of prime real estate" will face negative consequences (not that the residents of POORER areas will).

31) CORRECT ANSWER: C

The sentence must be coordinated so that the subject-verb phrase "that . . . are" is properly aligned: this alignment can be accomplished by setting off the intervening descriptive phrase with two commas. C properly does so, while A and B wrongly use only one comma each. D wrongly places a sentence fragment (not a full sentence or a set of items) after a colon and should thus be eliminated.

32) CORRECT ANSWER: C

The underlined portion should describe the non-corporate "personality" or vibrant "Character" of Newark: mentioning the "independent restaurants" of a well-defined area would effectively do so. Choose C and eliminate A (which presents "character" as part of a trade-off, rather than simply or clearly describing it) and B (which describes the "character" of Starbucks, not the "character" of Newark). D is problematic because it shifts focus to another New Jersey location, Paterson, without describing Newark itself.

33) CORRECT ANSWER: B

The underlined portion should form a standard phrase with "to balance": the proper usage for describing two factors that are being balanced is "to balance . . . with". B is the best answer: A and D are idiomatically incorrect and indicate direction, while C wrongly indicates comparison or analogy (not two factors or qualities that are balanced "with" each other).

Passage 4: Heavy Metal, Asteroid Style

34) CORRECT ANSWER: C

In the discussion that follows, the writer explains that 16 Psyche is "unique in composition", a judgment that is possible because its "exact contents" can be determined. C thus effectively sets up the discussion that follows, while the same reasoning can be used to eliminate A (which indicates that the composition of a "celestial body" such as 16 Psyche is UNKNOWN). B and D both wrongly focus on a minor topic (the human mind) that the writer uses to lead INTO the discussion of 16 Psyche and should be eliminated as detracting from the main topic.

35) CORRECT ANSWER: C

The information in the sentence must be coordinated using commas to present material in a logical fashion: C properly offsets the description of 16 Psyche (as a "metallic asteroid") in a manner that would create a grammatically correct sentence if this content were to be eliminated. A and D involve a faulty grouping that fails to offset the description (and wrongly indicate that an a "fact" of scientific procedure makes 16 Psyche metallic), and B creates an awkward linkage with "asteroid such" (words that should be separated with a comma).

36) CORRECT ANSWER: D

The words "speculate" and "that" describe a single action and should thus not be interrupted by punctuation: D is the best answer, while A, B, and C all break convention by inserting units of punctuation. In fact, "that" should not be separated from a verb to which it is linked unless a descriptive phrase (offset by two commas, dashes, or parentheses) intervenes.

37) CORRECT ANSWER: D

Sentence 5 both refers to the specific composition of 16 Psyche (mentioned in sentence 6 but NOT in sentence 4) and discusses protoplanets (a topic of the following paragraph). Thus, sentence 5 should be placed after sentence 6: choose D and eliminate A. Neither sentence 2 nor sentence 3 explains in detail the "key difference in composition" that separates 16 Psyche from other asteroids, a topic that only occurs later. For this reason, B and C should both be eliminated.

38) CORRECT ANSWER: C

The topic of "protoplanets" is discussed both in the paragraph that precedes and in the paragraphs that follow the underlined portion, which explains the term "protoplanet" itself. C rightly indicates that this definition of "protoplanet" should remain in the passage. This sentence does not actually discuss 16 Psyche (eliminating A), is the only sentence in which a "protoplanet" is defined (eliminating B), and provides objective information (rather than contributing to an argument, eliminating D).

39) CORRECT ANSWER: B

The phrase "usually through collisions with other objects" is a single thought that explains how protoplanets may "grow in size", and should not be interrupted by any punctuation. A, C, and D all wrongly insert units of punctuation that disrupt the phrase "usually . . . objects", while B properly sets this single though inessential idea off from the rest of the sentence by employing parentheses.

40) CORRECT ANSWER: C

The combined version of the sentences should place the "question" mentioned in the first segment after a colon and thus create a proper idea-and-illustration relationship. C fulfills these conditions. A creates a comma splice while B and D (instead of describing the question itself as "obvious") wrongly place the idea of obviousness as part of the question ITSELF.

41) CORRECT ANSWER: A

Elkins-Tanton claims that humans can "learn about inner space by visiting outer space", namely 16 Psyche: in other words, 16 Psyche can facilitate understanding of the "inner" nature or "composition and structure" of planets. A is the best choice. Neither other asteroids nor planetary explorations OUTSIDE the solar system are mentioned by Elkins-Tanton (eliminating B and D, respectively), while the idea of "visiting" 16 Psyche is raised by this expert (contradicting and thus eliminating C).

42) CORRECT ANSWER: B

In the paragraph that contains the underlined portion, the writer describes the projected events related to the mission and designated a few important years in the expected progress: the proposed sentence adds detail by mentioning an interval of "six months". B is the best choice, while the writer never introduces a negative tone of "difficulty" in this sentence (eliminating A). C neglects the fact that the writer has MOVED ON from discussing the nature of 16 Psyche to discussing the mission, while D introduces a note of doubt and should be eliminated as entailing a wrongly negative tone.

43) CORRECT ANSWER: D

A, B, and C all involve faulty constructions that indicate that NASA (NOT the "mission") is "targeted to launch". Only D properly indicates that the mission "is currently under development" and "is targeted to launch".

44) CORRECT ANSWER: D

Because the "technology" mentioned in the sentence utilizes previously-developed technology, new development costs are not needed and the mission is thus "relatively" affordable. D captures the correct "consequence" or cause-and-effect relationship. A wrongly indicates a situation that is unexpected or unusual, B wrongly indicates a contrast, and C indicates that the circumstances articulated in the sentence are similar or interchangeable, not that one CAUSES the other.

Test Three

Writing Test

35 MINUTES, 44 QUESTIONS

Turn to Section 2 of your answer sheet to answer the questions in this section.

DIRECTIONS

Each passage below is accompanied by a number of questions. For some questions, you will consider how the passage might be revised to improve the expression of ideas. For other questions, you will consider how the passage might be edited to correct errors in sentence structure, usage, or punctuation. A passage or a question may be accompanied by one or more graphics (such as a table or graph) that you will consider as you make revising and editing decisions.

Some questions will direct you to an underlined portion of a passage. Other questions will direct you to a location in a passage or ask you to think about the passage as a whole.

After reading each passage, choose the answer to each question that most effectively improves the quality of writing in the passage or that makes the passage conform to the conventions of standard written English. Many questions include a "NO CHANGE" option. Choose that option if you think the best choice is to leave the relevant portion of the passage as it is.

Questions 1-11 are based on the following passage.

No Predators, No Problem?

Think of the most fearsome animals on the face of the earth: the great white shark, the Bengal tiger, the saltwater crocodile. It may seem, **1** in other words, that animals such as these have little in common, other than the fact that they are some of the largest and deadliest creatures in their respective ecosystems. Yet biologists have developed **2** a term "apex predators," that encompasses a category of animals, distinguished mainly by their absence of natural enemies. These are organisms of all kinds—golden eagles, killer whales, lions, and Komodo dragons, **3** in addition to the different animals that prey on these organisms—that always seem to be on the hunt and are never (except in special yet crucial circumstances) themselves hunted.

1

A) NO CHANGE
B) upon some reflection,
C) to most experts,
D) at first glance,

2

A) NO CHANGE
B) a term, "apex predators," that encompasses a category of animals distinguished mainly by their absence
C) a term—"apex predators" that encompasses a category of animals distinguished mainly by their absence
D) a term, "apex predators," that encompasses a category of animals—distinguished mainly by their absence

3

Which choice best enables the writer to coordinate information in a logical manner?

A) NO CHANGE
B) in addition to organisms that resemble all of these,
C) in addition to some animals that are not normally carnivorous
D) in addition to those that have already been named

202

CONTINUE

Apex predators such as these fill a few important ecological roles. Some of them, particularly apex predator "big cats," hunt other large mammals; [4] despite this sort of population control, it is possible that creatures such as antelopes and buffalos would over-populate and over-graze their habitats, leading to resource shortages. [5] Yet such apex predators may also impart more indirect benefits. Recently, researchers led by José Hernán Sarasola have determined that cougars may play an important role in dispersing seeds, since (according to Sarasola's findings, published in *Scientific Reports*) cougars feast on the seed-eating Eared Dove. The seeds that this animal consumes pass through the [6] cougars' digestive tracts. These same seeds are scattered to new areas of the cougars' native ecosystems.

Despite their crucial ecological presence, [7] apex predators face one major enemy: which is humankind. The very "big cat" predators that are some of the most famous apex specimens are also the frequent targets of big game hunters, while other apex species—wolves, eagles, and more—may lose their habitats to logging or industrial development. [8] Moreover, the Komodo dragon, which has its range in a remote group of Indonesian islands, is now threatened by the encroachment of human settlements.

4
A) NO CHANGE
B) without
C) due to
D) under

5
Which choice offers the best transition to the content that follows?
A) NO CHANGE
B) However, well-adapted apex predators may also drive prey species to extinction.
C) Nonetheless, the diets of some "big cats" have changed radically over time.
D) Nor do poachers pose the threat to such ecosystems that they once did.

6
Which choice best combines the two sentences at the underlined portion?
A) cougars' digestive tracts, for which these same seeds
B) cougars' digestive tracts, in which these same seeds
C) cougars' digestive tracts, although these same seeds
D) cougars' digestive tracts, and these same seeds

7
A) NO CHANGE
B) apex predators face one major enemy: from humankind.
C) apex predators face one major enemy, from humankind.
D) apex predators face one major enemy: humankind.

8
The writer is considering deleting the underlined sentence. Should this content be kept or deleted?
A) Kept, because it offers a further example for one of the writer's points.
B) Kept, because it offers an important qualification of one of the writer's points.
C) Deleted, because it undermines the writer's claim that multiple apex predators are seldom found in one ecosystem.
D) Deleted, because it focuses on an apex predator with few important ecological roles.

CONTINUE

To protect apex predators—and to bolster apex predator populations that have been diminished—strategies of extreme sensitivity are necessary, since apex predators are so crucial to their ecosystems' [9] food chains which those ecosystems can change drastically once the apex predators disappear. [10] Adrian Stier of the University of California at Santa Barbara is aware of this tricky situation: "To recover apex predators we must first appreciate that the pathway to predator recovery may differ markedly from the pathway predators initially followed to decline" (as quoted for phys.org). [11] In light of the large number of environmental variables that must be considered, the strategies for recuperating apex predators must necessarily be as diverse as apex predators themselves.

9

A) NO CHANGE
B) food chains that those ecosystems
C) food chains when those ecosystems
D) food chains as those ecosystems

10

At this point in the paragraph, the writer is considering making the following addition.

> In this respect, the work of one young researcher offers a refreshing perspective.

Should the writer add this content here?
A) Yes, because it establishes that past research on apex predators is somewhat inaccurate.
B) Yes, because it efficiently introduces Stier and indicates that his work is significant.
C) No, because the paragraph has already explained how Stier arrived at his research topic.
D) No, because the writer expresses skepticism earlier on about the value of Stier's work.

11

Which choice best concludes the writer's discussion while also referring to a major point presented earlier in the passage?

A) NO CHANGE
B) It may, unfortunately, take the extinction of some of today's most prominent apex predators to spur not only environmental activists but also the public to truly take the initiative.
C) For Stier, protecting the seed-dispersing cougars of the Western Hemisphere is only a provisional first step.
D) Only then can apex predators reclaim their "apex" positions from more numerous, less vigorous species.

CONTINUE

Questions 12-22 are based on the following passage.

Laura Pawel: Dance, or Something Like It

The first time you see a performance by choreographer and performer Laura Pawel's dance troupe, you might find yourself confronting a rather pointed question: is this even dance? [12] This is an ignorant judgment. One representative Laura Pawel routine consists of middle-age to [13] elderly dancers moving, gingerly around the stage, sometimes waving their arms or breaking into wild gesticulations, sometimes speaking sentences about mundane topics: the weather, public transportation, or raising children. Pawel herself, rather than sitting on the sidelines like a more traditional choreographer, often participates.

All of this can seem strange, if not entirely nonsensical, if you are accustomed to clearly-structured traditional [14] ballets: such as *Firebird* and *Swan Lake*. Works such as these have well-defined narratives: they take the form of contests between good and evil, complete with central heroes who face specific obstacles. [15] Beyond an occasional utterance from a performer (and again, normally an utterance about something low-drama, if not completely unremarkable), a Laura Pawel composition has little to no narrative.

12

Which choice best articulates a stance that the writer develops as the passage proceeds?
A) NO CHANGE
B) This is an understandable reaction.
C) This is the first query of most experts.
D) This is the only logical response.

13

A) NO CHANGE
B) elderly dancers moving gingerly around the stage, sometimes, waving
C) elderly dancers moving gingerly around the stage, sometimes waving
D) elderly dancers moving gingerly around the stage sometimes waving

14

A) NO CHANGE
B) ballets, such as,
C) ballets, such as
D) ballets, as

15

A) NO CHANGE
B) In contrast to
C) On the basis of
D) In concordance with

CONTINUE

[16] As it turns out, Pawel's dance performances are best understood as extended responses to [17] a time of renewed reverence for "old-fashioned" dance routines: the period in the middle years of the 20th century when form, gesture, and ambiguous or indeterminate messages became central features of artistic expression.

[1] Pawel's approach to art was formed, to some extent, under the guidance of Merce Cunningham (1919-2009), [18] a midcentury choreographer, who blurred the lines—dividing dance, random gesture, and even abstract painting. [2] One famous Cunningham routine consists of dancers in bulbous costumes bobbing up and down. [3] The more than seventy dances that Pawel has composed for her company since 1968 do not respond to Cunningham in a rote or predictable manner. [4] However, they are certainly executed in the spirit of his work. [5] Signature Cunningham compositions also involved contributions from video artists such as Nam June Paik and satiric "pop" artists such as Andy Warhol. [6] Nuances of shape, rhythm, and color (as evidenced by the careful twilight-tinted lighting of some Pawel pieces) are elements of a shared vocabulary for the two choreographers. [19]

16

At this point in the passage, the writer is considering inserting the following sentence.

> However, the work of Laura Pawel should not be written off as nonsense.

Should the writer make this addition here?

A) Yes, because it aligns with the writer's dismissive tone towards much of Pawel's work.

B) Yes, because it serves to reinforce the writer's main argument.

C) No, because it raises an opinion that the writer finds mostly ludicrous.

D) No, because it departs from the colloquial and informal tone used earlier.

17

Which phrase most logically anticipates the content that follows?

A) NO CHANGE

B) a well-defined moment in the history of art

C) an era of political and artistic rebellion

D) an epoch that until recently was misunderstood

18

A) NO CHANGE

B) a midcentury choreographer who blurred the lines: dividing

C) a midcentury choreographer who blurred the lines dividing

D) a midcentury choreographer: who blurred the lines dividing

19

To make the order of ideas in the paragraph most logical, sentence 5 should be placed

A) where it is now.

B) after sentence 1.

C) after sentence 2.

D) after sentence 6.

CONTINUE

Pawel's other great inheritance from Cunningham may be a sense of community and collaboration. Her performances are not grand affairs: [20] many of them are held at the intimate Chen Dance Center in Manhattan's Chinatown. Some of the same viewers attend Pawel's performances year after year, [21] and talk in reverent tones about Merce Cunningham during intermissions. Pawel may not have much use for the thrill of flamboyant showmanship, [22] so long as her sense of dance as an art to be savored—and shared—has its own rewards.

20
A) NO CHANGE
B) holding many of them at
C) many held at
D) at

21
Which choice best supports the writer's characterization of the typical Pawel performance?
A) NO CHANGE
B) and find that the performance quality compensates for the small premises and unpredictable acoustics.
C) including dance critics who, at last, are bringing Pawel's work the attention it deserves.
D) including painters and performance artists who take Pawel as an unexpected inspiration.

22
A) NO CHANGE
B) because
C) unless
D) but

CONTINUE

Questions 23-33 are based on the following passage.

Marriages of Inconvenience

In some of the world's most affluent countries, marriage and childbirth rates are falling. [23] Similarly, for those who do choose to get married, the average age of first marriage has been pushed back considerably. This is very much the situation in Japan, a country known for its efficiently-run mass transit, world-famous technology and manufacturing companies, and historically low poverty rate. Despite all these social advantages, [24] only 38.7%, of unmarried 20- to 30-year-old Japanese men, have any interest in marrying, according to a 2016 study cited in *The Japan Times*. [25] The country's youth unemployment rate is now comparable to the rate that Japan witnessed after World War II; under such conditions, it will be difficult to prevent an automatic shrinking of the population.

23

A) NO CHANGE
B) Inversely,
C) Moreover,
D) Consequently,

24

A) NO CHANGE
B) only 38.7% of, unmarried 20- to 30-year-old, Japanese men
C) only 38.7%, of unmarried 20- to 30-year-old Japanese men
D) only 38.7% of unmarried 20- to 30-year-old Japanese men

25

Which of the following choices logically anticipates the assertion that ends the sentence?

A) NO CHANGE
B) The country's childbearing rate currently hovers around 1.4 children per adult woman;
C) The country's rate of late in life marriages (ages 40 and over) has risen modestly in the past decade;
D) The country's home ownership rate has remained virtually unchanged over the past thirty years;

CONTINUE

Japan is not alone in experiencing family-rearing malaise; Europe as a whole appears to be reeling. In 2014, a feature story in *The Guardian* presented the finding that "the number of weddings has fallen to historical lows in France and Spain **26** but has rebounded in other Catholic countries such as Italy, Ireland, Poland, and Portugal, according to national and European data." The authors of the article ("Marriage falls out of favour for young Europeans as austerity and apathy bite") did note that the number of weddings in Scandinavia has not seen a comparable decline. However, childbearing rates remain a Scandinavian problem, to such an **27** extent which Denmark launched a recent ad campaign to lift the national birthrate from its current 27-year low.

[1] For nations such as Japan, Italy, and Denmark, "affluent" may not in fact be the best label. [2] As different as some of these countries are, there are shared social and economic factors that explain why they follow many of the same broad trends. [3] Each of these countries has prosperous companies and a relatively high per-person annual income, but young adults are often left out of such prosperity. [4] A few years ago, a survey conducted by Eurofound determined that **28** almost half (48% of all European young adults, Europeans aged 18-30) can be found living with their parents. [5] This situation is occasionally explained by traditional, close-knit family structures. [6] More often, it is the result of unpleasant **29** modern realities: high youth unemployment figures and low, often stagnant wages for

26
Which choice most effectively fits the logic and structure of the writer's discussion at this point?
A) NO CHANGE
B) and has similarly tumbled
C) while remaining constant
D) despite skyrocketing

27
A) NO CHANGE
B) extent that Denmark
C) extent as Denmark
D) extent if Denmark

28
A) NO CHANGE
B) almost half (48%) of all (European young adults, Europeans aged 18-30)
C) almost half (48%) of all European young adults (Europeans aged 18-30)
D) almost half (48%) of (all European young adults) Europeans aged 18-30

29
A) NO CHANGE
B) modern realities, high youth unemployment
C) modern realities, that are high youth unemployment
D) modern realities: which are high youth unemployment

workers in their twenties and thirties. **30**

Similar economic **31** stresses—and similar blows to marriage and childbearing prospects—can be observed **32** thanks to formal studies commissioned by Japanese universities. For their part, Japanese singles who are fully dependent on their parents' resources and for whom marriage is virtually out of the question have been given their own category: "parasite singles," **33** a term devised by sociologist Masahiro Yamada. Any step towards getting these young people and their global counterparts out of their parents' houses, and into productive marriages, may need to start with treating marriage not as a romantic issue, but as an economic one.

30

To make the order of ideas in the paragraph most logical, sentence 3 should be placed
A) where it is now.
B) before sentence 1.
C) before sentence 5.
D) before sentence 6.

31

A) NO CHANGE
B) stresses—and similar blows to marriage and childbearing prospects can
C) stresses, and similar blows to marriage and childbearing prospects—can
D) stresses and similar blows to marriage and childbearing prospects, can

32

Which choice would best support the idea that the "economic stresses" mentioned by the writer can now be observed in a variety of national contexts?
A) NO CHANGE
B) in centers of commerce in the United States.
C) using recently-developed statistical models.
D) in the results of both interviews and questionnaires.

33

The writer is considering deleting the underlined portion and ending the sentence with a period. Should this part of the sentence be kept or deleted?
A) Kept, because it helps to explain a concept central to the writer's analysis.
B) Kept, because it justifies the writer's apparent disdain for the "Japanese singles".
C) Deleted, because it distracts from the paragraph's focus on specific new proposals.
D) Deleted, because it undermines the writer's critical stance towards modern sociology.

CONTINUE

Questions 34-44 are based on the following passage.

Yes, Even Billionaires Have Bad Days

Clay Cockrell is a Manhattan-based therapist whose practice is unusual in two respects. First, instead of sitting his patients down in an office and talking **[34]** to them about their problems, there (as most therapists do), he prefers to hold sessions while striding through New York City. Second, **[35]** and perhaps more unsettlingly, many of the men and women who book "walk and talk" sessions with Cockrell are among the wealthiest 1% of Americans.

Cockrell is by no means the first therapist or counselor to focus on a super-wealthy clientele: Hawaii-based Brad Klontz, to take but one, is a psychologist who counsels ultra-wealthy patients through his firm Your Mental Wealth Advisors. **[36]** There is evidently a small industry that caters to the psychological problems of **[37]** the ultra rich. Another matter—what, in exact terms, such an industry does—is not as easy to discern.

34

A) NO CHANGE
B) to them about their problems there (as most therapists do),
C) to them (about their problems) there as most therapists do,
D) to them (about their problems) there, as most therapists do,

35

A) NO CHANGE
B) and perhaps more remarkably,
C) and in a possible business liability,
D) and in a departure from Cockrell's earlier practices,

36

At this point in the passage, the writer is considering adding the following sentence.

> Such arrangements are a source of fascination and intrigue: in fact, the blockbuster television show *Billions* revolves around the relationship between one such counselor and the CEO of a hedge fund.

Should the writer insert this content here?

A) Yes, because it may help to make an otherwise disorienting topic more comprehensible.
B) Yes, because it anticipates the analysis of the media and journalism industries that arises later in the passage.
C) No, because the writer is discussing actual instances of counseling and therapy, not depictions in entertainment.
D) No, because the writer is explaining why therapists decide to take on extremely wealthy clients, not why such arrangements would inspire fascination.

37

Which choice best combines the two sentences at the underlined portion?

A) the ultra rich, even though another matter
B) the ultra rich, since another matter
C) the ultra rich, when another matter
D) the ultra rich: another matter

CONTINUE

[1] So what are the problems that multimillionaire and billionaire clients bring to specialists like Cockrell and Klontz? [2] Some patients fear that their funds or earning power may eventually vanish. [3] Ultra-wealthy business executives realize that their fortunes are often indebted to lucky timing, **38** <u>and that some therapists are considerably more expensive than others.</u> [4] This is not an idle worry. [5] Modern magnates have often watched **39** <u>where</u> seemingly invincible companies (Blackberry, Yahoo!) were reduced to ghosts of their former selves. [6] Such patients want to avoid—or at the very least give themselves reasonable ways to cope with—similar fates. **40**

38

Which choice best supports the writer's analysis of the fears that the ultra-wealthy face?
A) NO CHANGE
B) and that even minor scandals can quickly undermine a company's reputation.
C) and that the global marketplace can be volatile.
D) and that education does not guarantee success.

39

A) NO CHANGE
B) after
C) for
D) as

40

To make the order of ideas in the paragraph most logical, sentence 4 should be placed
A) where it is now.
B) after sentence 2.
C) after sentence 5.
D) after sentence 6.

CONTINUE

Other ultra-wealthy individuals find their wealth disorienting, incapable of imparting a sense of social or spiritual purpose to their lives in any meaningful manner. In a personal essay for the *New York Times*, Sam Polk, a former hedge fund trader [41] <u>who has written widely about the psychological dangers of immense wealth</u>, recalls "receiving an email from a hedge-fund trader who said that though he was making millions every year, he felt trapped and empty, but couldn't summon the courage to leave." Polk's own [42] <u>solution, (as documented) in his *Times* article "For the Love of Money,"</u> was to leave finance and use his immense past earnings to fund philanthropic projects. A therapist for the wealthy can help his or her clients determine when to balance the pursuit of money and the pursuit [43] <u>of meaning; while that balance</u> ever becomes hopelessly skewed towards money, the same therapist can guide a change of career or lifestyle.

Counseling of this sort, however, is far from traditional therapy in yet one [44] <u>more way: practitioners like</u> Cockrell and Klontz have finance backgrounds of their own. With the wealth of interconnected issues that therapists for the wealthy face, expertise in the world of money is essential for anyone who aims to help out America's ultra-rich.

41

The writer is considering deleting the underlined portion, adjusting the punctuation as needed. Should this portion of the sentence be kept or deleted?

A) Kept, because it clarifies Polk's ideas in a manner that provides context for the quotation that follows.
B) Kept, because it indicates an important similarity between Polk and the experts mentioned earlier.
C) Deleted, because it re-phrases information that is later provided about Polk.
D) Deleted, because it contradicts later statements about Polk's viewpoints.

42

A) NO CHANGE
B) solution, as documented, in his *Times* article "For the Love of Money,"
C) solution, as documented, in (his *Times* article) "For the Love of Money,"
D) solution, as documented in his *Times* article ("For the Love of Money"),

43

A) NO CHANGE
B) of meaning—while that balance
C) of meaning; if that balance
D) of meaning, if that balance

44

A) NO CHANGE
B) more way: because practitioners like
C) more way: practitioners, such as
D) more way, for practitioners:

STOP

Answer Key: TEST 3

Test 3

PASSAGE 1
No Predators, No Problem?

1. D
2. B
3. D
4. B
5. A
6. D
7. D
8. A
9. B
10. B
11. A

PASSAGE 2
Laura Pawel: Dance, or Something Like It

12. B
13. C
14. C
15. A
16. B
17. B
18. C
19. C
20. A
21. D
22. D

PASSAGE 3
Marriages of Inconvenience

23. C
24. D
25. B
26. B
27. B
28. C
29. A
30. A
31. A
32. B
33. A

PASSAGE 4
Yes, Even Billionaires Have Bad Days

34. B
35. B
36. C
37. A
38. C
39. D
40. B
41. A
42. D
43. C
44. A

Answer Explanations

SAT Practice Test #3

Passage 1: No Predators, No Problem?

1) CORRECT ANSWER: D
The paragraph explains that specific animals may seem to "have little in common" but in fact are part of a single category, "apex predators": it may thus appear "initially" or "at first glance" that these animals have little in common. Choose D and eliminate B, which introduces the OPPOSITE of the needed relationship. A would only be appropriate if the sentence that contains the underlined portion were to re-phrase the preceding sentence (which it does not), while C introduces the perspective of "experts", who are not considered until later and have developed a category that CONTRADICTS the idea that the animals are different.

2) CORRECT ANSWER: B
The phrase "apex predators" can be offset with two commas, since it modifies the word "term": B properly does so. A wrongly uses only ONE comma and breaks the linked phrase "term . . . that" with only a single unit of punctuation; C and D both use dash and comma combinations (NOT effectively paired commas) and should thus be eliminated.

3) CORRECT ANSWER: D
The underlined portion should continue the writer's list of animals "that always seem to be on the hunt" and are never "themselves hunted": some animals of this sort have been mentioned earlier in the paragraph. D is thus the best answer. A designates PREY (not predators), B wrongly indicates that powerful predators all resemble one another (a point that the writer rejects or at least complicates earlier), and C wrongly introduces animals that are not carnivorous and thus do not "hunt".

4) CORRECT ANSWER: B
The sentence that contains the underlined portion indicates that "population control" keeps certain animal species from over-populating; these species will thus over-populate "without" population control. B is the best answer. A, C, and D all indicate that the "population control" is PRESENT and that over-population occurs, and thus contradict the most logical meaning for the sentence.

215

5) CORRECT ANSWER: A

While the early portions of the paragraph explain how, in line with their expected hunter role, big cats "hunt other large mammals", later portions explain that big cats also spread seeds. A effectively shifts to this less expected and "indirect" benefit. B wrongly continues to emphasize the hunting role, C wrongly indicates a change in diet among species (NOT the actual shift in the roles analyzed in the passage), and D introduces the topic of "poachers" (which the paragraph avoids).

6) CORRECT ANSWER: D

The underlined portion should link two stages in a chronological description of how the seeds "are scattered": D properly connects the two stages with "and". A indicates that the seeds are scattered "for" or on behalf of the digestive tracts (not AFTER passing through them), B indicates that the seeds are scattered "in" the digestive tracts (not AFTER they leave), and C wrongly introduces a contrast.

7) CORRECT ANSWER: D

The sentence should designate the "enemy" of apex predators: "humankind". D concisely and efficiently presents this information as an item after a colon; A and B both introduce unnecessary transition words rather than concisely presenting the item "humanity", while C also involves needless and awkward phrasing (and implies direction or derivation with "from", RATHER than simply clarifying an idea).

8) CORRECT ANSWER: A

In the preceding sentences, the writer explains that "humankind" is a treat to various apex predators; the underlined sentence builds upon this idea by explaining that a specific apex predator, the Komodo dragon, is "threatened by the encroachment of human settlements". Choose A and eliminate B (since the sentence BUILDS upon an idea, rather than presenting an exception or "qualification). C uses problematic logic (because the presence of OTHER apex predators in the Komodo dragon's ecosystem is never addressed), while D raises an irrelevant issue (the ecological role of the Komodo dragon, as opposed to the THREATS that it faces).

9) CORRECT ANSWER: B

The sentence employs the standard phrase "so . . . that" to explain degree of importance: B creates the proper phrase while A switches in the word "which" (a trap because "which" and "that" can be mistaken as interchangeable). C ("when" for time) and D ("as" for comparison) also break the standard phrase and should thus be quickly eliminated.

10) CORRECT ANSWER: B

The sentence refers to a "young researcher", who is effectively identified in the sentence that follows as "Adrian Stier": B is the best answer while A assumes an inappropriate negative tone with the theme of "inaccurate" research. Keep in mind that Stier is only mentioned AFTER the proposed sentence position to eliminate C and D, which both wrongly indicate that he has been mentioned BEFORE.

11) CORRECT ANSWER: A

In the first paragraph, the writer explains that apex predators are "diverse organisms of all kinds": A returns to the idea of diversity in terms of apex predator species, and focuses on the "recuperating" process emphasized in the final paragraph. Choose this answer and eliminate B (which focuses on activists, NOT on the researchers emphasized in the passage). C wrongly links Stier to earlier content (the seed-dispersing "cougars") that is not in any way explicitly related to his own research, while D discusses apex predator competition with various other animal species (NOT, as is the passage's focus, the problems that apex predators face due to humans).

Passage 2: Laura Pawel: Dance, or Something Like It

12) CORRECT ANSWER: B

The writer argues that Pawel's version of dance "can seem strange": thus, asking if Pawel's dance is "even dance?" is a perfectly understandable question. Choose B and eliminate the negative answer A. C wrongly introduces the topic of experts (avoided in the first two paragraphs) while D wrongly indicates that ALL viewers should react one way (not, as the writer argues in a less extreme manner, that a doubting response is understandable).

13) CORRECT ANSWER: C

The writer should offset the unified description of dancers "sometimes moving . . . " with a single comma (much like the parallel description "sometimes waving . . . "). C properly does so. A wrongly splits the phrase "moving gingerly" (which describes a single action), B wrongly splits up the "sometimes moving . . . " construction, and D wrongly indicates that the STAGE is "sometimes waving" because this answer omits the needed comma for coordination.

14) CORRECT ANSWER: C

The underlined portion should set up the examples of "ballets": the use of "such as" in C creates an effective transition. A wrongly uses a colon (which would only work WITHOUT a transition phrase such as "such as"), B wrongly uses a comma to separate "such as" from the words that it should introduce, and D eliminates the word "such" to suggest a COMPARISON, not to introduce EXAMPLES.

15) CORRECT ANSWER: A

An "utterance" or verbal expression would be an example of "narrative", a quality that a Laura Pawel composition would normally lack "Beyond" a few examples. A is the best answer, while B creates an illogical comparison or contrast between an "utterance" and an entire "composition". In context, C and D both wrongly indicate that the passing and rare "utterances" determine or guide the ENTIRE composition, and should thus be eliminated.

16) CORRECT ANSWER: B

While the writer admits that Pawel's dances can seem "nonsensical", the writer also argues that such dances are related to meaningful "artistic expression." Eliminate answers such as A and C for their negative logic and choose B, which rightly indicates that the writer is somewhat positive towards Pawel's style of dance. D is problematic because the passage is not "colloquial" (or written to recall a casual conversation); instead, despite the writer's lively tone, the passage is a detailed overview of a somewhat scholarly topic.

17) CORRECT ANSWER: B

The writer states that Pawel's dances are linked to modes of artistic expression that flourished in "the middle years of the twentieth century": Pawel's compositions are thus connected to "a well-defined" art-historical moment. Choose B and eliminate A (since Pawel's dances are defined as non-traditional earlier) and C (since the writer is concerned with art but NOT with politics). D distorts content from the passage: Pawel's dances can inspire confusion or misunderstanding, but it does not follow that the entire "epoch" that formed her work inspires misunderstanding.

18) CORRECT ANSWER: C

The phrase "a midcentury choreographer who blurred the lines dividing" treats closely linked ideas and thus should not be broken up with commas or other punctuation. Only C treats the phrase as a single unit, while A, B, and D wrongly employ interrupting punctuation. B and D also involve faulty colon usage (since colons should only be followed by sets of items or entire independent clauses, NOT by new transitional phrases) and can be eliminated for this reason.

19) CORRECT ANSWER: C

Sentence 5 explains some features that "Cunningham compositions also involved" and should thus be placed after sentence 2, which lists the features of "One famous Cunningham routine". C is the best answer: A breaks a discussion of Pawel and Cunningham with a description of Cunningham alone, while B places sentence 2 after a sentence that refers to Cunningham's general ideas but does NOT build on a discussion of SPECIFIC compositions. D places the description of Cunningham's work alone after a concluding assessment of Cunningham and Pawel, and thus detracts from the comparative analysis that concludes the paragraph.

20) CORRECT ANSWER: A

The portion after the colon explains why Pawel's performances "are not grand affairs": namely, they are held at an "intimate" venue. A creates the proper colon relationship by placing an explanation formatted as an independent clause AFTER the colon. B, C, and D all phrase roughly the same information using sentence fragments after the colon, and should all be eliminated for faulty grammar.

21) CORRECT ANSWER: D

The writer points out that Pawel's form of dance is defined by "community and collaboration": the idea that Pawel is an "inspiration" for other artists would support this characterization. Choose D and eliminate A (since only PAWEL'S response to Cunningham, not that of the audience, is described by the writer). Both B and C wrongly treat Pawel's work as faulty or obscure; however, the only real negative that the writer discusses is the strange or disorienting nature of Pawel's compositions.

22) CORRECT ANSWER: D

The sentence begins by explaining that Pawel's work does not provide a certain type of "thrill", but that there are other "rewards" to experiencing her dances. The writer is thus presenting a contrast, so that D is the best answer. A (simultaneity), B (cause and effect), and trap answer C ("unless", which indicates a precondition or requirement) all present faulty linkages that do not properly contrast two DIFFERENT positives.

Passage 3: Marriages of Inconvenience

23) CORRECT ANSWER: C

While the first sentence presents one negative regarding marriages (a falling rate), the sentence that contains the underlined portion presents a second negative (a pushing-back in average age). C properly indicates an added fact, while A wrongly indicates that the two sentences are similar (when only the FIRST mentions "childbirth rates"). B wrongly indicates that the two sentences present opposite facts (NOT facts that take the same tone), while D establishes a cause-and-effect relationship that the writer has not clearly attempted to substantiate in any direct way.

24) CORRECT ANSWER: D

The underlined content is essential to the sentence and should NOT be separated out with commas, since it is unclear what the "38.7%" represents without the reference to "Japanese men". D properly avoids any comma usage; A and B wrongly treat the phrase "of unmarried . . . men" as inessential, while C wrongly breaks a subject-verb combination ("38.7% . . . have") with only one comma.

25) CORRECT ANSWER: B

The writer must explain why "an automatic shrinking of the population" is possible: a reference to a country's "childbearing rate" would logically link to the idea of a shrinking population. Choose B and eliminate A and D (which refer to ECONOMIC factors that may or may not have any relationship to population size). C may actually indicate a factor that acts AGAINST a shrinking population (if the number of marriages is increasing in one group) and should thus be eliminated.

26) CORRECT ANSWER: B

The writer explains that "Europe as a whole" faces declining rates related to marriage; like France and Spain, "other Catholic countries" in Europe would thus face a fall in the number of weddings. B properly reflects this logic, while A and D wrongly indicate rising rates in countries beyond France and Spain, and C wrongly indicates a constant rate (NOT a fall).

27) CORRECT ANSWER: B

The sentence must employ the standard phrase "to such . . . that" to describe extent or degree: B establishes the correct wording. A ("which", wrongly mistaken for "that"), C ("as"), and D ("if") all depart from the needed standard phrase and should thus be quickly eliminated.

28) CORRECT ANSWER: C

The sentence should describe the situation of "almost half . . . of European young adults"; the other phrases in the underlined portion are pieces of inessential content that explain these two pieces of principal content, and can be set off using parentheses. Choose C and eliminate A and B, which wrongly treat the reference to "European young adults" as inessential content. D wrongly assumes that a parenthetical phrase can INTRODUCE essential content (not EXPLAIN such content after it is introduced) and should be eliminated as a faulty construction.

29) CORRECT ANSWER: A

The content in the second portion of the sentence takes the form of a list of "unpleasant modern realities". Such a list can be effectively introduced by a colon as in A. Choose this answer and eliminate B (which wrongly uses a comma in the same position), C (which introduces a wordy and awkward transition), and D (which places a fragment beginning with a transition word, NOT a list, after the colon).

30) CORRECT ANSWER: A

While sentence 2 refers to "social and economic factors" that are common across countries, sentence 3 describes these factors and then introduces the topic of "young adults" who are left out of prosperity; this topic is continued in sentence 4. A is thus the best answer. B would wrongly separate the introductory reference to "young adults" from the discussion that continues in sentence 4, while C and D would wrongly detract from the negative discussion of young people by re-positioning the references to positive factors in prosperity and income.

31) CORRECT ANSWER: A

The inessential phrase "and similar . . . prospects" should be offset using two commas or two dashes: A employs the correct construction using dashes. B and D both wrongly separate the subject-verb combination "stresses . . . can be observed" using only ONE dash (B) or comma (D), while C wrongly uses one comma and one dash, not two units of the same punctuation.

32) CORRECT ANSWER: B

The writer has already discussed economic stresses in Japan and in various European countries: the presence of the same stresses in "the United States" would provide a new, broadening context. Choose B and eliminate A, C, and D, which describe HOW the stresses are measured, not where or in what national CONTEXTS they are prevalent.

33) CORRECT ANSWER: A

The underlined content indicates the origins of the term "parasite singles", a concept related to the writer's discussion of the problems faced by young adults. A is the best answer and captures the explanatory role of the underlined information; B and D both wrongly assume that the writer's intention is to argue against society (NOT, as here and elsewhere in the passage, to simply explain problems). C mistakes a minor topic in the paragraph (improving the lives of young people) for a focus on specific proposals in the entire paragraph, and should be eliminated for this reason.

Passage 4: Yes, Even Billionaires Have Bad Days

34) CORRECT ANSWER: B
The underlined portion should separate the essential description of Cockrell's work ("to them . . . there") from the secondary information about other therapists ("as most therapists do"). B uses parentheses to effectively coordinate these portions of the sentence. A breaks the first combined description using a comma, while C and D wrongly divide closely linked essential ideas (that Cockrell talks to his patients about their problems) with parentheses.

35) CORRECT ANSWER: B
The writer has established that Cockrell's practices and patients are "unusual" or unlike those of "most therapists"; he thus stands out from them or is "remarkable" in comparison. B is the best answer, while A and C both criticize Cockrell rather than simply noting a point of difference. D wrongly assumes that Cockrell was once more traditional or had different guidelines (a possibility that is not explicitly considered) and should be eliminated as out of scope.

36) CORRECT ANSWER: C
While the passage at this point is concerned mainly with how therapy for the ultra-wealthy works, the proposed sentence is concerned with the use of such therapy as a motif in a television show. The proposed content should thus not be inserted: C is the best answer, while D uses faulty logic (since the writer is still describing an industry in overall terms, NOT explaining the perspective of therapists in detail). The writer never clearly indicates that the topic of this clearly-written passage is inaccessible (eliminating A) and uses journalism only to help investigate the main theme of wealth (rather than investigating journalism or the media in depth, eliminating B).

37) CORRECT ANSWER: A
The writer needs to present a contrast between the fact that there is "evidently" a small industry and the fact that it is "not easy to discern" what the industry does. A creates the proper contrast transition. B (cause-and-effect), C (simultaneity), and D (idea and illustration) all link the sentences but do NOT indicate a contrast as the writer's ideas require.

38) CORRECT ANSWER: C
In the relevant paragraph, the writer focuses on one fear of ultra-wealthy individuals: that "their funds or earning power may eventually vanish". This fear would be present in an unpredictable or "volatile" economy. C is the best answer, while the ultra-wealthy do not harbor fears regarding therapists THEMSELVES (eliminating A) or the question of GAINING wealth (as opposed to losing it, eliminating D). B is a trap answer: it is never made clear that the ultra-wealthy individuals considered here are company owners, so fears regarding company "reputation" are out of the scope of the discussion.

39) CORRECT ANSWER: D

The "magnates" have watched something happen, or watched "as" it happened: D is thus the idiomatically correct answer. A wrongly refers to location (NOT time), B indicates that the watching occurs "after" companies have deteriorated (NOT simultaneously), and C indicates that the magnates are looking out for or "watching for" the companies, not (as demanded by the passage's content) that they have passively witnessed companies fall apart.

40) CORRECT ANSWER: B

While sentence 4 states that a particular "worry" is justifiable, sentence 2 introduces possibilities that the ultra-wealthy "fear". Sentence 4 would build off this description to offer the writer's evaluation: choose B and eliminate A, C, and D, since any of these placements would interrupt the discussion of the fears of the ultra-wealthy (which sentence 4 should lead into) with a distracting general statement.

41) CORRECT ANSWER: A

The underlined portion explains that Polk has written about the dangers of "immense wealth"; in the content that follows, Polk is quoted discussing some of these dangers and his own approach is explained. Choose A, since the underlined portion provides helpful context, and eliminate B (since Polk, who is a writer, and the therapists do not pursue the same activities). C wrongly indicates that Polk has been described earlier when in fact he has just been introduced; D wrongly indicates that the underlined portion, rather than supporting or clarifying the later content regarding Polk, goes AGAINST Polk's ideas.

42) CORRECT ANSWER: D

Polk's solution was "documented in his *Times* article": a single, unbroken phrase should be used to designate a source in an efficient manner. D offers the correct punctuation, while A, B, and C all interrupt the writing using commas or parentheses.

43) CORRECT ANSWER: C

The sentence that contains the underlined portion describes a situation that is hypothetical, and in which a therapist "can help": it would be best to describe what can happen "if" the balance described becomes skewed. C captures this hypothetical condition: A and B both introduce contrasts (and assume that the balance is DEFINITELY skewed) with "while", and D creates a comma splice.

44) CORRECT ANSWER: A

The content after the colon should explain the "way" in which therapy for the ultra-wealthy differs from traditional therapy, and should do so using a full sentence. A fulfills both requirements. B places a fragment after the colon, C separates a subject-verb combination ("practitioners . . . have") with a comma, and D introduces an awkward construction that only describes "Cockrell and Klontz," rather than explaining the larger "way" in which they and OTHER practitioners differ from traditional therapists.

Test Four

Writing Test
35 MINUTES, 44 QUESTIONS

Turn to Section 2 of your answer sheet to answer the questions in this section.

DIRECTIONS

Each passage below is accompanied by a number of questions. For some questions, you will consider how the passage might be revised to improve the expression of ideas. For other questions, you will consider how the passage might be edited to correct errors in sentence structure, usage, or punctuation. A passage or a question may be accompanied by one or more graphics (such as a table or graph) that you will consider as you make revising and editing decisions.

Some questions will direct you to an underlined portion of a passage. Other questions will direct you to a location in a passage or ask you to think about the passage as a whole.

After reading each passage, choose the answer to each question that most effectively improves the quality of writing in the passage or that makes the passage conform to the conventions of standard written English. Many questions include a "NO CHANGE" option. Choose that option if you think the best choice is to leave the relevant portion of the passage as it is.

Questions 1-11 are based on the following passage.

Venice Wasn't Built in a Day

The city of Venice, **1** which is today regarded as one of the cultural and architectural marvels of northern Italy, evolved into its current form over the course of centuries. **2** As this once-dominant power collapsed under the pressure of barbarian invasions, wealthy Romans sought safety and security. Around 400 A.D., some of these Romans settled on the island of Torcello in the Venetian lagoon. This situation— **3** a lifestyle entirely free from violence, along with easy access to waterways—would help Venice to emerge as a powerful center of European trade and commerce.

1

A) NO CHANGE
B) that is today
C) as is today
D) is today

2

Which choice, if inserted here, best anticipates the content that follows?

A) Venice emerged through competition with the Roman empire.
B) Venice had long existed in harmony with the mainland Roman empire.
C) Venice rose to prosperity by closely imitating the Roman empire.
D) Venice's beginnings coincide with the fall of the Roman empire.

3

Which is the most logical description of Venice's situation at this point in the passage?

A) NO CHANGE
B) a culture based on rationality and self-reflection,
C) technological advancement that rivaled Rome's,
D) complete security against land-based attacks,

226

CONTINUE ➡

After choosing the site of their new settlement, the Venetians decided on a structural engineering method that would help them build a prosperous city outward. The islands in the lagoon were too **4** marshy—to serve as foundations for durable stone structures. Thus, the Venetians set in place their own foundation system by driving wooden stakes into the watery soil, then by building wooden platforms atop the stakes. **5** These platforms support the stone squares, bridges, and palaces that define Venice's appearance even today.

[1] Naturally, the people of Venice needed to source an enormous amount **6** of lumber: due to one seventeenth-century estimate, over 1.1 million wooden stakes were driven underwater. [2] The wooden stakes **7** were sourced from forests near the Crimean coast, and would eventually harden to resemble petrified wood or even stone. [3] Fortunately for Venice, once these stakes had been positioned, they would be safe from decay. [4] This is not the only way in which the stakes were prevented from deterioration. [5] In the open air, wood tends to decompose because microorganisms and insects attack its fibers. [6] However, underwater wood is shut off from the air supply that such organisms would need to survive and is thus protected from the major threat to its structural soundness. **8**

4
A) NO CHANGE
B) marshy; to serve
C) marshy, to serve
D) marshy to serve

5
The writer is considering deleting the underlined sentence. Should this sentence be kept or deleted?
A) Kept, because it helps to explain the precise function of the wooden platforms.
B) Kept, because it helps to explain why the wooden stakes have not decayed over time.
C) Deleted, because the information in this sentence is reiterated in the discussion that follows.
D) Deleted, because it detracts from the writer's discussion of why the Venetians chose the lagoon for a building site.

6
A) NO CHANGE
B) of lumber: by one
C) of lumber: as one
D) of lumber: one

7
Which choice provides the most helpful and relevant information at this point in the passage?
A) NO CHANGE
B) are seen by some as a symbol of Venice's ingenuity,
C) were positioned in orderly, almost grid-like arrangements,
D) would gradually absorb minerals from the lagoon water,

8
To make the order of ideas in the paragraph most logical, sentence 3 should be placed
A) where it is now.
B) before sentence 2.
C) before sentence 6.
D) after sentence 6.

CONTINUE

The architecture of Venice is just as distinctive as the engineering and layout of the island city. One of Venice's iconic structures is St. Mark's basilica, which combines elements of a few different architectural styles—gold mosaics reminiscent of those found in Byzantine churches, spires and arches that recall [9] those—of Gothic cathedrals, to create a structure of remarkable opulence. Venice's prowess in shipping and warfare also helped to form St. Mark's: some of its bronze and gold decorations were looted from Constantinople, another port city, and transported over the Mediterranean Sea. These feats of engineering, architecture, and artistry built a [10] city that in (its final form) spans more than 100 separate islands. Now connected to the mainland by a bus route— [11] and in other ways reshaped by recently-adopted technology—the modern Venice is accessible yet still rich in history.

9

A) NO CHANGE
B) those of Gothic cathedrals—to create a structure of remarkable opulence.
C) those of Gothic cathedrals, to create—a structure of remarkable opulence.
D) those of Gothic cathedrals, to create a structure—of remarkable opulence.

10

A) NO CHANGE
B) city that (in its final form) spans
C) city and in (its final form) spans
D) city and (in its final form) spans

11

The writer wishes to conclude the passage by referring to a topic raised earlier. Which choice most effectively and appropriately completes this goal?

A) NO CHANGE
B) and currently undergoing massive publics works renovations
C) and famed as a site of romance, mystery, and intrigue
D) and no longer, of course, a refuge from barbarians

CONTINUE

Questions 12-22 are based on the following passage.

No Need to Be So Salty

[12] The task, of turning salty seawater into drinkable water, may not seem especially mysterious. Removing salt from water, a process known as "desalination," can take any one of a few different forms, all of which resemble processes that should be familiar from everyday life. One of these processes is distillation; the seawater will be heated until the water evaporates (leaving a salt deposit behind) and will then be condensed back into purified water. [13] (Distillation is often explored in junior high school sciences classes, and is also common in brewing alcoholic beverages.) Another process that is common in purifying seawater is filtration, a method which simply entails passing the water [14] through—sieves or filters, glorified versions of kitchen implements—until any minerals are removed.

12

A) NO CHANGE
B) The task of turning salty seawater (into drinkable water) may
C) The task (of turning salty seawater into drinkable water) may
D) The task of turning salty seawater into drinkable water may

13

The writer is considering deleting the underlined parenthetical content. Should the sentence in parentheses be kept or deleted?

A) Kept, because it helps to clarify the differences between different forms of desalination.
B) Kept, because it supports the writer's point that processes such as distillation can be observed in everyday contexts.
C) Deleted, because it contradicts the writer's argument that desalination uses a special form of distillation.
D) Deleted, because it undermines the detached and scholarly tone of the passage.

14

A) NO CHANGE
B) through sieves or filters—glorified versions of kitchen implements—until any minerals
C) through sieves or filters glorified versions of kitchen implements, until any minerals
D) through sieves or filters, glorified versions of kitchen implements; until any minerals

CONTINUE

But like most human technologies, the technology of desalination has evolved considerably over time. In recent years, researchers have developed new devices that exploit the chemical properties of salt water to generate drinkable water with increased efficiency. **15**

One ingenious apparatus was crafted by researchers at the Massachusetts Institute of Technology (MIT), who worked in partnership with Jain Irrigation Systems. The MIT team's device uses solar power to charge two electrodes, one positive and one negative. Saltwater is then directed in a channel that runs between **16** the electrodes, provided that each electrode attracts one type of salt ion **17** (or atom with a positive or negative charge). **18** Likewise, as the water flows, extremely salty water is concentrated near the electrodes, while the central stream of water is remarkably pure.

15

The writer is considering adding the following sentence at this point in the passage

Fears that desalination technology will "cease to evolve" have ultimately proven unfounded.

Should the writer make this addition here?
A) Yes, because it indicates a likely motive for the continued research in desalination technology.
B) Yes, because it balances out some of the mildly critical statements that appear in the previous paragraph.
C) No, because it introduces a perspective that most readers would automatically find illogical.
D) No, because it introduces a perspective that does not fit the context of the discussion.

16

A) NO CHANGE
B) the electrodes, as soon as each
C) the electrodes, because each
D) the electrodes and each

17

A) NO CHANGE
B) (or atom with) a positive or negative charge.
C) or atom (with a positive or negative) charge.
D) or atom with (a positive or negative charge).

18

A) NO CHANGE
B) Nonetheless,
C) Conversely,
D) Thus,

CONTINUE

[1] The MIT method cannot be neatly classified as either filtration or distillation. [2] However, another recent breakthrough in desalination is a sophisticated version, more or less, of classic saltwater filtration. [3] Lockheed Martin, a company perhaps most famous for its work in aerospace and weapons engineering, has developed **19** a filter that consists of carbon atoms bonded, to one another, or a "graphene" network. [4] Although the arrangement's underlying filtration concept is traditional, the effectiveness is revolutionary. [5] John Stetson, the engineer behind this saltwater filtration method, has told news outlets including Reuters and Gizmodo that each graphene sheet is "500 times thinner than the best filter on the market today and a thousand times stronger." **20**

Indeed, such technologies are impressive. But there may also be an irony to their recent emergence: **21** they were developed in wealthy countries but are really only needed in poorer nations. In fact, another invention that has emerged from MIT in recent years is a solar-powered device that extracts and condenses water from the humidity in the air. Whether such devices will exist in synergy with saltwater **22** purification methods, which can successfully deploy solar power themselves or render desalination superfluous, remains an open question.

19

A) NO CHANGE

B) a filter that consists of carbon atoms, bonded to one another or

C) a filter, that consists of carbon atoms bonded to one another in

D) a filter that consists of carbon atoms bonded to one another in

20

To make the order of ideas in the paragraph most logical, sentence 4 should be placed

A) where it is now.

B) after sentence 1.

C) after sentence 2.

D) after sentence 5.

21

Which of the following is an "irony" that is appropriate to the context of the writer's discussion?

A) NO CHANGE

B) their practical benefits are disproportionate to the positive press that MIT and Lockheed Martin have received.

C) they have attracted the attention of non-specialists but are regarded by chemists as only minor achievements.

D) they may soon be completely replaced by drinking water generation methods that entirely avoid desalination.

22

A) NO CHANGE

B) purification methods, which can successfully deploy solar power (themselves or render desalination superfluous),

C) purification methods (which can successfully deploy solar power themselves) or render desalination superfluous

D) purification methods, which can successfully deploy solar power (themselves or render desalination superfluous),

CONTINUE

Questions 23-33 are based on the following passage.

Mastering Your Future

    For young adults who want to secure high salaries and respected positions, a basic four-year undergraduate (or bachelor's) degree [23] can prove to be completely useless. In order to break into a variety of prestigious fields—including business management and university teaching—a college graduate who possesses a bachelor's degree will often need to obtain a further two-year degree known as a master's. Such a degree [24] naturally involves academic challenges, but, combines these with a challenge that has nothing to do with technical writing or scholarly research: the challenge of managing and allocating time, money, and energy.

    It is best to think of a master's not simply as a degree, [25] or as an investment. This is certainly the necessary mentality for anybody who wants to obtain one of the most coveted degrees in the world of modern enterprise and entrepreneurship, the Master's of Business Administration. The career advancement that the typical two-year MBA can offer comes at a [26] hefty price. Each year of this Master's can cost a total of $40,000 in tuition and $20,000 in room, board, and

---

23

Which choice best reflects the writer's argument in the paragraph that follows?
A) NO CHANGE
B) spells the difference between success and failure.
C) may not be worth the money spent.
D) is often just the beginning.

24

A) NO CHANGE
B) naturally involves academic challenges, but combines these, with a challenge
C) naturally involves academic challenges but combines these, with a challenge
D) naturally involes academic challenges, but combines these with a challenge

25

A) NO CHANGE
B) despite being an
C) but as an
D) to be an

26

Which choice best combines the two sentences at the underlined portion?
A) hefty price: each year
B) hefty price, even though each year
C) hefty price; in consequence, each year
D) hefty price: as each year

CONTINUE

miscellaneous expenses, [27] giving the entire MBA experience a $120,000 upfront price tag, more than most American households earn in two years.

[1] Other master's degrees may have much lower upfront costs. [2] Indeed, the tens of thousands of dollars that a student could have made in a given year will be "lost" to master's program classes and projects. [3] A situation of this sort can be observed in high-profile Master's of Fine Arts programs in creative writing. [4] An MFA in fiction or poetry is the highest possible [28] degree: that an aspiring writer can obtain, but that same writer could choose to spend the two years of the typical MFA [29] working as a high school teacher or freelance editor. [5] The $45,000 or so that such employment might earn will be sacrificed even in MFA programs—such as those offered by the Iowa Writer's Workshop and the Johns Hopkins Writing Seminars—that do not charge any tuition. [6] They do, however, involve the "hidden" costs of taking their students out of the workforce. [30]

27

The writer is considering deleting the underlined portion and ending the sentence with a period after "expenses". Should the underlined portion be kept or deleted?

A) Kept, because it concludes this stage of the writer's discussion with a single dollar figure that puts the issue in perspective.

B) Kept, because it uses a single dollar figure to prompt the reader to reflect on the inadvisability of pursuing a typical master's degree.

C) Deleted, because it introduces an overly critical tone into an otherwise objective discussion.

D) Deleted, because it employs a method of comparison that the writer elsewhere rejects.

28

A) NO CHANGE
B) degree, that an aspiring writer can obtain, but
C) degree that an aspiring writer can obtain, but
D) degree that an aspiring writer can obtain: but

29

Which choice provides the most logical and relevant example at this point in the writer's discussion?

A) NO CHANGE
B) traveling and gaining new writing material.
C) applying for poetry or playwriting grants.
D) independently creating a body of writing comparable to an MFA thesis.

30

To make the order of ideas in the paragraph most logical, sentence 6 should be placed

A) where it is now
B) after sentence 1.
C) after sentence 2.
D) after sentence 3.

CONTINUE

These daunting figures should not, however, deter pragmatic and hardworking students **31** against pursuing master's degrees. After all, a student with an MBA can possess earning power that a student with only a bachelor's in business or economics will never experience. **32** When "lost" wages are factored in, an MBA can run to over $250,000 for some students, yet that MBA might be the ticket to securing a $300,000 to $500,000 per year job.

As it turns out, the math behind master's programs can be sensible. Even more important are the connections to seasoned professionals **33** and possible mentors, connections deeper than any that a simple undergraduate degree can foster—that a master's program enables. In education, as in much of life, you get what you pay for.

31

A) NO CHANGE
B) from pursuing
C) if pursuing
D) to pursue

32

The writer is considering adding the following sentence at this point in the passage.

> Nor will these bachelor's students enjoy the rewards of the kind of intellectual community that only an MBA can provide.

Should the writer make this addition here?

A) Yes, because it demonstrates that intellectual benefits can often be assigned specific prices.
B) Yes, because it anticipates an important distinction between MBA and MFA programs.
C) No, because it raises a topic that is only a focus earlier in the passage.
D) No, because it clouds the focus on the finances of MBA programs.

33

A) NO CHANGE
B) and possible mentors, connections, deeper than any, that a simple
C) and possible mentors—connections deeper than any that a simple
D) and possible mentors—connections deeper than any, that a simple

CONTINUE

Questions 34-44 are based on the following passage.

How the West Was Filmed

With their gripping conflicts between lawmen and outlaws, films that depict the American Wild West can be enjoyed as suspense-filled adventure tales. Yet for all their thrills, the most famous Westerns are also pointed statements on such themes as duty, responsibility, and individualism; they endure because they offer something much more insightful than the usual good guys versus bad guys, cowboys versus bandits setup that some viewers associate with Western films. **34**

Some of the westerns that appeared in the 1950s, just as the genre was getting a foothold, reveal the moral nuances in apparent "good versus evil" conflicts. In the black-and-white classic *High Noon* (1952), a U.S. marshal named Will Kane must face down four outlaws who threaten a small town. Kane emerges **35** victorious, and his struggle comes with a twist: the townspeople whom Kane protects refuse to help him in any way. Their complacency offers a harsh commentary on the rarity of heroism, and raises **36** the idea, that a true hero struggles without expectation of assistance, reward, or acknowledgment. The

34

At this point, the writer is considering adding the following sentence.

Such dichotomies may seem simple, but were inspired by a series of dramatic historical events.

Should the writer make this addition here?
A) Yes, because it anticipates a topic that appears in the final paragraphs.
B) Yes, because it establishes the writer as a credible source.
C) No, because several of the films that the writer discusses are in fact historically inaccurate.
D) No, because it detracts from the writer's focus on the moral messages in Western films.

35
A) NO CHANGE
B) victorious, and his struggle comes with a twist, where
C) victorious, but his struggle comes with a twist:
D) victorious, but his struggle comes with a twist, where

36
A) NO CHANGE
B) the idea that a true hero struggles
C) the idea, which a true hero struggles
D) the idea which a true hero struggles

CONTINUE

concept of solitary heroism is central to another seminal

western from roughly the same period, *The Searchers* (1956).

[37] Moreover, a veteran of the Civil War must track down his

scattered relatives, [38] forming a noble figure in a plot that

occasionally descends into slapstick comedy.

　　With some of the most famous westerns of the 1960s, a new

breed of western hero—or rather anti-hero—began to emerge.

[39] Since the main characters of *High Noon* and *The Searchers*

were motivated by lofty values such as community, family, and

justice, western protagonists now valued money and vengeance

to a much greater extent. [40] The director who was solely

responsible for this transformation was Sergio Leone. In Leone

masterpieces such as *A Fistful of Dollars* and *The Good, the Bad,*

and the Ugly, [41] (the protagonist an unnamed gunslinger played

by) Clint Eastwood indulges in dark humor and hunts for hidden

wealth. In his values and his brutal methods, this "Man with No

Name" can be difficult to distinguish from his foes.

37

A) NO CHANGE
B) As in *High Noon,*
C) In this adventure film,
D) According to this argument,

38

Which choice best supports the writer's argument about how 1950s westerns depict heroism?

A) NO CHANGE
B) emerging as a symbol of American pride and responsibility in an increasingly chaotic 20th century.
C) reuniting his family members but not expecting to join the community they form.
D) committing acts of brutality that, though regrettable, ensure his survival.

39

A) NO CHANGE
B) Before
C) Wherever
D) While

40

Which choice most effectively and accurately anticipates the writer's argument in the remaining sentences of the paragraph?

A) NO CHANGE
B) As a director, Sergio Leone created parody versions of *High Noon* and *The Searchers*.
C) Sergio Leone, a prominent 1960s director, disregarded the work of his predecessors.
D) This shift is particularly evident in the films directed by Sergio Leone.

41

A) NO CHANGE
B) the protagonist (an unnamed gunslinger played by Clint Eastwood)
C) the protagonist an unnamed gunslinger (played by Clint Eastwood)
D) the protagonist an unnamed gunslinger, played by Clint Eastwood

CONTINUE

[1] Westerns that complicate and undermine the very idea of heroism have proliferated in more recent years. [2] *Unforgiven* (1992), **42** where it featured Eastwood as both its director and its leading actor, revolves around the theme that western "heroism" may be a facade or a myth. [3] Many of the characters in *Unforgiven* are driven **43** by traits such as cruelty and empty pride. [4] *Unforgiven* may seem like a dark take on the American west. [5] Eastwood's character, for his part, is a lonely, retired gunslinger, driven by a pessimistic view of the world and capable of stunning brutality. [6] However, it is not impossible that the western—an ever-shifting genre—will one day return to its more straightforwardly heroic roots. **44**

42

A) NO CHANGE
B) as it featured Eastwood
C) which featured Eastwood
D) that featured Eastwood

43

A) NO CHANGE
B) by traits such as cruelty (and empty pride).
C) by traits (such as cruelty) and empty pride.
D) by traits (such as cruelty and empty pride).

44

To make the order of ideas in the paragraph most logical, sentence 5 should be placed

A) where it is now.
B) after sentence 2.
C) after sentence 3.
D) after sentence 6.

STOP

Answer Key: TEST 4

Test 4

PASSAGE 1
Venice Wasn't Built in a Day

1.   A
2.   D
3.   D
4.   D
5.   A
6.   B
7.   D
8.   B
9.   B
10. B
11. D

PASSAGE 2
No Need to Be So Salty

12. D
13. B
14. B
15. D
16. D
17. A
18. D
19. D
20. A
21. D
22. C

PASSAGE 3
Mastering Your Future

23. D
24. D
25. C
26. A
27. A
28. C
29. A
30. B
31. B
32. D
33. C

PASSAGE 4
How the West Was Filmed

34. D
35. C
36. B
37. C
38. C
39. D
40. D
41. B
42. C
43. A
44. C

Answer Explanations

SAT Practice Test #4

Passage 1: Venice Wasn't Built in a Day

1) CORRECT ANSWER: A
The underlined content must refer back to "Venice": the pronoun "which" effectively does so when placed after the comma. Choose A and eliminate B (which wrongly uses "that" after a comma, instead of connecting "that" directly to the noun), C (which wrongly indicates comparison with "as"), and D (which does not involve a linking pronoun or any other transition word).

2) CORRECT ANSWER: D
The writer explains that Venice was created because wealthy Romans "sought safety and security": the collapse or fall of the Roman empire would cause them to seek security and would thus happen almost simultaneously with or "coincide with" the creation of Venice. Choose D and eliminate A and B, both of which wrongly indicate that Venice existed during the SAME period as the Roman empire. C is problematic because Venice (which is water based) represented a shift away from the tactics of the apparently land-based Roman empire.

3) CORRECT ANSWER: D
An island city such as Venice would offer natural security against "land-based attacks", since attackers could only reach the island by boat. D is thus the best answer; A is problematic because the people who live in Venice could still commit violence against ONE ANOTHER (and be attacked by boat). B (cultural values) and C (high technological advancement) raise topics that are not directly considered, since the writer is mostly concerned at this point with the location and safety of Venice.

4) CORRECT ANSWER: D
For a consolidated and effectively-worded explanation, the islands should be described as "too marshy to serve". D properly presents this phrase without interruption, while A, B, and C all wrongly insert units of punctuation that break the standard phrase "too . . . to". B also misuses a semicolon, since a semicolon CANNOT be followed by a fragment.

5) CORRECT ANSWER: A
The underlined sentence explains that the platforms "support" various buildings and thus explains their function or purpose: A is the best answer, while the durability of the platforms is only discussed in the NEXT paragraph (eliminating B). This shift in topic can be used to eliminate C (which wrongly assumes that the content is reiterated), while D should be eliminated because the choice of the lagoon as a building site is mainly discussed in the PREVIOUS paragraph.

6) CORRECT ANSWER: B

The content after the colon should explain the "enormous amount of lumber", which was given a set figure "by one estimate". B is the logically and idiomatically correct answer, while A (cause-and-effect) and C (comparison) set up relationships other than explanation or elaboration. D simply and awkwardly sets out the phrase "one estimate" without any transition to establish a relationship, and should thus be eliminated.

7) CORRECT ANSWER: D

In context, the underlined portion should help to explain how the stakes "would eventually harden". The absorption of "minerals" would help to change the composition of the stakes and to thus harden them, so that D is the best answer. The origins (A), symbolic meaning (B), and positioning (C) of the stakes are not clear, direct explanations for the hardening process, so that all of the other answers should be eliminated as introducing details irrelevant to the sentence.

8) CORRECT ANSWER: B

While sentence 3 explains that the stakes would be "safe from decay", sentence 2 explains HOW the stakes became safe from decay. Sentence 3 should thus introduce sentence 2 and its detailed description of a process: choose B and eliminate A (which wrongly provides the explanation BEFORE the issue is introduced). C and D both position sentence 3 late in the paragraph, AFTER the fact that the stakes are "safe from decay" should be well-established, and should be eliminated for this reason.

9) CORRECT ANSWER: B

The secondary content between dashes should involve parallel descriptive phrases which reference features of "Byzantine churches" and "Gothic cathedrals". B places the needed references between dashes, while A wrongly places the reference to "Gothic cathedrals" outside the dashes. C creates a non-grammatical phrase ("styles a structure") if the content between dashes is factored out, while D wrongly places the infinitive "to create" (which must link with the verb "combines") inside the dashes and thus separates it from other essential content.

10) CORRECT ANSWER: B

The sentence must be grammatically correct if the content between parentheses is disregarded: B, under these conditions, would correctly create the phrase "that spans". Choose this answer and eliminate A ("in spans") as problematic in construction. C and D would both use "and" to create a faulty meaning and improper grammar, indicating that the feats "spans" separate islands.

11) CORRECT ANSWER: D

Earlier in the passage, the writer explains that the "pressure of barbarian invasions" led to the founding Venice: D thus returns to an earlier topic as demanded by the question. Choose this answer and eliminate A and B (since RECENT developments in Venice are not mentioned until the final paragraph itself). C is problematic because the writer never explicitly characterizes Venice or its culture as exciting, and focuses instead on how and why Venice was constructed.

Passage 2: No Need to Be So Salty

12) CORRECT ANSWER: D

This sentence needs to explain what exactly the "task" is as part of its essential content, in order to keep the passage from being unclear. D properly avoids any punctuation that would divide up a description of the "task of turning salty seawater into drinkable water". A wrongly introduces a single comma that splits the subject-verb combination "task . . . may", while C and D wrongly break up the essential content using parentheses.

13) CORRECT ANSWER: B

Earlier, the writer explains that desalination is premised on "processes that should be familiar from everyday life": in describing distillation, the sentence refers to the everyday contexts of "high school" and "beverages" and thus supports this idea. Choose B and eliminate A and C (since the writer is explaining distillation ITSELF, not designating different FORMS of distillation). D relies on a misreading of the content: the writer is discussing everyday topics, but is not doing so in an everyday "conversational" tone that would undermine the detached and composed tone used elsewhere.

14) CORRECT ANSWER: B

The essential content of the sentence must explain what the water passes "through", namely "sieves or filters", which can be described using the inessential phrase "glorified versions of kitchen implements". B is the best answer, while A wrongly places the essential information "sieves and filters" between the dashes and C uses ONLY one unit of punctuation for the inessential descriptive phrase. D wrongly places a fragment after a semicolon and should be eliminated for this reason.

15) CORRECT ANSWER: D

At this point in the passage, the writer is mainly discussing changes in desalination technology: a negative perspective that entails "fears" is inappropriate to this mostly neutral and factual discussion. Choose D and eliminate A (which assumes that the negative tone is highly relevant) and B (which wrongly identifies the writer's earlier objective statements as "critical"). C wrongly considers the perspective of the reader (an issue that the writer does not explicitly raise) and should be eliminated as out of scope.

16) CORRECT ANSWER: D

The underlined portion should link two chronological stages of a process in which saltwater is "directed" before salt ions are "attracted": "and" would be an appropriate transition for one item that follows another in time. Choose D and eliminate A and B (which both wrongly treat the SECOND event as a PRECONDITION). C wrongly reverses the process, and uses a faulty cause-and-effect relationship.

17) CORRECT ANSWER: A

The parentheses should be used to offset a description of an "ion", which is a type of "atom"; the sentence should also display proper construction if the parenthetical content is factored out. A fits both conditions. B ("ion a") and C ("atom charge") create non-grammatical word pairings in the absence of the parenthetical content; D ends the sentence with "with" and wrongly does not link this preposition to a noun.

18) CORRECT ANSWER: D

The previous sentence has explained that each electrode attracts "one type of salt ion": the sentence that contains the underlined portion explains the outcome of this process, or what "thus" happens. Choose D and eliminate A (which indicates that the sentences are similar and comparable, NOT that they have a cause-and-effect relationship). B and C both indicate reversals or negative shifts, not expected outcomes, and should be eliminated.

19) CORRECT ANSWER: D

Punctuation should not interrupt unified phrases such as "filter that consists" or "atoms bonded to one another". A and B both wrongly break up the second phrase, while C breaks up the first. Only D avoids any punctuation that would disrupt the sentence's presentation of connected ideas.

20) CORRECT ANSWER: A

Sentence 4 both refers back to the "network" or arrangement discussed in sentence 3 and sets up the idea of "revolutionary" effectiveness that John Stetson expands upon in sentence 5. The sentence is thus best in its current placement: choose A and eliminate B and C (which would discuss the "arrangement" used in the filter BEFORE the filter is introduced in sentence 3). D would wrongly place the reference to "effectiveness" AFTER the example that this reference should set up.

21) CORRECT ANSWER: D

The paragraph discusses water purification methods that do not rely on desalination; it would thus be ironic if, despite the "impressive" desalination technology, desalination is soon rendered unnecessary. Choose D and eliminate A (which refers to nations and economics, topics that are avoided here). B (positive press) and C (specialists and non-specialists) reference issues from EARLIER paragraphs that are not entirely relevant to the writer's discussion at this point, and should thus be eliminated.

22) CORRECT ANSWER: C

The sentence should lay out two alternatives, existing in "synergy" and becoming "superfluous", that are essential to the sentence's meaning and thus should NOT be placed between parentheses. Eliminate B and D for this reason, and eliminate A because it treats "synergy" and becoming "superfluous" as linked or synonymous conditions, NOT as alternatives. Only C pairs off these alternatives using proper punctuation and properly uses the phrase "which . . . themselves" to describe "purification methods".

Passage 3: Mastering Your Future

23) CORRECT ANSWER: D

In the paragraph that follows, the writer explains that a master's degree can help young adults "to break into a variety of prestigious fields": a basic "undergraduate" degree is a necessary and positive step towards obtaining a master's, so that D is the best answer. Eliminate negative answers such as A and C, as well as the ambivalent or undecided answer B.

24) CORRECT ANSWER: D

The sentence that contains the underlined portion should set out two different and contrasting types of "challenge", which can be described in phrases separated by a comma. D rightly places a comma after the description of "academic challenges" and leads into the description of a non-academic "challenge" with the transition "but." A wrongly places a comma AFTER "but" as well, and B and C wrongly break up the unified phrase "combines these with" with a comma.

25) CORRECT ANSWER: C

The sentence that contains the underlined portion should present a qualifying relationship using the standard phrase "not simply . . . but" to explain how a master's degree should be understood. C is the best answer: A wrongly DENIES that a master's degree is an investment, B provides an awkward and wordy alternative to the standard phrase, and D both breaks the standard phrase and introduces an inappropriate case of parallelism with "to think".

26) CORRECT ANSWER: A

The content in the second sentence explains the "hefty price" referenced in the first: such a sentence relationship can be effectively presented using a colon alone. Choose A and eliminate the other answers, which do not actually involve idea and explanation relationships. B presents a contrast, C presents a case of cause-and-effect, and D wrongly places a fragment after the colon.

27) CORRECT ANSWER: A

In the relevant paragraph, the writer explains that a master's degree is a considerable "investment": the underlined portion uses a dollar figure to explain the significance of investing in an MBA. A appropriately reflects this logic, while B and C wrongly apply a negative tone to the writer's evidence (which is simply used to explain a situation). D is inaccurate because the writer does not argue AGAINST comparing educational costs to other dollar figures, and in fact lists other dollar figures related to education elsewhere in the passage.

28) CORRECT ANSWER: C

The phrase "degree that" is closely connected and should NOT be broken by punctuation. Eliminate A and B for this reason, then eliminate D as a choice that misuses a colon (which can only be followed by a set of items or an explanatory independent clause, NOT by a fragment that involves a contrast). C both avoids disrupting punctuation and properly leads into the phrase "but that" with a single comma.

29) CORRECT ANSWER: A

The underlined portion should refer to an alternative to pursuing an MFA degree, one that would classify as money-earning "employment". Work in teaching or editing would be a logical example of such employment: choose A and eliminate B and D, since these activities are connected to the intellectual (NOT financial) issues involved in MFA degrees. C is problematic because applying for grants may or may NOT bring in income, while teaching and editing would logically guarantee some sort of income stream.

30) CORRECT ANSWER: B

Sentence 6 refers to the hidden "costs of taking students out of the workforce"; these costs could effectively be contrasted with the "upfront costs" mentioned in sentence 1. Choose B and eliminate A, C, and D as answers that disrupt the discussion of "lost" income with a statement that should INTRODUCE this discussion by describing "hidden" costs.

31) CORRECT ANSWER: B

The proper idiomatic phrase is "deter . . . from"; choose B as introducing the only possible correct usage. A suggests the idea of going "against" but does not involve the correct pairing for the phrase "deter . . . from", while C (possibility) and D (necessity) both break the idiom and suggest meanings inappropriate to the context.

32) CORRECT ANSWER: D

At this point in the passage, the writer is concerned entirely with "earning power" and specific dollar figures: a discussion of an "intellectual community" blurs this focus. Choose D and eliminate C because intellectual community is not the writer's primary focus at ANY point in the passage, which mostly examines finances and career prospects. A wrongly focuses on intellectual benefits as well, while B wrongly returns to the topic of an MFA, while the writer analyzes MBA programs in the relevant paragraph.

33) CORRECT ANSWER: C

The phrase "connections to seasoned . . . that a master's" should be separated by content that is offset by two identical units of punctuation. A and B wrongly use only ONE dash for the intervening content, while D wrongly uses a comma to separate the connected phrase "any that" WITHIN the intervening content itself. Only C avoids these errors and properly uses two dashes to coordinate the intervening description.

Passage 4: How the West Was Filmed

34) CORRECT ANSWER: D

In the relevant paragraph, the writer is mostly concerned with how Westerns served as "pointed statements" on moral and ethical themes; whether specific "events" inspired such Westerns is never a focus. Choose D and eliminate A and C (which wrongly assume that the writer DOES eventually shift focus to historical accuracy, whether to argue for it or against it). B is problematic because the writer's own background and credentials are not referenced, so that "credibility" cannot be effectively determined.

35) CORRECT ANSWER: C

The sentence should present a contrast between the fact that Kane "emerges victorious" yet faces a negative "twist", and should also use a colon to introduce an explanation of the "twist" itself. C fits both of the needed conditions; A wrongly uses "and" and thus fails to indicate a contrast, while B and D both use "where" (and wrongly indicate place) instead of the needed colon.

36) CORRECT ANSWER: B

The sentence should explain an idea about a "true hero": phrasing the content as "idea that a true hero struggles" effectively presents this unified idea using an appropriate transition. B is the best answer: A wrongly uses a comma to divide "that" from the content that it should introduce, while C and D both wrongly use "which" to create awkward and illogical constructions (which suggest that the hero struggles against the idea ITSELF).

37) CORRECT ANSWER: C

The sentence that contains the underlined portion refers to a "veteran of the Civil War" who, in context, would be the hero of *The Searchers*. C refers back to the film mentioned in the previous sentence and is thus the best answer. A indicates that the two sentences are similar (not that one INTRODUCES the other), B creates a faulty parallel (since the hero of *High Noon* must protect a town, not find his relatives), and D refers to an "argument" even though no specific analysis or "argument" (as opposed to a set of principles) motivates the hero of *The Searchers*.

38) CORRECT ANSWER: C

The writer explains that the hero of *The Searchers* is a figure of "solitary heroism"; reuniting a family but not joining it would be an action that fits this concept. Choose C and eliminate A (which introduces the irrelevant topic of comedy), B (which relates *The Searchers* to historical context, not to the writer's ideas about heroism), and D (which wrongly criticizes the hero of the film, who is not criticized elsewhere).

39) CORRECT ANSWER: D

The sentence should create a contrast between the "lofty values" of some Western characters and the principles of "money and vengeance" favored by others. D properly captures this contrast, while A wrongly creates a cause-and-effect relationship and B REVERSES the proper relationship, since the "lofty values" came BEFORE the prioritization of "money and vengeance". C wrongly refers to place and consistency rather than directly creating a contrast.

40) CORRECT ANSWER: D

The writer follows the discussion of a general shift in the values articulated by Western films with a consideration of how Sergio Leone's films made the new values especially apparent. D is the best answer, while A wrongly indicates that Leone was the ONLY director to put a broad shift into effect (not simply one important director). B and C both indicate that Leone was negatively inclined towards the work of earlier Western filmmakers: in fact, all that is known is that his films were different, not that he was antagonistic or indifferent to earlier work.

41) CORRECT ANSWER: B

The parenthetical content should explain who the "protagonist" is. B properly designates the protagonist's role and names the actor who played him in parentheses. A wrongly places the word "protagonist" (which takes the verb "indulges") in parentheses, C wrongly runs together "protagonist" and part of the description outside the parentheses, and D wrongly incorporates a single comma that breaks the subject-verb combination "protagonist . . . indulges".

42) CORRECT ANSWER: C

The underlined portion should refer directly back to *Unforgiven*, a film "which" featured Eastwood. C is thus the best answer. A designates a place, B would set up a comparison, and trap answer D uses "that" in an awkward and incorrect construction, wrongly using a comma to split "that" and the noun that it should reference.

43) CORRECT ANSWER: A

To make the sentence as clear as possible, the writer should explain what "traits" drive the characters as part of the essential content (NOT in parentheses). Only A lists the needed traits, "cruelty and empty pride", outside parentheses, while B, C, and D wrongly place one or both of these important items in parentheses.

44) CORRECT ANSWER: C

Sentence 5 discusses "Eastwood's character" and his values, thus adding detail to the discussion of the "characters in *Unforgiven*" in sentence 3. C effectively coordinates these two sentences, while A and D both separate the sentences that discuss the "characters". B is a trap answer: while the reference to "Eastwood's character" might seem to indicate that sentence 5 should be placed after sentence 2, the phrase "for his part" indicates that sentence 5 should build off an EARLIER statement about characters, such as that in sentence 3.

Test Five

Writing Test

35 MINUTES, 44 QUESTIONS

Turn to Section 2 of your answer sheet to answer the questions in this section.

DIRECTIONS

Each passage below is accompanied by a number of questions. For some questions, you will consider how the passage might be revised to improve the expression of ideas. For other questions, you will consider how the passage might be edited to correct errors in sentence structure, usage, or punctuation. A passage or a question may be accompanied by one or more graphics (such as a table or graph) that you will consider as you make revising and editing decisions.

Some questions will direct you to an underlined portion of a passage. Other questions will direct you to a location in a passage or ask you to think about the passage as a whole.

After reading each passage, choose the answer to each question that most effectively improves the quality of writing in the passage or that makes the passage conform to the conventions of standard written English. Many questions include a "NO CHANGE" option. Choose that option if you think the best choice is to leave the relevant portion of the passage as it is.

Questions 1-11 are based on the following passage.

Dressed for Success: Fashion Design Careers

[1] The art of dressing well involves selecting and coordinating entire outfits. These are the skills that are typically emphasized by fashion and lifestyle magazines such as *Vogue* and *Esquire*, and that entail awareness of how different colors, fabric textures, and fabric patterns balance one another. While a professional fashion designer must be aware of such intricacies [2] of coordination, which the typical fashion designer does goes well beyond pairing blouses and skirts.

1

Which sentence most effectively anticipates the content that follows in this paragraph?

A) NO CHANGE
B) The talents involved in dressing well can be applied to a variety of non-fashion disciplines.
C) Today's cultural critics lament the "decline" of the aptitudes involved in dressing well.
D) Almost none of the abilities associated with the art of dressing well can be learned through formal study.

2

A) NO CHANGE
B) of coordination which the
C) of coordination, what the
D) of coordination, that the

CONTINUE

A fashion designer is responsible for building an outfit from the ground up. It is a designer's responsibility to devise individual garments that might, eventually, make their way into a harmonious ensemble. Creativity, ingenuity, and a sense of the "big picture" are of course useful skills for aspiring designers, yet the field of fashion design **3** itself—also requires professional aptitudes including the ability to communicate effectively with superiors—that can appear somewhat less glamorous.

Typically, a budding fashion designer will begin by obtaining a bachelor's degree in an appropriate field. Many institutions offer degrees that combine fashion studies with merchandising and **4** marketing coursework. Yet the most specialized fashion schools offer precisely subdivided bachelor's of fine arts programs. The Fashion Institute of Technology in Manhattan—perhaps the best-known name in fashion education—offers BFA concentrations **5** in areas, such as accessories design, fashion-related entrepreneurship, and fabric styling. **6** Fashion design is one of the few professions in which such minute subdivisions are not self-defeating.

3
A) NO CHANGE
B) itself also requires—professional aptitudes including the ability
C) itself also requires professional aptitudes—including the ability
D) itself also requires professional aptitudes including the ability—

4
Which choice effectively combines the two sentences at the underlined portion?
A) marketing coursework, although, the most
B) marketing coursework; although, the most
C) marketing coursework, however, the most
D) marketing coursework; however, the most

5
A) NO CHANGE
B) in areas such as
C) in areas such as,
D) in areas: such as

6
The writer is considering deleting the underlined portion of the passage. Should this sentence be kept or deleted?
A) Kept, because it effectively tempers the writer's enthusiasm for fashion design programs.
B) Kept, because it anticipates an objection to fashion education that many readers would have.
C) Deleted, because it does little more than reiterate content from elsewhere.
D) Deleted, because it raises a line of argument that the writer does not pursue.

CONTINUE

[1] Such precise subdivisions can quite effectively prepare students for the reality of working in the fashion industry, and perhaps for some of the limits that such work involves. [2] For an internship or an entry-level position, **7** a budding designer will perform various duties that have nothing to do with fashion design. [3] However, this sense of focus should not be seen as a limitation of the profession, since even designers who are revered as creative geniuses can have somewhat narrow fixations. [4] The task of a novice designer is not to determine the creative direction of an entire brand. [5] **8** A celebrated designer like Tom Ford, for instance is known primarily for custom-made power suits and tuxedos—and for little else. **9**

With a median salary in the neighborhood of $60,000, a position as a fashion designer can bring financial security. Moreover, with the growing importance of trend forecasting and industry **10** analysis, web sites such as WGSN in the fashion world, work in fashion design certainly fosters technical savvy and higher-order thinking skills. Along with these benefits comes the aspect of fashion design that continues to be its greatest **11** creative attraction: the potential to transform a unique sartorial vision into real, remarkable clothes.

7

Which choice most logically supports the writer's description of the role of a young designer?
A) NO CHANGE
B) a budding designer's primary responsibility is often the marketing that defines an entire company's identity.
C) a budding designer's main role is to bring a few discrete projects to fruition.
D) a budding designer often completes work that has few practical applications.

8

A) NO CHANGE
B) A celebrated designer like Tom Ford for instance, is known,
C) A celebrated designer like Tom Ford for instance is known,
D) A celebrated designer like Tom Ford, for instance, is known

9

To make the order of ideas in the paragraph most logical, sentence 4 should be placed
A) where it is now.
B) before sentence 1.
C) before sentence 2.
D) after sentence 5.

10

A) NO CHANGE
B) analysis, web sites such as WGSN in the fashion world
C) analysis web sites such as WGSN in the fashion world,
D) analysis web sites such as WGSN in the fashion world

11

A) NO CHANGE
B) creative attraction; the potential
C) creative attraction, to the potential
D) creative attraction, of the potential

CONTINUE

Questions 12-22 are based on the following passage.

Is It All a (Video) Game?

Video games may strike some observers as the ultimate "useless" technology. Though they provide entertainment, they don't necessarily do anything that makes life more efficient or [12] more comfortable, which they are at best a pleasing diversion from everyday reality. Yet it turns out that the technologies that video game companies have developed—and the habits of thought that video games foster— [13] are a source of controversy that hurt most businesses that adopt them.

Among the companies that have aggressively adapted video game conventions to other contexts (a process known as "gamification") are ridesharing [14] providers particularly: Uber and Lyft. Both of these multibillion-dollar firms recruit drivers who own their own cars, set their own hours, [15] and take as many (or as few) passenger assignments as they want. [16] The goal for Uber and Lyft is to find new markets where ridesharing can flourish. To do so, these companies have adopted some of the same psychological gimmicks that cause players to log hours upon hours exploring a single video game.

[12]
A) NO CHANGE
B) more comfortable that they are
C) more comfortable—where they are
D) more comfortable; they are

[13]
Which choice accurately and logically anticipates the content that immediately follows?
A) NO CHANGE
B) are still being investigated, surprisingly, by respected social scientists.
C) are central to some of the success stories in modern business.
D) are indeed of scholarly interest to those who regularly use video game platforms.

[14]
A) NO CHANGE
B) providers; particularly
C) providers, particularly
D) providers particularly—

[15]
A) NO CHANGE
B) and take (as many or as few) passenger assignments
C) and take as many, or as few passenger assignments
D) and take as many or as few, passenger assignments

[16]
Which choice describes a business objective that would be appropriate to the writer's discussion?
A) NO CHANGE
B) The trick for Uber and Lyft is to keep the drivers on the road.
C) The challenge for Uber and Lyft is to make "gamification" good for public relations.
D) The plan for Uber and Lyft is to systematically eliminate smaller rivals.

CONTINUE

[1] For instance, the most immersive video games tend to create dynamic visual environments and involve intricate systems of goals, awards, and achievements. [2] Lyft, **17** <u>which like Uber operates through a touchscreen interface complete with absorbing moving graphics,</u> awards its most dedicated and top-earning drivers the kind of digital "achievement" badges that are a video game staple. [3] Many adventure and role-playing video games also create endless, sprawling environments. [4] Instead of fighting towards a single accomplishment and logging off after attaining victory, gamers **18** <u>will keep playing, constantly: aware</u> that there are more prizes to win and more foes to defeat. [5] Uber to some extent takes advantage of this mentality by routinely alerting a driver to new passengers, sometimes even before a current ride is completed. [6] There is always another digital treasure chest—or, in this case, another $22 commission—just around the corner. **19**

17

The writer is considering deleting the underlined portion and adjusting the punctuation as needed (namely, by deleting the comma immediately after "Lyft"). Should this portion of the sentence be kept or deleted?
A) Kept, because it helps to underscore the point that Uber and Lyft are identical in almost all respects.
B) Kept, because it helps to explain how Lyft and Uber are able to deploy features that recall video games.
C) Deleted, because the writer's intended readers are deeply familiar with both Lyft and Uber.
D) Deleted, because it reiterates content from earlier in the passage.

18

A) NO CHANGE
B) will keep playing, constantly aware,
C) will keep playing, constantly aware
D) will keep playing constantly aware

19

To make the order of ideas in the paragraph most logical, sentence 6 should be placed
A) where it is now.
B) after sentence 1.
C) after sentence 3.
D) after sentence 4.

CONTINUE

These video game methods have drawn press criticism from sources such as [20] the *New York Times. This newspaper called* attention to the potentially exploitative effects of "gamification" in the feature story "How Uber Uses Psychological Tricks to Push Its Drivers' Buttons." Gamification, however, can also be applied to modern industries in ways that are virtually free of controversy.

[21] Nonetheless, the role of gamification in education is instructive. Some of the classic software programs used in grammar schools, including Reading Rabbit and Oregon Trail, are formatted almost exactly like colorful videogames. Moreover, high school students can be motivated to spend time with online standardized testing platforms if right answers yield digital "achievements." [22] Video games aren't good for nothing, or good only for dumbing us down. Their methods, if applied correctly, can be both entertaining and mind-enhancing.

20

Which choice best combines the two sentences at the underlined portion?

A) the *New York Times*, called
B) the *New York Times*: as calling
C) the *New York Times*, as it called
D) the *New York Times*, which called

21

A) NO CHANGE
B) Though unusual,
C) In this respect,
D) As this evidence shows,

22

At this point in the passage, the writer is considering adding the following sentence.

> A student who gets an "achievement badge" for answering five consecutive math problems correctly will, in all likelihood, continue on to keep the streak going.

Should the writer make this insertion here?

A) Yes, because it offers a concrete example of the pattern of behavior discussed in this paragraph.
B) Yes, because it anticipates and addresses an argument against the ideas present in this paragraph.
C) No, because it detracts from the writer's focus on ridesharing companies.
D) No, because it detracts from the writer's increasingly negative stance on gamification.

CONTINUE

Questions 23-33 are based on the following passage.

Just Say "Noh"

[23] Before their emergence in the 14th century, Japanese noh plays have delighted their viewers with colorful costumes, striking stories, and skillful music. The word "noh," in fact, can be loosely translated as "aptitude," indicating perhaps [24] the alienating and seemingly incomprehensible subject matter essential to even the briefest of Japan's noh performances. However, the kinds [25] of aptitudes—involved and the dramatic structure that talented noh actors and musicians must master— may surprise viewers who are newcomers to noh, especially if those viewers are familiar with realistic European and American plays.

Rather than depicting scenes from daily life or attempting to comment on social or political issues, the typical work of noh theater depicts a single protagonist from myth or legend, such as a god or a warrior. [26] Indeed, the most famous Greek dramas address similarly lofty characters. This central figure is known as the "shite" and communicates his or her story primarily through gesture and dance. An effective shite performance is an act of resourcefulness: the shite does not speak, and cannot even rely on changes of facial expression, since a traditional shite will wear a mask that conveys a single sentiment (such anger, sadness, or elation).

23
A) NO CHANGE
B) Since
C) Despite
D) Alongside

24
Which choice best supports the writer's overall characterization of noh theater?
A) NO CHANGE
B) the rare and expensive costume craftsmanship
C) the high level of onstage practice and coordination
D) the difficulty of conjuring the realistic scenarios

25
A) NO CHANGE
B) of aptitudes involved—and the dramatic structure that
C) of aptitudes involved and the dramatic structure—that
D) of aptitudes involved and the dramatic structure that

26
The writer is considering deleting the underlined sentence. Should this sentence be kept or deleted?
A) Kept, because it explains why noh plays and Greek dramas embrace similar material.
B) Kept, because it addresses and corrects a possible flaw in the writer's argument.
C) Deleted, because it raises a topic that is only a primary focus elsewhere in the passage.
D) Deleted, because it undermines the argument that noh and Greek drama are entirely incompatible.

CONTINUE

The movements of the shite will be accompanied and complemented by the activity of a few [27] other performers, that help the audience to understand the shite's narrative. Secondary characters known as "waki" may [28] emerge onstage. One of these waki may open the play by explaining the setting. Thus, this speaker sets the context for the action that follows, [29] as will later take on a gestural role that is closer in design to that of the shite. Members of a chorus will also appear. These noh performers can comment on the action and may even speak lines attributed to the central noh personages. All of this action is painstakingly rehearsed [30] and coordinated: while powerful turns of expression are valued, improvisation is not.

27

A) NO CHANGE
B) other performers that help the audience, to understand
C) other performers who help the audience to understand
D) other performers, who help the audience, to understand

28

Which choice best combines the two sentences at the underlined portion?

A) emerge onstage, one of whom may
B) emerge onstage, that one may
C) emerge onstage; may
D) emerge onstage:

29

A) NO CHANGE
B) but
C) or
D) DELETE the underlined portion.

30

A) NO CHANGE
B) and coordinated, while powerful
C) and coordinated—powerful
D) and coordinated: powerful

257

CONTINUE

[1] Although noh is a distinctive art form, there are a few surface-level similarities between noh theater and various European theatrical genres. [2] Greek tragedies commonly used choruses. [3] The members of these groups would often be side participants in the main action of a Greek drama and would offer clarifying commentary, much as a noh chorus does. [4] For their part, noh personages embody specific strong traits. [5] It is also possible to draw parallels between the highly symbolic masterpieces of noh theater and the morality plays of the middle ages. [6] These plays feature characters who are important mainly as embodiments of particular virtues. **31**

Yet noh is set apart from these other theatrical forms by its reliance on dance and by its centralized, pavilion-like performance space. **32** <u>Perhaps most importantly noh plays continue to be performed</u> with many of their original trappings. **33** Even today, noh productions transport audiences back to the 14th century, or into the realm of Japanese folklore and heroism.

31

To make the order of ideas in the paragraph most logical, sentence 4 should be placed

A) where it is now.
B) before sentence 3.
C) after sentence 5.
D) after sentence 6.

32

A) NO CHANGE
B) Perhaps most importantly noh plays continue, to be performed
C) Perhaps most importantly, noh plays continue to be performed
D) Perhaps most importantly, noh plays continue to be performed,

33

At this point, the writer is considering adding the following sentence.

> This adherence to tradition seems designed to drive away audiences; however, it is not especially difficult for a contemporary noh troupe to turn a profit.

Should the writer make this addition here?

A) Yes, because it returns to an earlier argument regarding the finances of noh plays.
B) Yes, because it supports the argument that noh plays will only become more popular over time.
C) No, because it conflicts with the writer's idea that Greek dramas are more popular than noh plays.
D) No, because the profitability of noh plays is not a primary focus of the passage.

CONTINUE

Questions 34-44 are based on the following passage.

On the Lighter Side: Glow-in-the-Dark Mushrooms

It's a sight that you might find in a fantasy epic, in an after-school cartoon, or on the cover of a 1970s folk rock album: a cluster of mushrooms that glow in the dark. However, mushrooms that turn bright green or yellow once the lights are turned off are not simply the inventions of whimsical artists or animators. These mushrooms are real, and have recently become a source of serious scientific study. **34**

35 Despite the 100,000 species of fungi currently known to biologists, only 70 to 80 can emit their own light or are "bioluminescent." These bioluminescent mushrooms are scattered around **36** the globe. Two that have piqued the interest of an international research team can be found, respectively, in Brazil and Vietnam. As reported by Bob Yirka of Phys. org, the researchers examining these two fungi species solved the longstanding "mystery" of how some bioluminescent mushrooms glow. **37** Apparently—"bioluminescence occurred in the mushrooms when luciferin molecules interacted with a luciferase enzyme in the presence of oxygen; the reaction resulted in the production of a light-emitting substance called oxyluciferin."

34

At this point, the writer is considering inserting the following sentence.

> The phenomenon of "glowing" mushrooms itself calls attention to the often-harmonious relationships between artists and scientists.

Should the writer make this addition here?

A) Yes, because it explains the motives behind the collaborative developments that are cited earlier in this paragraph.
B) Yes, because it anticipates the writer's later argument that the public is paying attention to research on bioluminescence.
C) No, because it shifts attention to a group that is not discussed in the following paragraph.
D) No, because it would be more effectively placed at a later point in the passage.

35

A) NO CHANGE
B) From
C) Of
D) As

36

Which choice best combines the two sentences at the underlined portion?

A) the globe, and two that
B) the globe, while two that
C) the globe: whereas two that
D) the globe: as two that

37

A) NO CHANGE
B) Apparently: "bioluminescence
C) Apparently; "bioluminescence
D) Apparently, "bioluminescence

CONTINUE

Insights such as these are regarded as breakthroughs among fungus experts, and among the journalists who report on fungus-oriented research. Writing for the NPR Weekend Edition, Nell Greenfield-Boyce documented the solution to a [38] further "ancient mystery," surrounding glowing mushrooms: not *how* but *why* these mushrooms emit light in the first place. This issue was to some extent resolved by Jay Dunlap of the Geisel School of Medicine, who determined that mushrooms glow not to repel animals that might feast on them [39] (including some insects that are of little interest to scientists otherwise) [40] except to attract animals that might spread mushroom spores. Because the Brazilian mushrooms involved in Dunlap's study are native to a "dense forest, where there's little wind," these mushrooms can only spread if [41] the small insects, which are drawn to them unwittingly act as spore carriers.

38

A) NO CHANGE
B) further "ancient mystery" surrounding glowing mushrooms:
C) further "ancient mystery," surrounding glowing mushrooms,
D) further "ancient mystery" surrounding glowing mushrooms,

39

Which parenthetical phrase would add the most relevant and logical information to the passage?
A) NO CHANGE
B) (a common tactic among stationary organisms that take on vivid colors)
C) (or to blend in with non-luminous foliage once darkness falls)
D) (since the scientists behind the study had never seriously considered this possibility)

40

A) NO CHANGE
B) unless
C) instead
D) but

41

A) NO CHANGE
B) the small insects, that
C) the small insects that
D) the small insects as

CONTINUE

[1] Glowing-in-the-dark mushrooms [42] may have piqued the interest of researchers, yet these mushrooms are not especially hard to find. [2] Dunlap himself came across "his first glowing fungi as a kid, when he was on a camping trip and slept in a rustic shelter." [3] Some of [43] the most striking, bioluminescent fungi species can be found in North America and Europe. [4] For instance, two species that are commonly referred to as "jack-o-lantern" mushrooms can be found in the northern hemisphere: the North American *Omphalotus illudens* and the European *Omphalotus olearius*. [5] Indeed, you just might discover glowing mushrooms of your own in a "rustic shelter" near you. [6] Other species are equally abundant. [44]

42

Which choice best reflects one of the writer's main points about the "mushrooms" discussed in the passage?

A) NO CHANGE
B) are mostly figments of overactive imaginations,
C) are of little evident practical use to humans,
D) may be transforming some remote ecosystems,

43

A) NO CHANGE
B) the most striking, bioluminescent fungi species, can be found
C) the most striking bioluminescent fungi species can be found,
D) the most striking bioluminescent fungi species can be found

44

To make the order of ideas in the paragraph most logical, sentence 5 should be placed

A) where it is now.
B) after sentence 1.
C) after sentence 3.
D) after sentence 6.

STOP

Answer Key: TEST 5

Test 5

PASSAGE 1
Dressed for Success: Fashion Design Careers

1. A
2. C
3. C
4. D
5. B
6. D
7. C
8. D
9. C
10. C
11. A

PASSAGE 2
Is It All a (Video) Game?

12. D
13. C
14. C
15. A
16. B
17. B
18. C
19. A
20. D
21. C
22. A

PASSAGE 3
Just Say "Noh"

23. B
24. C
25. B
26. C
27. C
28. A
29. B
30. A
31. D
32. C
33. D

PASSAGE 4
On the Lighter Side: Glow-in-the-Dark Mushrooms

34. C
35. C
36. A
37. D
38. B
39. B
40. D
41. C
42. A
43. D
44. D

Answer Explanations

SAT Practice Test #5

Passage 1: Dressed for Success: Fashion Design Careers

1) CORRECT ANSWER: A
The sentence should introduce the topic of the "intricacies" of arranging an outfit, which is the main focus of this paragraph. A is an effective answer while B mentions non-fashion careers (which are not a focus of the passage) and C applies a wrongly negative tone to this mostly objective discussion. D raises the topic of "formal study", which the passage only addresses LATER, and should be eliminated as out of scope.

2) CORRECT ANSWER: C
The sentence must involve a proper subject-verb combination with "goes beyond" as the verb; the idea "what . . . does" can be taken as a single subject, so that C is the best answer. A, B, and D all introduce transition words that do NOT yield an effective main subject-verb combination, and thus create sentence fragments.

3) CORRECT ANSWER: C
The sentence must be coordinated so that the sentence would make sense if the content between dashes were to be factored out. C would create the phrase "aptitudes that" under these conditions, and properly uses the content between dashes to describe "aptitudes". Choose this answer and eliminate A ("itself that"), B ("requires that"), and D ("ability that") as creating awkward constructions if the intervening phrase is eliminated, or (for D) as not placing the word "including" between dashes in a manner that properly begins the description.

4) CORRECT ANSWER: D
The combined sentence should contrast the general and combined curricula at "Many institutions" with the subdivided curricula at "the most specialized fashion schools". D reflects the contrast with a grammatically correct use of "however". A and B both use a comma to wrongly split "although" from the phrase that it should introduce, while C creates a comma splice, since "however" must be preceded by a semicolon when it introduces an independent clause.

5) CORRECT ANSWER: B
The phrase "in areas such as accessories design" is a unified thought that, for the sake effective transition, should not be interrupted by commas. B avoids unnecessary punctuation, while A and C both insert unneeded commas and D wrongly uses a colon (which should NEVER be immediately followed by a transition such as "such as").

6) CORRECT ANSWER: D

The sentence indicates "professions" other than fashion design, yet fashion design is the only profession that the writer considers at any length. Choose D because the writer does not pursue this topic and eliminate C, which assumes that the writer does so elsewhere in the passage. A wrongly indicates that the statement takes a NEGATIVE stance towards fashion design (not towards other professions), while B wrongly considers the perspective of the readers (who are not directly referenced by the writer here) and is thus out of scope.

7) CORRECT ANSWER: C

In the paragraph that contains the underlined portion, the writer calls attention to the "limits" of design work and cites a "sense of focus" as important to an early fashion design role. C properly reflects the idea of projects that are "discrete" or informed by focus, while A and B wrongly characterize a budding designer's role as LACKING a relatively small focus. D wrongly assumes that the budding designer's work is impractical; instead, such work is limited in SCOPE of responsibilities, not in whether it is USEFUL.

8) CORRECT ANSWER: D

The sentence must be coordinated so that the subject-verb combination "designer . . . is known" is not interrupted by a single comma. D properly sets off the phrase "for instance" using two commas; A and B both break the subject-verb combination with a single comma, while C wrongly interrupts the phrase "is known primarily for" with a single comma.

9) CORRECT ANSWER: C

Sentence 4 describes what the task of a novice designer "is not"; this qualifying information could effectively lead into a clarification of what a "budding designer" does, as explained in sentence 2. Choose C and eliminate A and D, which would place a general statement within the discussion of design duties that it should help to INTRODUCE. B would place sentence 4 before sentence 1, which should introduce the ENTIRE topic of limits that sentence 4 examines in greater specificity, and should be eliminated for this reason.

10) CORRECT ANSWER: C

The phrase "with . . . fashion world" is a single idea that describes the importance of specific web sites and should be offset by commas, NOT itself broken up by commas. Choose C and eliminate A and B for this reason; D should be eliminated because it fails to separate "fashion world" and the subject "work" with a comma and thus causes different ideas to wrongly flow together.

11) CORRECT ANSWER: A

The content in the second part of the sentence should describe an "aspect" of fashion design; a colon can be effectively used to set up an item, such as "potential", that aligns with an earlier noun ("aspect"). Choose A and eliminate B, since a semicolon cannot introduce content that lacks a full subject-verb combination. C (direction) and D (possession) introduce prepositions that distort the meaning of the sentence (which mostly explains an idea) and should thus be eliminated.

Passage 2: Is It All a (Video) Game?

12) CORRECT ANSWER: D
The sentence should transition from a consideration of the limitations of video games to a discussion of their status as a "pleasing diversion". D uses a semicolon to create this transition in a grammatically correct manner, while A and B both employ awkward transition pronouns ("which" and "that", respectively) that do not have clear references. C wrongly uses a dash (which is closer to a comma in function) in place of a semicolon and wrongly designates place with "where", and can be eliminated for these reasons.

13) CORRECT ANSWER: C
The writer explains that technologies related to video games have been used to the advantage of "multibillion-dollar firms". Thus, factors related to video games are linked to business success stories: choose C and eliminate the negative answer A. B and D both refer to experts who may in fact have investigated video games but are not DIRECTLY mentioned in the content that "immediately follows", and should thus be eliminated as inappropriate to the requirements of the question.

14) CORRECT ANSWER: C
The sentence should designate ridesharing "providers" using correct punctuation: the word "particularly" refers to "Uber and Lyft" and should thus not be separated by punctuation from the words it references. Eliminate A and D for this reason, then eliminate B because a semicolon can ONLY be followed by an independent clause (not by a group of nouns). C effectively groups the ideas in the sentence and properly uses a comma in doing so.

15) CORRECT ANSWER: A
The phrase "as many . . . as" is a linked standard phrase that should help to explain the passenger assignments, and that should NOT be divided using only one unit of punctuation. Eliminate C and D (which wrongly insert single commas to break the phrase). Then, consider that the sentence should make sense if any parenthetical content is factored out. B would wrongly introduce the non-grammatical phrase "take passenger assignments as", while A would properly coordinate both the standard phrase and the parenthetical content, and is thus the best answer.

16) CORRECT ANSWER: B
The writer explains that Uber and Lyft have deployed psychological "gimmicks" to cause drivers to "log hours upon hours" in a manner that calls to mind video games. B properly refers to the idea of keeping "drivers on the road", while A and D refer to DIFFERENT profit-related issues (markets and rivals, respectively). C wrongly refers to "public relations", a topic that is only considered in a much LATER paragraph.

17) CORRECT ANSWER: B

The writer states that a video game involves a "dynamic visual environment"; the Uber and Lyft interfaces similarly involve "absorbing moving graphics". B rightly indicates a point of similarity involving Uber, Lyft, and video games, while A wrongly indicates that Uber and Lyft are almost ENTIRELY identical (not that they are identical in a FEW aspects that recall video games). C is problematic because it considers the perspective of the reader (who is not directly referenced at this point), while D misstates the function of the content. The author is building upon a comparison, but has not in fact described the "touchscreen interface" EARLIER and thus cannot reiterate content.

18) CORRECT ANSWER: C

The phrase beginning with "constantly aware" should describe "gamers", and can be offset using a comma to fulfill this requirement. C properly inserts a comma before "constantly". A misuses a colon (which should only introduce an explanatory clause or a set of items), B wrongly separates the linked phrase "aware that" using a comma, and D avoids punctuation and, in doing so, creates an awkward construction that wrongly suggests that "playing" is "constantly aware".

19) CORRECT ANSWER: A

Sentence 6 describes a "$22 commission", which would be pursued as the result of responding to Uber's gamification format and accepting "new passengers" as described in sentence 5. Thus, sentence 6 is effectively placed in its current position. Choose A and eliminate B (which wrongly places this example of gamification in the early stages of the paragraph, when the PREMISES behind ridesharing gamification are being explained) as well as C and D (which would wrongly place the reference to a "$22 commission" after sentences that do not directly refer to ridesharing).

20) CORRECT ANSWER: D

An effective transition would refer back to the *New York Times*, a newspaper "which" called attention to certain gamification effects. D is an excellent answer, while A creates a case of improper verb reference which suggests that the "methods" (not the *New York Times*) called attention. B and C both wrongly use "as" to indicate a comparison as opposed to a direct reference, while B also wrongly places a fragment that begins with a transition after a colon.

21) CORRECT ANSWER: C

The sentence that precedes the underlined portion points to positive uses of gamification in "modern industries"; "gamification in education" is such a positive case. C, "In this respect", properly indicates that the writer is introducing an example that supports a specific idea. A wrongly indicates a contrast, B wrongly criticizes gamification in education, and D wrongly refers to the earlier general statement on gamification as "evidence" (when in fact evidence is only presented AFTERWARDS).

22) CORRECT ANSWER: A

The proposed sentence adds new and precise details to the preceding sentence's discussion of how "high school students can be motivated" by gamification formats. A is thus the best answer, while the proposed content ONLY supports the writer's ideas rather than addressing arguments against these ideas (eliminating B). C wrongly refers to a topic (ridesharing) that the writer has moved beyond, while D reverses the writer's actual stance, which is clearly POSITIVE in the final paragraph.

Passage 3: Just Say "Noh"

23) CORRECT ANSWER: B

The sentence should describe how Japanese noh plays first emerged and then "delighted their viewers"; "Since" is a sentence opening that designates a point of beginning. B is the best answer, while A creates an illogical relationship, suggesting that noh plays delighted viewers BEFORE noh plays even emerged. C wrongly indicates a contrast, and D wrongly indicates place or simultaneity, not an EARLIER event.

24) CORRECT ANSWER: C

The writer explains that noh theater involves "skillful music" and is linked to the concept of "aptitude": C, which refers to practice and coordination, correctly captures the theme of skill. A and D are both wrongly negative, while B focuses on rarity and expensiveness (different exceptional qualities from SKILL) and thus avoids the proper main idea.

25) CORRECT ANSWER: B

The sentence contains the subject-verb pairing "kinds . . . may surprise", which should only be separated by an intervening phrase that is placed between two dashes. B exhibits proper use of dashes and also connects the description "involved" to "aptitudes". A wrongly splits the unified phrase "aptitudes involved", C wrongly splits the unified phrase "structure that", and D wrongly places ONE dash between "kinds" and "may surprise".

26) CORRECT ANSWER: C

Although the writer's main focus at this point is the "typical work of noh theater", the proposed content introduces a distracting reference to the "most famous Greek dramas", which are only examined in a later paragraph. Choose C and eliminate D (because the writer in fact argues LATER that noh and Greek drama are in some ways similar). A uses faulty logic (since the reasons BEHIND the similarity are never addressed in the sentence), while B assumes that Greek drama is at this point an essential topic in the writer's argument (when in fact such drama is only addressed later).

27) CORRECT ANSWER: C

The reference to what the "performers" do ("help the audience to understand") should be connected directly to the word "performers". C creates a proper transition using "who". A uses "that" (which is less appropriate than "who" when referring to people) and wrongly separates "that" from the noun it references with a comma. B and D both wrongly use a comma to break the phrase "help the audience to understand", which articulates a single idea.

28) CORRECT ANSWER: A

The combined sentence must contain a transition that refers back to one of the "waki". A involves a proper reference to the "waki", "one of whom" may open the play. B creates an awkward construction that can be read ("that may" forming an independent clause) as a comma splice, C places a fragment after a semicolon, and D misuses a colon (which can only be followed by a set of items or by a full sentence).

29) CORRECT ANSWER: B

The sentence that contains the underlined portion should present a contrast involving a waki performer, who first acts as a "speaker" but then takes on a "gestural role". B is the best answer, while A and C wrongly indicate that the waki performer's two roles are similar or interchangeable. D creates an awkward construction (and makes it unclear what noun "will take" references) by eliminating any transition whatsoever, and should thus be eliminated.

30) CORRECT ANSWER: A

The content after the colon helps to explain the rehearsed and coordinated "action" of noh theater, which involves "expression" but not "improvisation". A uses a colon to properly set up an explanatory relationship. B introduces a comma splice, as do C and D, since "turns . . . are" and "improvisation is" are two independent clauses.

31) CORRECT ANSWER: D

Sentence 4 describes "noh personages", but uses the phrase "For their part" to indicate that this sentence should follow a discussion of OTHER characters with strong traits. Morality play "characters" that embody "particular virtues" are discussed in sentence 6; choose D and eliminate A and B (since it is not clear that the characters in a Greek chorus have strong traits). C is problematic because sentence 5 introduces "morality plays" but does not explicitly explain morality play "characters" in the manner of sentence 6.

32) CORRECT ANSWER: C

The introductory and inessential phrase "Perhaps most importantly" should be separated from the rest of the sentence with a single comma. C employs the correct punctuation; A and B cause the phrases to flow together (and wrongly indicate that "most" modifies "plays", not "importantly"), while D wrongly breaks the connected words "performed with" with a comma.

33) CORRECT ANSWER: D

At this point, the writer is most concerned with how noh plays are performed and with how audiences react to these plays; whether a play will "turn a profit" is not the focus in any way. Choose D and eliminate A (since the finances of noh plays are not a focus elsewhere) and B (since the writer only ever indicates that noh plays are currently popular and appreciated, not that they WILL BECOME more popular in the future). C wrongly indicates an audience preference for Greek dramas over noh plays; the writer only compares the two forms of theater in terms of format and technique, and in any case Greek drama is not directly mentioned in the proposed content.

Passage 4: On the Lighter Side: Glow-in-the-Dark Mushrooms

34) CORRECT ANSWER: C

Although the writer briefly mentions forms of art or self-expression in the first paragraph, the topic of "artists" is not discussed in the content that follows. C is the best answer, while D can be eliminated because the topic of art is mentioned ONLY in the first paragraph. A wrongly identifies a correspondence between the mushrooms and particular images as a "collaboration" involving people, while B is out of scope because the proposed content mentions only artists and scientists, not "the public".

35) CORRECT ANSWER: C

The writer is describing a sample related to a group, or a selection "Of" the 100,000 species. C indicates part of a group and is the best answer, while A sets up a contrast, B (when inserted into the sentence) would indicate direction instead of a sampling, and D sets up a comparison.

36) CORRECT ANSWER: A

The underlined content should transition into a discussion of "two" of the bioluminescent mushrooms mentioned earlier; "and" would be an appropriate transition for related facts that do not entail a shift in tone. A is the best answer, while B and C both incorrectly introduce contrasts, and C and D both wrongly place fragments (as opposed to items or independent clauses) after a colon.

37) CORRECT ANSWER: D

To set aside a brief introductory phrase such as "Apparently", a comma is the appropriate unit of punctuation. Choose D and eliminate A (since a single dash in such circumstances often indicates a strong shift in tone). B wrongly places a single word (as opposed to the required sentence) before a colon, while C commits a similar error using a semicolon.

38) CORRECT ANSWER: B

The phrase ""ancient mystery" surrounding glowing mushrooms" articulates a single idea about "mushrooms" and should be grouped without a comma; moreover, a colon should be used to introduce the explanation of the "mystery". B is the best answer, while A and C wrongly use a comma to split the phrase and C and D wrongly introduce the explanation of the "mystery" with a comma, not a colon.

39) CORRECT ANSWER: B

The ultimately discarded idea that the mushrooms glow "to repel animals" would initially arise because repelling animals is a "common tactic" among organisms similar to the stationary mushrooms. B is the best answer since it explains a logical origin for the idea of repelling animals. A describes the perspective of scientists and focuses on insects themselves, C shifts focus to a DIFFERENT idea, and D is illogical because the scientists DID consider and reject the idea that the mushrooms glow to repel animals.

40) CORRECT ANSWER: D

The sentence should describe two contrasting ideas, one rejected and one accepted. The phrase "not to . . . but to" would create a proper parallel construction for such a contrast. Choose D and eliminate A, B, and C, all of which indicate forms of difference but none of which form the EXACT standard phrase that the sentence requires with "not . . . but".

41) CORRECT ANSWER: C

The subject-verb combination "insects . . . act" cannot be interrupted by a single unit of punctuation. C properly avoids such interruption while A and B both interrupt the subject-verb combination with a single comma. D introduces the wrong sentence relationship: "as" indicates a comparison, while the sentence should directly refer back to insects "that" are drawn to mushrooms.

42) CORRECT ANSWER: A

The passage as a whole demonstrates that the glowing mushrooms are of considerable interest (or have "piqued" the interest) of researchers such as Jay Dunlap, so that A is the best answer. Both B and C wrongly apply clear negative tones to the mushroom, while D mistakes the passage's focus on how the mushrooms THEMSELVES function for how the mushrooms INFLUENCE the ecosystems around them.

43) CORRECT ANSWER: D

The phrase "most striking bioluminescent fungi species" is essential content because it explains what "Some" (the subject of the sentence) refers to. D properly avoids offsetting this content with commas and thus treats it as essential. A (and which breaks the subject and verb with a comma) and B wrongly attempt to offset the phrase, while C wrongly uses a comma to separate the single idea that the species can be "found in" specific areas.

44) CORRECT ANSWER: D

Sentence 5 splits sentence 4 (which describes specific mushroom species) from sentence 6 (which describes "other species"); re-positioning sentence 5 after sentence 6 would bring the references to species together, and would allow the paragraph to return to an earlier idea (the "rustic shelter") in a unifying concluding statement. Choose D and eliminate A. B would wrongly place the second reference to the "rustic shelter" BEFORE the introducing reference in sentence 2, while C places sentence 5 after sentence 3, which does not explain WHY "you just might" find glowing mushrooms. In contrast, sentence 6 explains that glowing mushrooms are abundant and indicates why you might discover "glowing mushrooms" as described in sentence 5.

Made in the USA
San Bernardino, CA
26 January 2020

63628030R00153